Task of Theology Today III

Sin and Salvation

The Task of Theology Today Series is a publication of the Australian Theological Forum. Each volume is a collection of essays emanating from a colloquium organised by the Forum. The essays address a particular theological theme and draw upon the expertise of various branches of theology in this endeavour, including biblical scholars, systematic and philosophical theologians.

Series Editor
Hilary Regan

ATF Press

Task of Theology Today I, *Doctrines and Dogmas*, edited by Victor Pfitzner and Hilary Regan, ATF, 1998

Task of Theology Today II, *Starting with the Spirit*, edited by Stephen Pickard and Gordon Preece, ATF, 2001

Sin and Salvation

EDITED BY

Duncan Reid and Mark Worthing

ATF Press

First published May 2003

Cover design by Mark Thomas. Painting on the front cover by Wes Campbell entitled *Crucifixion in the Gulf,* 1991.

National Library of Australia
Cataloguing-in-Publication data

Sin & Salvation

Includes Index
ISBN 1 920691 04 9

1. Salvation. 2. Sin I. Reid, Duncan, 1950-. II. Worthing, Mark William. III. Title: Sin and salvation.
(Series: Task of theology today; III).

234

Published by
ATF Press
An imprint of the Australian Theological Forum
PO Box 504
Hindmarsh
SA 5007
AUSTRALIA

www.atfpress.com Fax + 61 8 8340 34 50

Printed by Openbook Print, Adelaide, Australia

Contents

Introduction

Duncan Reid and Mark Worthing

The current theological context is one in which the sense of human brokenness cannot be ignored. We live in the aftermath of September 11, the war in Afghanistan, the terrorist attack in Bali, the continuing conflicts between Israelis and Palestinians and—at the time of writing—the real prospect of war in Iraq. It is within precisely this context that the present volume, the third in the ATF's Task of Theology Today Series,[1] seeks to contribute to the discussion of the nature, origin and impact of human sinfulness, and its resolution in the hope of salvation.

The colloquium was organised by the ATF in partnership with the Science and Religion Course program of CTNS in Berkeley, California and in association with the Centre for Theology, Science and Culture of Flinders University / Adelaide College of Divinity. The ATF thanks both bodies for the assistance that was given in running the event.

The volume begins appropriately with a chapter from the noted German Lutheran theologian Hans Schwarz. This opening contribution gives an insightful and comprehensive overview of the question of sin, evil and the evil one in the biblical and theological traditions, with an emphasis on contemporary trends within these discussions.

Peter Lockwood plumbs what might seem an unlikely source of insight into salvation, the story of the rape of Dinah. A more conventional approach might have seen sin as a primary theme here, but Lockwood's real interest is in what the story tells us about salvation. He offers two very divergent readings of the passage, and has the reader well down the path of uncritically accepting the received interpretation before dramatically unveiling a diametrically opposed reading, one that opens up the way of salvation to the non-Israelite players in the drama. Salvation may well be from the God of Jacob, but it does not require us to be like Jacob. The strongest

---

1. Task of Theology Today II, *Starting with the Spirit*, edited by Stephen Pickard and Gordon Preece (Adelaide: ATF, 2001).

condemnation is for Jacob's sons, whose fanaticism would exclude non-Israelites from life. But even the unattractive figure of Jacob emerges at the end as one whose far from sinless life, despite everything, is redeemable.

Brendan Byrne's chapter continues the biblical exploration of sin and salvation by revisiting the Adam myth, as it is presented and used in the Letter to the Romans. In doing so, Byrne rethinks the Augustinian doctrine of original sin. The Adam myth has implications for a contemporary understanding of sin and salvation, but only if we can unlearn this all-pervasive doctrinal gloss and look afresh at what Paul actually says. We may also, in this process, find that Augustine has unexpected things to teach us. But again, we need to listen to Augustine himself, and not our standard readings of him.

Wes Campbell's chapter is a personal exploration of what it is to be an artist and a theologian—a religious artist and a Protestant theologian—with all that the epithet 'Protestant' can imply about distrust of religious imagery. The chapter is necessarily schematic because at the conference it was illustrated by reference to Campbell's own artistic work. He explores this theme theologically, making extensive use of Jüngel's theological aesthetics. The problem is that, contrary to the well-known aphorism by Keats, truth is not always beautiful, nor beauty truthful. Wes Campbell refuses to avoid this problem, either in his artwork or in his theological reflection on it. But in the end, he argues, plasticity is demanded—not just by our increasingly icon-oriented culture, but more importantly by the Christian scriptures themselves. God's work of salvation is a work of art, and must call forth from us an artistic response.

Rosalie Hudson takes a practical and pastoral approach to our theme. Her interest is highly personal, beginning in her own experience as a community hospice nurse. She cites two cases in order to explore the difference between a Socratic and a Christian approach to dying. Pastoral practice, she argues, must be grounded in theological belief, and theological belief does not separate itself from specific pastoral practice. Hudson critiques our cultural trivialising of the weightiness of death. Death is not to be treated as merely heroic. Life is to be affirmed, but not by means of desperate metaphysical optimism. Life is to be affirmed because, and only because, Jesus Christ has died, and has overcome the offensiveness of death.

In an era heavily influenced by the insights of the physical sciences, an examination of the nature and origins of human sin would be incomplete without reference to the scientific contributions to these questions. Ted Peters, prominent in the theology and science dialogue of the last decade, examines the question of the genesis and genetics of sin. Building on previous work on the theological implications of human genetics, Peters tackles the difficult but recurring question of whether human brokenness might in some way be explained by our genetic makeup.

In a similar vein, Mark Worthing looks at the question of the origin of guilt and sin, and the closely related human experience of guilt, from the perspective of human evolutionary history. While it is often asserted that evolution knows nothing of morality, Worthing asks the surprising question whether perhaps guilt has bestowed on human beings an evolutionary advantage. It is precisely the biological evolution of human beings, he argues, that has produced our sense of guilt and sin. Guilt is a development that 'needs to be understood in a comparable manner to all other developments in the evolutionary development of humanity'. The biblical story of the fall, far from being incompatible with evolutionary theory, thus points to a significant quality about ourselves as human beings, and becomes even more intelligible in the light of recent developments in evolutionary biology.

In the third of the contributions focusing on the science-theology dialogue, Bob Russell, founder and head of the Center for Theology and Natural Sciences in Berkeley, examines the question of sin, salvation and cosmology. He focuses specifically on the difficulty we have in relating current scientific eschatologies to our theological models of human sin and the final manifestation of salvation. Russell poses some difficult questions that do not find easy answers. But they are issues that cannot be put aside by a theological community that is serious about both its eschatological hope and its engagement with modern scientific worldviews.

Peter Lockhart's chapter argues for a non-trivial understanding of sin—as opposed to sin as it tends to be understood in popular culture. Our recognition of sin comes only as a consequence of salvation. Without the apprehension that we are redeemable, if not actually redeemed, we would have no way of knowing we were sinners. Salvation reveals sin for what it is—estrangement from God. This estrangement is revealed by the incarnation, in its directionality towards our salvation. The author then considers atonement, or reconciliation, understood as new being for humanity, before looking at our situation in the church of the twenty-first century. The emphasis here is on the classical theological themes of sin, law, covenant, and the possible limits of God's grace—the question of salvation outside the church.

Duncan Reid examines an issue that has been causing a great deal of discussion recently among Luther scholars, namely, the thesis of a number of Finnish theologians that Luther's doctrine of salvation has a great deal in common with the Eastern theological notion of theosis. Stemming from the thought of Tuomo Mannermaa, this school of thought has produced both ardent defenders and staunch critics. Reid demonstrates, without passing judgment on the correctness of the thesis, that the renewed discussion of precisely how Luther understood salvation is proving a healthy exercise for theologians interested in both Eastern and Western conceptions of salvation.

Denis Edwards picks up the theme of the salvation of 'outsiders', of those who have never heard the good news: our own Neanderthal and Indigenous Australian predecessors. Edwards' chapter relies heavily on Karl Rahner's universalising vision of salvation, taking this vision in an explicitly pneumatological direction. Before the historical incarnation, in Judea in the time of Caesar Augustus, it was the Spirit who was ever-present as life-giver. Edwards is cautious about any naïve reliance on experience, but nevertheless claims the Spirit is at work wherever we are touched by experiences of beauty, goodness or mystery—not excluding our painful experiences of these things. Further, the Spirit who brings life is none other than that Spirit who can also be identified as the Spirit of Christ. This Spirit manifests—non-verbally if you like—an inner directionality towards the Word who in time is to be made flesh. A final section of the chapter explores more intentionally the link between the Spirit of Christ and non-Christian religions. The Spirit of God is the one who graciously fills the universe and accomplishes and celebrates the emergence of life.

The volume concludes with a second contribution by Hans Schwarz, in which he takes up the question of salvation as an eschatological, other-worldly expectation. He treats particularly scientific visions arising out of evolutionary theory and the writings of physicist Frank Tipler as well as millennial expectations. Schwarz contends that other-worldly expectations of salvation, while given at time to extremes, cannot simply be dismissed as pie-in-the-sky hopes, but are grounded biblically in this present created order.

The original colloquium, which took place in Adelaide, Australia, only a few weeks after the September 11 2001 terrorist attacks in the United States, was very much aware of the concrete reality of human brokenness and the pain and anguish that result. Yet it was also clear that it was theologically and pastorally incomplete to hold a meeting on sin without also talking about the possibility and indeed the reality of salvation. Only a couple of the papers make salvation their specific theme, but few of the others fail to come back to the message of hope. While biblical, theological, cultural and scientific aspects of the nature of sin are treated in this volume, a significant and vital part of its contribution to the current theological discussion is that the message of hope in Christ is never far from the surface. In a world that is unable to escape the tragedy of human-initiated pain and suffering, this volume seeks to provide a timely and much needed contribution to our reflections on the underlying questions of sin and salvation.

Duncan Reid, Melbourne
Mark Worthing, Adelaide

1

Evil and the Evil One

Hans Schwarz

'The Lord saw that the wickedness of humankind was great in the earth, and that every inclination of the thoughts of their hearts was only evil continually' (Gen 6:5). Then the flood came and wiped the slate clean. But the same condition that in the prologue to the flood is the foundation for God's judgment becomes in the epilogue the reason for God's grace and indulgence. This, because he said in his heart: 'I will never again curse the ground because of humankind, for the inclination of the human heart is evil from youth' (Gen 8:21). The human condition is characterised by evil inclinations which are not changed even through divine chastisement. In the New Testament, Paul even dramatises this situation, saying: '. . . I am of the flesh, sold into slavery under sin . . . For I know that nothing good dwells within me, that is, in my flesh. I can will what is right, but I cannot do it. For I do not do the good I want, but the evil I do not want is what I do' (Rom 7:14, 18-19.). As Rudolf Bultmann has rightly shown, flesh and sin are seen as powers to which humanity has succumbed. Humanity is powerless against them, and the personification of these powers shows that humanity is no longer in control of its own actions.[1] Several questions emerge from these biblical quotations: Are sin and evil identical? How could sin or evil emerge if that which God created was 'very good', as at least the priestly creation account states? And last, but not least, how are these personified powers related to God?

1. Evil and sin

While good and evil are ethical opposites, there is no immediate opposite word recognisable to sin, since sin is a religious concept and not primarily an ethical one. Sin is that which stands against the will or

---

1.   Rudolf Bultmann, *Theology and the New Testament*, § 23.

wishes of the Godhead and a sinful act is always an act that does not find divine approval. One cannot sin against one's nature or against another person, but only against God. For instance, when David was confronted by Nathan on account of David's adultery, the king did not confess that he had sinned against Uriah the Hittite, whose wife he had taken, but said: 'I have sinned against the Lord' (2 Sam 12:13). Sinful behaviour is always directed against God and therefore separates us from God and his will.

Breaking a religious taboo or a cultic law can also be sin, without being ethically evil. For instance, eating an ostrich is certainly not evil, but since this bird is considered unclean, such action would be sinful (cf Deut 14:15). Yet sin and evil often go together in theological reflection, as we can see in Paul's discourse on sin in Romans 7. Evil in the Old Testament, denoted by *ra* or *raah*, can also be something that is simply considered as negative, such as brackish water (2 Kgs 2:19), a miserable place (Num 20:5) or simply wild animals (Gen 37:20).

As soon as we move from the natural world to that of humanity, evil takes on a moral dimension by those 'who plan evil things in their minds' (Ps 140:2f). When evil denotes a human act or attitude, it stands in opposition to God and his will. It is nothing natural, but something intentional, which is ultimately directed against God. In reaction to this, God responds correspondingly, as he says through the prophet Jeremiah: 'Hear, O earth; I am going to bring disaster [evil (*raah*)] on this people, the fruit of their schemes' (Jer 6:19). Therefore the punishment of God for individuals or an entire people when they deviate from God's ways is perceived as something that is evil or a calamity. The path of alienation from God then leads to destruction. Being in tune with God, the psalmist can say: 'I fear no evil; for you are with me' (Ps 23:4). We notice here that evil, especially in its ethical dimension, is intimately connected with sin. The evil that a person does always transcends the interpersonal or natural realm and therefore is something sinful.

The most frequently used word for sin in the Hebrew language is 'chattat' or 'chet'. In its profane use it means 'missing the target' or 'straying from the path'. This use of the word, which occurs seldom, already illustrates the fundamental religious meaning of the term. Yet sin is not 'missing' a norm or an expressed law or commandment of God, but is rather primarily and basically an offence against God. Sin awakens the wrath of God and unleashes God's reaction, provided a third party does not intervene and turn aside this reaction, as Abraham attempted on behalf of the people of Sodom (Gen 18:23).

Another Hebrew word for the concept of sin, the noun 'avon', is taken up in the prophetic and cultic literature of the exilic and post-exilic period as the primary term for human guilt and disaster.[2] It addresses idolatry (Ezek 14:3f), a lack of concern for the poor (Ezek 16:49), a dishonest behaviour (Ezek 18:8), and other offences. The one who has committed sin and become burdened with guilt wastes away and is doomed to ruin (Lev 26:39). The guilt of the people can even be transferred to a scapegoat (Lev 16:21f) or they can humble themselves before God and confess their sin so that God once more remembers his covenant with them (Lev 26:40ff).

A third important term covering the area of sin is the Hebrew noun 'pesha', which in its substantive form indicates an offence, crime, or similar phenomena. It can simply be a misdeed, as in the story of Jacob and Laban, when Jacob is accused by Laban of having stolen his idols. Jacob, unaware of any misdeed, asks Laban: 'What is my offence [pesha]? What is my sin, that you have hotly pursued me?' (Gen 31:36). Often it occurs in parallel relationship to *chattat* (Ps 32:1) or *avon* (1 Sam 25:28) or to both, as in Ezekiel 21:24, where Yahweh says to Israel: 'Because you have brought your guilt [*avon*] to remembrance, and that your transgressions [*pesha*] are uncovered, so that in all your deeds your sins [*chattat*] appear—because you have come to a remembrance, you shall be taken captive.' Again the offences of the individual and of the people provoke Yahweh's action.

In the New Testament evil is described primarily by two adjectives or substantival terms, 'kakos' and 'poneros'. While 'kakos' is limited to the human realm (Jas 1:13f), 'poneros' confronts us first of all in the sense of the Old Testament *raah*, as that which is not useful or suitable, for instance, when we read that an evil or bad tree produces bad fruit (Mt 7:18). *Poneros* can also, however, mean 'bad', 'dangerous', or 'disastrous', again in relation to natural occurrences. More frequently, *poneros* is used in relationship to evil people (Mt 7:11) who stand in contrast to God, who alone is good. Thus Jesus speaks of an 'evil and adulterous generation' (Mt 12:39). When people are evil in their basic orientation, they will be fatefully drawn ever further into the web of evil. Evil people stand in contrast to God and therefore, at the end of

---

2.   So Klaus Koch, 'Awon', in *TWAT* 5:1160.

the world, those who are evil will be separated from the righteous (Mt 13:49).

When we look for the Greek equivalent to 'chattat', 'avon', and 'pesha', we find 'harmatia' (sin), in both its substantival and verbal forms. This term appears much less frequently in the four gospels than in the other New Testament writings. This fact should not surprise us, if we remember that Jesus of Nazareth did not appear as a prophet of God's judgment, but rather as the one to redeem the world. Yet as we can glean from the Sermon on the Mount, Jesus was aware of the reality of sin. He came as the conqueror of sin and therefore could say: 'I have come to call not the righteous but sinners' (Mt 9:13). Jesus desires to lead individuals back to God and to establish fellowship with them so that they leave their evil and sinful ways to be received into a new community with God. Yet such change is no automatism. As Paul emphatically states, humans have no chance to escape from their evil ways. Their own efforts lead them even more deeply into sin. It is rather 'the law of the Spirit of life in Christ Jesus [that] has set you free from the law of sin' (Rom 8:2). For that new possibility Jesus' death and resurrection, as Paul has pointed out, is decisive, something to be remembered and re-enacted in the Eucharist and in baptism. Paul writes: 'For if we have been united with him in a death like his, we will certainly be united with him in a resurrection like his. We know that our own self was crucified with him so that the body of sin might be destroyed, and we might no longer be enslaved to sin' (Rom 6:5-6). Yet how did humanity get into this enslavement in the first place? The origin and reality of evil is theologically speaking one of the most vexing problems.

2. The origin and reality of evil

When considering the origin of evil, one thinks instinctively of the fall narrative in Genesis 3. Yet this narrative is remarkably isolated from the rest of the Old Testament. It is taken up neither by the psalmist nor by the prophets nor by any other Old Testament writer.[3] This does mean that in the rest of the Old Testament we do not hear of evil and sin, to the contrary. But no causal connection is made between this first sin and subsequent sins or between this sin and the resultant evil,

---

3. So Gerhard von Rad, *Genesis: A Commentary*, revised edition, originally translated by JH Marks (Philadelphia: Westminster, 1972), 102.

except to say, as we hear in the conclusion of the fall narrative in picturesque terms, that drudgery, pain, and death were the consequences of this first sin. Yet pictures and narratives are not the means for a logical explanation. Therefore this narrative is 'simply unfit to explain the origin of evil in rational terms'.[4] It rather asserts in its own circumscribable way that evil does not come from God, since creation prior to and after the fall was still good. In this way, the origin of evil remains shrouded in mystery. One might recall what behavioural psychology determined concerning the phenomenon of aggression. Aggressive drives are also found among animals. These drives normally serve to facilitate the survival of a species. This applies to aggression directed toward other species, as in the case of defence or hunting; and even within species, as in the establishment of hierarchies, defensive behaviour or the selection of mates. As soon as human beings appeared, however, and began to exercise dominion over one another and their environment, and to develop increasingly sophisticated tools and weapons, the aggressive drives became more and more ambivalent. They increased the potential for good as well as for evil. Many animal species were annihilated and others domesticated. Human civilisations were destroyed and others forcefully merged through local takeovers. As psychoanalysis shows, the activities of humans are highly ambivalent; they comprise the drive for life while at the same time spreading fear and death.

The appearance of evil cannot be compared to a natural catastrophe against which humanity was helpless. Evil does not appear within man or woman, but rather from the outside, as the serpent shows in the fall narrative. Humanity was not sinful from the very beginning, but temptation originated externally. The cause of evil, however, is not some God-opposing principle external to God's creation, even though this view was held within Gnosticism. The serpent, which becomes the tempter, is described as an animal and thereby as part of God's creation, but not as part of the heavenly court.[5]

The primeval history gives no answer to the fundamental question of where evil comes from. Along with the rest of the Old Testament, not the slightest attempt is made to take refuge in either a dualistic or pluralistic worldview. It is beyond the interest of the Yahwist why a

---

4.   Johan B Hygen, article entitled 'Böse, Das', in *TRE* 7:12.
5.   See Johannes Fichtner, 'Ophis (Gen 3)', in *TDNT* 5:573, who emphasises the created nature of the serpent.

creature of God's good creation became the tempter, because the answer to this question would not contribute to the description of human sinfulness. The guilt, in all its severity, is allowed to stand as unexplained guilt.

When we leave the fall narrative in Genesis and seek to determine the cause of evil from other Old Testament sources, our task becomes even more difficult.[6] For instance, we find in Amos that Yahweh asks his people: 'Does disaster [that is, evil] befall a city, unless the Lord has done it?' (Amos 3:6). God stands behind the evil and the good. After Job is hit by misfortune, he is convinced of God's omnipotence and says to his wife: 'Shall we receive good at the hand of God, and shall we not receive the bad?' (Job 2:10). His wife, however, appears to take no comfort in this, for she warns her husband to renounce and even to curse God, because he is the cause of all evil that has befallen Job. In Deutero-Isaiah the pressing question of whether God is the cause of evil is likewise answered in the affirmative, for there we hear the Lord say: 'I form light and create darkness, I make weal and create woe, I the Lord do all these things' (Isa 45:7). In other texts we discover that the Lord can even incite one person against another (see 1 Sam 26:19).

God is the only God who knows good and evil, and everything depends on him. But there is also a spirit of evil that is to be distinguished from Yahweh that afflicts the people (1 Sam 16:14f.). Nevertheless such a statement does not diminish the understanding that God is the only genuine power, for it is God who sends the evil spirit.[7] One might want to speak here of a demonic God, in light of whose actions no one can be secure. Or one might assume that the Israelites ascribed good and evil to Yahweh in order to preserve a monotheistic understanding of God. These attempts at a solution, however, fail. God is not a demon, and his works are always directed toward the triumph of his kingdom and the advance of his plan of redemption. Thus the Psalmist is correct when he confesses: 'For his

---

6. See for this and the following Theodorus C Vriezen, *An Outline of Old Testament Theology*, second edition (Oxford: Blackwell, 1970), who also notices the difficulty of introducing evil into a monotheistic religion without associating it directly with God.

7. See Werner Foerster, 'Daimon', in *TDNT* 2:11, who, in reference to this text, writes: 'OT monotheism is thus maintained, since no power to which man might turn in any matter is outside the one God of Israel.'

anger is but for a moment; his favour is for a lifetime' (Ps 30:5). Israel was nevertheless convinced that Yahweh ordains for individuals as well as an entire people tests, afflictions, or even judgment. In this sense God does 'evil'.[8] From this perspective one can understand the story of Job, who was afflicted by God and was led thereby to a deeper understanding of God. God is never, however, understood as a capricious God whose deeds one must fear, but rather as a holy God before whom one dare not appear as if an equal or in a demanding manner. Behind the statements of the incomparable circumspection of a God who creates good and evil stands the recognition of the absolute sovereignty of God over life and death, fortune and misfortune, well-being and calamity.

Up to and including the time of the great writing prophets like Isaiah, God is viewed as an absolutely sovereign God from whom comes both good and evil. The question of theodicy or how a just God can also cause evil without thereby himself becoming evil, is not posed in this form. The emphasis, in fact, is upon God's sovereignty, since only because he is sovereign can one expect from him the mighty acts that show him to be the Lord of history. Consequently, all the facets of life, the dark as well as the light, the frightening as well as the joyous, the threatening as well as the saving, are transferred to Yahweh. He is the final ground of all things and the sole causality of life.

Once Jerusalem was destroyed and the Israelite elite led into captivity, and as even the resettlement plans did not bring about the New Jerusalem in its expected glory, it became more and more difficult to see the great acts of God in a clear and discernible line of historical events. To the contrary, one increasingly saw oneself within the broadening historical context as a pawn of historical world powers. Therefore it was no longer so easy to attribute everything to God and to continue, nevertheless, to hold fast to his promises of salvation. If God were to remain in the future the one upon whom salvation ultimately depends, then he could not continue to be understood as the author of both good and evil. Evil was, so to speak, excluded from God. Without God evil just became one power among others in the process. Thus one distinguishes between evil as an act or thing and its underlying causal force that is distinct from God.

When we hear in the intertestamental period of the fall of angels, humans still remain responsible for their own sins even if sin can be

---

8. See Herbert Hag, *Vor dem Bösen ratlos?* (Munich: Piper, 1978), 23.

traced back to the fall of Adam or of angels as the historical inception of sin.[9] Evil came through the appearance of the first man and the first woman, and it continues to reveal itself in conjunction with the appearance of humans.

When we now take a brief look at the New Testament, we notice that Paul, its most prominent theological author, affirmed that sin came into the world through Adam. This attributed the origin of sin in line with Judaism. This first human being set itself against God, and thus sin was born. With sin, death also came into the world, for it is, so to speak, the consequence of sin, because there is no life in separation from God. Through the reign of death the universality of sin is to be seen, for all people are marked by death. Death, however, is not a power from which there is no escape, as was the thinking in Hellenism and Greek culture. Instead, it is the individual human being who pursues sin. Thereby death gains its mastery. Sin is thus the author of everything evil.

For Paul sin is not only a single deed but also a universal context within which all persons find themselves. Humans are from the very beginning of their lives placed within a condition of collective sinfulness so that they no longer have the freedom to choose whether they do good or evil. An inseparable connection therefore exists between Adam's action and our own condition. But Paul did not develop a doctrine of original sin in which it would be spelt out that sin is passed from one person to the next. He sees all of humanity alienated from God, which makes it impossible for humanity to return to God on its own accord.

Yet there is an escape from this context of sin as shown in the Christ event. Christ has given us the triumph so that death is swallowed up in victory (1 Cor 15:45ff). However, if we cannot escape on our own accord from our alienation from God and therefore from evil which accompanies this alienation, and if Christ does indeed extricate us from that condition, the question of why Christ has left us so long in darkness and evil unavoidably emerges. Here the issue of theodicy seems unavoidable. As Immanuel Kant has recognised, however, when he attempted to solve the issue of theodicy, it is 'basically nothing but a

---

9.   Cf Hans Schwarz, *Evil: A Historical and Theological Perspective*, translated by Mark W Worthing (Minneapolis: Fortress, 1995), 66.

matter of our arrogant reason, thereby ignoring its boundaries'.[10] It would be an attempt to read the mind of God or, to speak with Luther, to bring to light the *deus absconditus*, the hidden God. To determine why God has not relieved us from evil from the beginning or not earlier in the salvational deed of Jesus of Nazareth, would be to second-guess God's actions. Such attempts, however, must always remain hypothetical constructs. But do we get any further when we try to discern what this phenonomen of evil is that in the process of Old Testament reflection was excluded from the perception of God?

3. A non-synthesisable paradox

In the *Life of Adam and Eve* which originated perhaps around the time of Jesus of Nazareth, we read that the devil who had his place in the midst of angels was disobedient to God and even threatened God: 'If he be wrathful with me, I will set my throne above the stars of heaven and will be like the Most High' (Vita 15:3). When he was consequently expelled from heaven and cast down onto the earth, he assailed Adam's wife and made Adam to be expelled through her from the joys of his bliss just as Satan had been expelled from his own glory (Vita 16:3). This picturesque story does not explain the origin of evil, but only pushes it one step further back from Adam and Eve to the devil. At the same time it attests to the irrationality of evil and the cosmic dimension of evil in its destructiveness of God's good creation.[11]

Already much earlier in the imagery of the poetic writings and also of the prophets, Leviathan, a multiheaded largely mythical primal creature, becomes the embodiment of evil who opposes God (Isa 27:1).[12] Rahab seems to play a similarly threatening role (Isa 13:7; but also Isa 51:9). More persistent is the figure of Satan who changes his function from initially being part of God's heavenly court, as in the ancient passage concerning Balaam and his donkey (Num 22:22ff), to the one who seeks to destroy the relationship between God and

---

10.   Immanuel Kant, *Über das Mißlingen aller philosophischen Versuche in der Theodizee*, in *Werke in zehn Bänden*, edited by Wilhelm Weischedel (Darmstadt: Wissenschaftliche Buchgesellschaft, 1968), 9:105.

11.   Cf Johan B Hygen, 7:12f.

12.   Yet according to Psalm 74:13f. Leviathan was killed by the creator of the cosmos or has been abidingly subdued (Ps 104:26f).

humanity, as held by the Judaism of the immediate pre-Christian area.[13]

Moreover, the Old Testament conception of Satan was continued and enlarged during the period of late Judaism. There is a multitude of satans led by Satan whose function it is to accuse human beings before God (1 Enoch 69:6), to attempt to incite humans to evil (1 Enoch 69:6), and to act as angels of judgment (1 Enoch 53:3). In the *Book of Jubilees* we read that these evil spirits 'practice all error and sin and all transgression' and that they 'destroy, cause to perish and pour out blood upon the earth' (Jub 11:5). In Judaism of the pre-Christian era Satan, Beliar, Mastem, or Azazel, as these evil powers were called, were understood to battle against God and to bring his honour into dispute.[14] From beginning to end the New Testament message, too, is characterised by the conflict between good and evil, God and the world, Jesus and Satan. The question now must be addressed whether we can continue such a dualistically sounding worldview in the face of God's salvific action in Jesus Christ.

Karl Barth especially emphasised God's gracious will so strongly that that which strives and works against this will cannot be accorded genuine existence. Ultimately, everything will be received into the salvific scope of God. Barth argues from the grace of God, from God's covenant with humanity. Evil is the opposite of that which God wills. Nevertheless, it becomes the object of God's *opus alienum*, that is, the work that is not proper to him, that of anger and judgment. The negation of the grace of God is

> chaos, the world which He did not choose or will, which He could not and did not create, but which, as He created the actual world, He passed over and set aside, marking and excluding it as the eternal past, the eternal yesterday. And this is evil in the Christian sense, namely what is alien and adverse to grace, and therefore without it.[15]

---

13. So Werner Foerster, 'Diabolos (The Later Jewish View of Satan)', in *TDNT* 2:76.
14. See HH Rowley, *The Relevance of Apocalyptic: A Study of Jewish and Christian Apocalypse from Daniel to Revelation* (New York: Association Press, 1963), 172.
15. Karl Barth, Church Dogmatics III/3 (Edinburgh: T&T Clark, 1957/1964), 353.

Nothingness opposes the grace of God inasmuch as it offends God and threatens his creation and breaks into the creation as sin, evil, and death, and produces chaos.

Barth emphasises that one cannot deal with nothingness in a frivolous manner. It is such a threatening power that the conflict with it, its conquest, removal and settlement, is primarily a matter for God. Nothingness, therefore, is above all God's own problem.[16] Humans are only affected by nothingness insofar as they fall willingly victim to it and thus become sinners. In this way suffering, want and destruction come to humanity. Yet Barth is optimistic in the face of the destructive power of nothingness since the 'kingdom of nothingness' is already destroyed.

> But its dominion, even though it was only a semblance of dominion, is now objectively defeated as such in Jesus Christ. What it still is in the world, it is in virtue of the blindness of our eyes and the cover which is still over us, obscuring the prospect of the kingdom of God already established as the only kingdom undisputed by evil.[17]

When one reads these words one must quite naturally ask to whom this blindness applies. These lines were published just five years after the close of World War II in which the anti-Godly powers, in their destructive and dehumanising way, celebrated one victory after another. Barth can, of course, refer to the gospels in which Jesus comments that Satan has fallen from heaven and has lost his position as our accuser at the right hand of God. Also, Martin Luther wrote in his hymn, 'A mighty fortress is our God' that the 'old evil foe' can be subdued by 'one little word.' But, nevertheless, both the gospel writers and Luther took this nothingness, this propagator of chaos, with utmost seriousness.

Barth, however, wishes to remain a biblical realist. Thus in connection with nothingness he also spoke of demons. In his treatment of demons Barth proceeds in a way similar to his classification of nothingness, for one dare not understand demons as the opposite of

---

16.   *Ibid*, 355.
17.   *Ibid*, 367.

angels.[18] Just as heaven and hell have nothing in common, Barth instructs us that we cannot speak in the same breath of God and the devil, or of angels and demons.

> The demons are the opponents of the heavenly ambassadors of God, as the latter are the champions of the kingdom of heaven and therefore the kingdom of God on earth. Angels and demons are related as creation and chaos, as the free grace of God and nothingness, as good and evil, as life and death, as the light of revelation and the darkness which will not receive it, as redemption and perdition, as kerygma and myth.[19]

Barth does not want to introduce a dualism here, but wishes rather to make clear than one must speak of demons in an entirely different way than of angels. The origin and form of the devil and demons is nothingness, whereby Barth once more makes reference to the left hand of God through which they receive their 'improper' existence.[20] They are ungodly and against God, and because God did not create them they are also not creaturely. They are not other than nothingness, but rather have their origin in nothingness. Because of the death and resurrection of Jesus and his elevation to the right hand of God, nothingness and demons 'have nothing to declare'. Therefore we are able to celebrate with Christ 'our liberation from demons'.[21]

While Barth points to these anti-Godly powers of destruction, for him the battle is already won. For Barth and contrary to John 14:13, the devil is no longer the ruler of this world. Therefore Barth cannot do justice to the phenomena of the negative and perverse within our world. But evil is not an accompanying apparition of the salvific activity of God, so that it could be synthesised with God's activity. It is rather a power that, from our human perspective, leaves open the question of who will prevail in the end. The Judeo-Christian tradition has also always emphasised that evil cannot be God's evil, but is

---

18.   *Ibid*, 519f.
19.   *Ibid*, 520.
20.   *Ibid*, 522f.
21.   *Ibid*, 530.

secondary to God. To prevent our concept of God from being perverted to one of a demonic power, evil has been gradually excluded from God. Yet how do these destructive forces of evil confront us?

If evil were just an impersonal 'it', we would have no choice but to view it as a fate or destiny to which we are helplessly handed over and from which there is no escape. But this view of evil is deficient for at least two reasons: To demonstrate the first reason, it is not even necessary to go to the extreme and point to black masses or satanic cults whose followers, in pseudo-religious devotion, consciously dedicate themselves to the forces of evil. We should simply look at the everyday behaviour of human beings. Humans do not confront evil as an unalterable fate. They continually give themselves and others over to evil with a strange and destructive desire, even though they realise that they should not do so and that in the end they will inflict harm on themselves. Second, some of the characteristics of the phenomenon of aggression, as examined by Konrad Lorenz and others, show that human beings are virtually addicted to evil. As the interest in the occult and New Age reveals, humans yearn after powers that promise them the experience of new wholeness. Humans subject their 'weak wills' willingly and longingly to these powers. Human beings, however, need not remain under the influence of these partly illusory, partly real and destructive powers of evil. The Christian faith testifies to the fact that Jesus liberates human beings to their true selves and gives them genuine freedom and wholeness. Paul says as much when he says that we can become a new creation (Rom 6).

We are not confronted with an impersonal fate or destiny that we experience to be evil, but rather with the influence of a will to which we subordinate our own will and from which we cannot escape through our own strength. We encounter evil as a threatening and overpowering opponent that desires to bring and keep us in its sphere of influence. A personal conception of these various destructive forces as *anti-Godly powers* emphasises their manifoldness while at the same time takes into account their common purpose through which they always oppose the good, namely God. With the term 'anti-Godly powers' we avoid the potential misunderstanding that we are speaking here of Satan or the devil in a way analogous to myths and fairy tales. This would also make it clear that these powers are not to be located within humanity at either the individual or collective level. Rather they find their limit before God. If God, however, is their limit, can they not be included in God's overreaching plan? No, because we can neither attest to their gradual waning nor to their domestication.

Seen from our angle, the progress of history is ambivalent. Any evolutionary or humanistic optimism must keep in mind that infinity is only a mathematical concept, not a physical or biological reality. Even Teilhard, who talked about evil as a by-product of evolution, did not dare to suggest that the noosphere would evolve toward the Christosphere. Evil is not simply a deficiency of the good (*privatio boni*) but also a suppression of good and its opposition. In this way, evil cannot be synthesised with the good. Yet how do we know that we do not end up with an ultimate dualism between good and evil? Here again, our conclusions must be rather modest. We cannot know it by analogy to scientific knowledge. Yet we can know it subjectively on the basis of what we have seen and experienced as members of the Judeo-Christian tradition. In this way, we can join Paul who trusted that 'the creation itself will be set free from its bondage to decay and will obtain the freedom of the glory of the children of God' (Rom 8:21). This is the kind of trust that the Judeo-Christian message elicits, hoping, praying, and in its own actions anticipating that the non-synthesiseable paradox between good and evil will finally be resolved.

2

Disentangled from the Web of Deceit: Sin and Salvation in the Story of Shechem and Dinah (Genesis 34)

Peter Lockwood

1. Introduction

Speaking of the account of Shechem's rape of Dinah and her retrieval by her brothers, Walter Brueggemann has wryly observed: 'This narrative will surely not be widely used in theological exposition.'[1] Indeed, theological questions have rarely been addressed to the story, especially questions of sin and salvation. But is it not worth dusting off the Bible's difficult texts and asking whether God speaks even through them in such a way that readers of today are addressed in matters of ultimate importance, matters affecting their life and their death? With its emphasis on the I-Thou encounter, and speech-act textual theory, the New Hermeneutics has certainly made a significant impact on biblical scholarship. But it still has to be admitted that the general tendency is to keep the text of the Hebrew scriptures at arm's length by regarding it chiefly as an object of literary enquiry or as providing insights into the society of ancient Israel and its religious beliefs and practices.

Genesis 34 is no exception. Earlier expositors read it as little more than a morality play, indicating the 'irregularities' that arise when children are raised in 'a home where bigamy ruled',[2] or expanding on the tragic results which follow when young girls 'form the habit of

---

1. Brueggemann, *Genesis Interpretation* (Atlanta: John Knox Press, 1982), 279.
2. H C Leupold, *Exposition of Genesis*, Vol 2 (Grand Rapids: Baker Book House, 1942), 911-12.

strolling about and looking out of the window' and go places 'without the permission of their parents or without companions'.[3]

In the modern era it became customary to read the text as a geo-political aetiology, giving the reason for the sad fate of the tribes of Simeon and Levi.[4] The story is also read[5] as a cautionary tale warning Israel, on the verge of the return from exile, against assimilating with the peoples of the surrounding nations. In fact, the text goes so far as to demand their extermination, because of the risk of apostasy caused by intermarriage (Deut 7:1-6). Others read the text as a socio-political tract. As a weaker group for most of their history, the ancient Israelites were compelled to offer sexual favours as a regular practice, to 'guarantee smooth relations in a situation of political and economic dependence'.[6] Others read Dinah's rape metaphorically. The violence done to her represents 'Israel's vulnerability to being dominated, taken over and absorbed by the other peoples'.[7]

A tradition-history reading would suggest that the text has been extensively recast in the interests of those with the power to shape ideology in post-exilic Israel. An old idyllic tale of the love of an Israelite girl for a non-Israelite man has been recast in such a way that the outsider is made over into a rapist and an extortionist. Originally Dinah was a fun-loving Israelite woman who established a loving relationship with a Canaanite man. Her liaison, however, threatened the inward-looking and self-protecting chauvinism of post-exilic Israel, so her partner had to be converted into a monster. According to this interpretation, the text has been given its final shape by a xenophobic minority engaged in a desperate and ill-conceived ideological struggle for survival.[8]

Brueggemann's approach has a certain appeal. He also regards Genesis 34 as a socio-political document, presenting in an even-handed manner both sides of an ongoing debate in Israel about the preferred manner of dealing with people of other faiths and cultures. Within the

3. Martin Luther, *Luther's Works,* Vol 6 (St Louis: Concordia Publishing House, 1958), 192.

4. Gerhard von Rad, *Genesis* (London: SCM, 1970), 330.

5. Claus Westermann, *Genesis 12-36* (Philadelphia: Fortress Press, 1976), 537.

6. Julian Pitt-Rivers, *The Fate of Shechem or the Politics of Sex* (Cambridge: Cambridge University Press, 1977), 160.

7. Alice A Keefe, 'Rapes of Women/Wars of Men', *Semeia* 61:79-97 (1993): 84.

8. So Ita Sheres, *Dinah's Rebellion* (New York: Crossroad, 1990), 70-73.

story, Jacob represents the broader and more pragmatic approach of tolerance, assimilation, and cooperation, whereas Jacob's sons represent the religious passion, even fanaticism, of those who are willing to take a stand on matters affecting orthodox worship and practice. By a narrow margin, Brueggemann maintains, the author prefers the approach taken by Jacob and the men of Shechem.[9]

Can texts like Genesis 34 contribute anything towards an enquiry into matters of ultimate concern, matters of theology, in particular the theological matters that lie at the heart of this conference, sin and salvation? Two radically divergent readings of Genesis 34 have moved the history of the text's interpretation several significant steps forward. In the final analysis, however, both readings would appear to be informed by specific ideological perspectives, and matters of sin and salvation, sinners and the saved, are construed in ways that conform with the ideologies of the scholars in question. After describing the two readings of the text, and some slight variations on each, I shall explore the possibility of breaking through the impasse by reading the text theologically within the context of the Jacob cycle at large.

2. External threats to faith and nation

Meir Sternberg has written an extended close textual reading of Genesis 34.[10] He is persuaded that the 'foolproof composition' of any and every biblical text allows unprejudiced readers to make 'tolerable sense of the world (they) are in . . . and the point of it all'.[11] Dinah, together with Levi and Simeon who snatch her from Shechem's house, are the characters most to be admired. On the other hand, nothing can excuse the behaviour of Shechem and Hamor, or Jacob and his other ten sons. The narrator of Genesis 34 has taken on the task of making Shechem's rape of Dinah outweigh in criminality and horror the measures taken by Jacob's sons to redress the situation. Jacob's sons deceive the inhabitants of the city of Shechem, rendering them incapable of defending themselves against Jacob's sons when they embark on a rampage of murder and destruction. Any objective analysis would conclude that the punishment is totally out of proportion to the crime. The rape of one girl, especially given the

---

9.   Brueggemann, *op cit*, 278.

10.   Meir Sternberg, 'Delicate Balance in the Rape of Dinah', *The Poetics of Biblical Narrative* (Bloomington: Indiana University Press, 1987), 445-81.

11.   *Ibid*, 50-51.

sudden turn in affections on the part of the rapist, hardly justifies the assault on the city that follows. In the telling, however, the narrator has amplified the initial crime to such an extent that not only does the punishment fit the crime, but in the final analysis the punishment, properly understood, pales beside the initial crime. The author has told the story in such a way that the initial rape is far worse than the deception, mass murder, and looting and pillage that follow. The task is made harder by spending little time on the rape itself and dwelling on the deeds of the sons of Jacob for an extended period.

After catching sight of Dinah, the text states that Shechem 'took her, laid her and raped her' (verse 2). From the outset he is depicted as lustful and violent, she as a victim of the worst form of sexual violence. But then the reader learns that Shechem's soul cleaved to Dinah, he loved her and he spoke to her tenderly (verse 3). Three verbs of violence are followed immediately by three verbs of tenderness. His sudden affection for Dinah is told in the words of the narrator, not in the words of Shechem. So we have it on the best authority. In the final analysis, however, the latter verbs fall short of counteracting the effect of the first three. The rapist may be a tender rapist, but he remains a rapist.

Then, Shechem is shown speaking to his father: 'Get me this girl to be my wife' (verse 4). His words are a brusque imperative. The word 'get', literally 'take', reminds the reader of the rape. Shechem is a spoilt brat, used to getting his own way. His father is expected to meet whatever demands Shechem makes of him. And the words that Shechem uses for Dinah, 'this girl' (*hayaldah hazot*) indicate that he thinks of her as little more than a plaything, to be used for his enjoyment.

Next, Jacob is introduced. He is described as hearing that Shechem had defiled his daughter (verse 5). This word indicates cultic defilement, defilement before God. It is a defilement that screams to high heaven to be purged and cleansed. The rape is no longer an isolated offence against one person, but a horrendous offence against the elemental depths of the universe.

Even though this is shown to be Jacob's perception of what has transpired, he is silent, he holds his peace. He says nothing and does nothing. After all, Dinah is the daughter of Leah, his non-preferred wife, not the daughter of Rachel, his favourite. The verb 'to be silent' (*charesh*) has no inherently negative connotations. It can imply holding one's peace when words are inappropriate (eg 2 Kgs 18:36; Isa 41:1), or in a different context it can signify a blameworthy silence (eg Pss 28:1; 32:3; 35:22; 39:12; 50:3). That is how it is with Jacob. Surely Jacob should denounce the rapist angrily and demand that he be punished appropriately. Even King David was capable of getting angry when Amnon raped his sister Tamar (2 Sam 13:21). But Jacob fails to react to the news about Dinah. We are not even told that he summons his sons to leave their work and come home. It well may be that he is content to wait until they have finished their day's work. They can take charge of the situation.

But where is Jacob's sense of outrage, his desire for settlement? It is not as if he is too old to feel deeply or too infirm to react to difficult situations. When evidence is brought to him that Joseph is dead, Jacob's son by Rachel, his grief knows no bounds (Gen 37:33-35). On this occasion, however, he fails completely to take parental responsibility for Dinah in the hour of her greatest need. His silence in the face of Dinah's dilemma is a double fault, failure to speak and failure to act. The frantic activity of Hamor, the other father in the story, clamouring to secure the best interests of his self-serving son (verses 6, 8-10), highlights Jacob's callous indifference.

Even when Shechem's father Hamor pays Jacob a special visit to talk matters over with him, Jacob does not care enough to engage him in conversation (verse 6). Jacob is the head of the household, the father of the raped child, the geographical centre of all the comings and goings in the text. His name and his relationship to his children, and by implication his responsibility towards them, are mentioned time and time again. But when the time comes to speak, or act, nothing is forthcoming.

The contrast between Jacob and his sons when they come in from the field could not be greater (verse 7). As soon as they hear what has happened, they are grief-stricken and angry, because Shechem has committed a 'folly' (*nevalah*) in Israel.[12] The crime has defiled Dinah and exposed Shechem as a fool.

Accordingly, the crime's ramifications continue to expand under the narrator's deft hand. The words 'in Israel' can also be translated 'against Israel'. In other words, far more than Dinah has been besmirched. The rape has contaminated the whole land of Israel, and all

---

12.   The fool says there is no God (Ps 14:1; 53:1) and acts accordingly (Deut 22:21; Judg 19:23,24; 20:6; 2 Sam 13:12; Jer 29:23).

its people. Furthermore, the words 'against Israel' can also imply 'against Jacob'. Jacob was renamed Israel after the wrestling match with the spectre of the night at the River Jabbok (32:28). As far as the narrator is concerned, not only the land and all its people have been adversely affected by the rape of Dinah, but so also has Jacob himself. As the paterfamilias, he is the one who bears the brunt of Shechem's assault on his daughter. But Jacob is oblivious to the fact, and his indifference to her plight is compounded accordingly. To blacken Shechem's portrait still more, the authoritative narrator observes that 'by lying with Jacob's daughter' Shechem was doing something that simply 'ought not to be done' (verse 7).

Partners in crime, Hamor and Shechem plead with the Israelites for Dinah's hand in marriage (verses 8-12). As the ruling nobility they can speak for all their people as they provide a range of incentives. This is hard bargaining. The father, Hamor, holds out the prospect of intermarriage between Hivites and Israelites, Israelite access to Hivite land, and Israelite business and trading rights among the indigenous peoples. The offers sound generous in the extreme. The son, Shechem, is impatient to get to the matter of real concern, the hand of Dinah in marriage. He goes so far as to say, 'No matter how large the dowry you require, no matter how expensive the bridal gift,[13] it will be granted' (verse 12).

But again the narrator seeks to colour the reader's assessment of the hard-working father and son team. The Hivite demands are placed strategically before and after the magnanimous concessions and magnificent gifts. Diplomatically, but no less forcefully, Hamor says, 'The heart of my son Shechem longs for (*chashaq*) your daughter; please give her to him in marriage' (verse 8). And Shechem concludes the bargaining process by repeating his request, in strident words, 'Only give me the girl to be my wife' (verse 12). They are interested in nobody's welfare but their own. An easy touch, the father spoils his son recklessly. For his part, the son exploits his father's weak-kneed desire to please. They make a shameless pair.

Jacob's sons now take centre stage. They answer deceitfully, the narrator informs us (verse 13a), with the result that the reader's

---

13. 'Here it seems likely that Shechem is offering both a "marriage present" to Jacob and "a gift" to Dinah.' Gordon J Wenham, *Genesis 16-50* (Dallas: Word, 1994), 313.

sympathy sways towards the Hivites. To counter the resurgence of sympathy, the narrator makes two allusions to the rape with which the story began. The immediate reason given for the brothers' deceptive ploy is that Dinah has been defiled (verse 13b). The reader is reminded of the violence done to Dinah, the dimensions of her suffering, the folly of the perpetrator, its ultimate target, Jacob himself, and the violation of the whole land of Israel and its people. When the brothers say, 'we cannot do (*'asah*) this thing', that is, 'give our sister to one who is uncircumcised' (verse 14), they are making a veiled reference to that which 'ought not to be done' (*'asah*), which means the rape itself (verse 2).

Sternberg says that the narrator continues to place at risk the reader's sympathy for Jacob's sons. Their condition for complying with the request for Dinah's hand in marriage is the circumcision of all the males of the city. The essential mark of Israelite identity and faith (Gen 17:10) has become an instrument of social control. How can this strategem be justified? At once the narrator is seen steering sympathy back in favour of Jacob's sons. If the Hivites refuse to be circumcised, the brothers say, 'then we will take our daughter and be gone' (verse 17). Our hearts start to go out to them once more, on two counts. First, Dinah has virtually become her brothers' daughter. They have in a sense adopted her because of Jacob's abdication of paternal responsibility. Secondly and more significantly, however, suddenly the reader discovers a new piece of information. Rather than returning home after she was raped, it now becomes apparent that Dinah is being held hostage, and the Hivites are practising blackmail. They have no intention of giving her back; it is only a question of whether they will keep her peaceably or forcibly, with consent or without it. Their generosity is fraudulent. All the cards are in their hands—numerical and military superiority, and Dinah as hostage in their home. The negotiations are not being conducted on a level playing field, and the brothers' deceit starts to look increasingly justifiable.

When Hamor and Shechem convey the proposal to their townsfolk (verses 20-23), they pretend that they are motivated by nothing but disinterested concern for the general welfare. In reality they are intent on nothing but deception. Whereas Jacob's sons had stressed circumcision again and again, treating it as the non-negotiable conditon of intermarriage, Hamor and Shechem mention it only in passing. While highlighting the advantages to be gained by their townsfolk—intermarriage, trade—they entirely fail to mention two vital matters. They do not mention their promise that the Israelites could acquire some of their land, and they do not mention their sole objective, their private stake in the arrangement, Dinah's hand in marriage. The narrator does not comment on Hamor and Shechem's practice of deception. But that does not mean that they are not planning to act deceitfully, even more deceitfully than the sons of Jacob. They are not only scheming to hoodwink their own people; they have also targeted the Israelites. 'Will not their livestock, their animals, and all their property, be ours?' (verse 23). Plans are afoot to acquire by force the Israelites' goods and chattels, whether by theft, extortion, or some other kind of thuggery.

Following the tension-laden and protracted negotiations between the Hivites and Israelites (verses 4-24), the story rushes to its close (verses 25-31). Simeon and Levi take their swords (just as Shechem had 'taken' Dinah), make a lightning raid on the unsuspecting city (just as Dinah had been taken unawares), kill all the male defenders of the city, including Hamor and Shechem (essential if two men are to rescue one woman from an armed city), snatch Dinah from Shechem's house, and make their escape (verses 25, 26). As ruthlessly efficient as a crack commando unit specially trained to free passengers from a hijacked airliner, the two men make no preparations in advance and take no precautions that are incidental to their one objective, the liberation of Dinah.

After the departure of Simeon and Levi, the rest of the brothers embark on a senseless orgy of looting and destruction, in city and countryside. Cowards, they come upon the slain, with nobody to resist but women, children and livestock. On a scale of morality, they slide to the same level as Hamor and Shechem, who for their part had been intent on the confiscation of Israelite property and livestock (verse 23). The highly principled actions of Simeon and Levi, which lead to the recapture of Dinah, are followed by the self-serving behaviour of their brothers. One can only conclude that they kill indiscriminately, terrorise children, rape women, and take prisoners and booty. This reverses the way the reader regards the rape and its sequel; the rape with outrage, its sequel with pleasant surprise. Now, admiration for Simeon and Levi gives way to outrage at their brothers.

If Jacob's silence throughout the story is incriminating, now his speech is damning. He singles out Simeon and Levi and reproaches them for damaging his reputation and putting his life in jeopardy (verse 30). The voice of egocentricity and cowardice rings out shrilly.[14] He does not castigate the men for their cruelty. Nor does he thank them for rescuing Dinah. All he can think about is the damage he may suffer at the hands of the locals. And if that is his problem, surely the ten other brothers, who went on a wanton spree of smash and grab, have done far more than Simeon and Levi to tarnish his name and jeopardise his life.

The closing retort of the young men has a menacing ring: 'Should he treat our sister as a harlot?' At first blush they are still speaking to Jacob and they are speaking about Shechem. In raping Dinah he treated her as an object of self-gratification, and in offering a dowry and wedding gift, with no limit to the price, she became a commodity to be bought; in short, a harlot. But the text is ambiguous, allowing for the possibility that the brothers have left Jacob's presence and are speaking about him: 'Should he (that is, Jacob) treat our sister as a harlot?' Jacob is just as much a whore-maker as Shechem, using his daughter as an instrument of social policy, treating her as expendable in the interests of harmonious relations with the native population of Canaan. This reading of Genesis 34 casts Jacob, Hamor and Shechem as the tale's least sympathetic characters, and Dinah, Simeon and Levi as its most sympathetic.[15]

3. The gift of the stranger

Starting from a totally different ideological perspective, Danna Nolan Fewell and David M Gunn have argued[16] that the narrator has portrayed Jacob, Hamor and Shechem as the characters most to be admired. These scholars argue that the key to understanding the chapter is supplied by Jacob's final pronouncement on Simeon and

---

14.   The first person pronoun appears eight times in Jacob's speech to Simeon and Levi. 'You have brought trouble on me by making me odious to the inhabitants of the land, the Canaanites and the Perizzites; my numbers are few, and if they gather themselves against me and attack me, I shall be destroyed, both I and my household.'

15.   Laurence A Turner (*Genesis Readings* [Sheffield:Sheffield Academic Press, 2000]) and Gordon J Wenham (*op cit*) have followed Sternberg in their interpretations of Genesis 34.

16.   Dana Nolan Fewell and David M Gunn, 'Tipping the Balance: Sternberg's Reader and the Rape of Dinah', *JBL* 110/2 (1991), 193-211.

Levi, in which he consigns their tribes to a troubled existence because of their violent anger (Gen 49:5-7).

Fewell and Gunn claim that the text is finally interested in the harmonious cohabitation of Israelites and Canaanites, implying inter-marriage and mutually beneficial trade and commerce arrangements. The villains of the piece are the sons of Jacob, fanatical in their determination to keep the Canaanites at arm's length. Like religious fundamentalists they want to avoid mingling with and marriage to outsiders at all costs because of the threat posed to racial purity and religious integrity.[17] The violence done to the Hivites is a further instance of Israel's failure to serve as a channel of God's blessing to 'all the families of the earth' (Gen 12:3b; see also 12:17; 20:9,18).

With this in mind the chapter is read in a different way altogether. Shechem's violence towards Dinah is completely outweighed by the affection and tender care that he subsequently lavishes on her. Shechem's 'soul clung to Dinah' (verse 3), suggesting that he loved her as much as the ideal husband loves his wife (Gen 2:24). 'He loved the girl, and he spoke to her heart' (verse 3), presupposing deep affection (Gen 50:21; Judg 19:3; 2 Sam 19:7; Isa 40:2).

Fewell and Gunn suggest that it is quite reasonable to suppose that Dinah has actually fallen in love with the popular young Canaanite prince. Unwanted as Leah's daughter in Jacob's family, Dinah may well have found kindred spirits and a welcoming home among her happy-go-lucky neighbours. The text does not say that she is being held hostage (contra Sternberg). Far from demanding a ransom payment in return for her release, the Hivites offer to pay as much as the Israelites demand for her hand in marriage, no matter how much it may exceed the stipulations of the law. According to Exodus 22:16-17 a rapist was required to marry his victim after paying a dowry set by the father (limited to 50 shekels at Deuteronomy 22:29), and he was forbidden from divorcing her. Shechem is willing to go far beyond outward compliance with the letter of the law. He has embraced the spirit of the law with gusto. His generosity knows no bounds; his love is exemplary.

---

17. According to Terence Fretheim: 'Perhaps most important, the sharp and unambiguous judgment (indeed, a curse!) by Jacob on the violence of Simeon and Levi must stand as the primary clue about how we should interpret this chapter.' *The New Interpreter's Bible*, Vol 1 (Abingdon Press, 1994), 577.

Jacob earned Sternberg's rebuke for his silence in the face of Leah's rape. But is it not possible that his initial response is a mark of his profound distress at Dinah's plight, not his indifference?[18] Then he remains silent until his sons come in from the fields because he wants to enter into serious negotiations with his neighbours. He does not want to act unilaterally. Before making a hasty decision, he wants his sons to gather and all parties to sit down around the table. They need to talk about what has happened. The Israelites need to weigh the Shechemite proposal calmly and carefully.

Hamor and Shechem work as a team, united in their desire for cooperation and cohabitation with the Israelites. While Jacob, Hamor and Shechem are bent on cooperation and cohabitation, and the omniscient author at no stage says anything negative about them, the author does observe that Jacob's sons act deceitfully (verse 13). They are willing to employ circumcision, symbol of conversion, belonging, and commitment to the faith of Israel, to cripple the enemy and render them defenceless in the face of attack. Canaanite goodwill is met by Israelite duplicity. And given that the reader cannot rule out the possibility that the Hivites have converted to the faith and practices of Israel, Israel's offence screams to high heaven.

Nor can it be said that Dinah's brothers appear to be particularly concerned about her welfare. Instead of speaking about the violence of rape and the injury to Dinah, they speak about the folly of a non-Israelite lying with Jacob's daughter. Such a thing was simply not done (verse 7). If they were to consent to marriage, they would be the ones who suffered disgrace as a result of their sister's union with an uncircumcised man (verse 14). And when the city is attacked and its defenders killed, including Shechem and Hamor, Dinah's wishes are not consulted. Her new companions are mowed down in cold blood, without any attempt on the part of her brothers to find out whether she is being held against her will or is perfectly happy in her new surroundings.

The impetuous and bloody attack on the city is a further incident in Israel's sorry history of failure to bring the blessing of God to their neighbours. The villains in the piece are Jacob's sons. After a life spent

---

18.   Luther asks: 'Why, then, does God permit the holy patriarch to be burdened with
this cross just as if he were not a saint, acceptable and welcome in God's sight? It
was done for our sake, that we may learn patience and consolation in adversity
and may stop our mouth if similar calamities befall us too.' *Luther's Works*, *op
cit*, vol 6, 192.

looking after number one, Jacob finally understands. His last words in the chapter are a plaintive plea, expressing frustration that Israel consistently fails to come alongside their neighbours, overcome barriers of race and religion, gain a good name, and as a result build a protective barrier against the threat of external aggression.

The insolence of the final throwaway line spoken by Simeon and Levi should not be overlooked, according to this reading. If the twosome are accusing both Shechem and Jacob of prostituting Dinah for personal gain, they have missed the mark by a long shot. The Shechemites and Jacob have readily agreed that Shechem should not have raped Dinah. But they also know that the situation has changed radically since the initial assault. A deep affection has developed. Previously unloved, Dinah has now found hearth, and home, and husband.

4. A theological reading

Three observations lie behind the proposal that follows. First, the stage movement of Simeon and Levi gives a telling indication of their status within the story. Starting off-stage and voiceless, they are given the last word.[19] It is highly likely that their voice, condemning Shechem and Jacob, corresponds to the authoritative voice of the author.

Secondly, despite Jacob's twenty years in Haran, the leopard has not changed his spots. Commentators who regard Jacob as a character to be admired for his supposed spirit of cooperation and admirable desire for cohabitation with the Canaanites fail to see that he has not improved one iota. Even his prayers proceed from distrust (28:20-22) or abject fear (32:9-12; see 32:7,20). Despite God's firm promises to care for him and bring him safely home again, Jacob does not believe God can be trusted. Jacob's whole life is testimony to the belief that it is up to him to make things happen. Trickery and theft are always valid options. It is said that in contrast to his complicity in the theft of the birthright and blessing, he plays no part in Rachel's theft of Laban's *terafim*. Rachel knows he is a changed man and therefore she does not engage his services. In fact, the author depicts Jacob as more of a 'taker' during and after his Haran period than he was before. Not only is he accused of taking everything that belongs to Laban (31:2), but also of

---

19.   Sternberg has drawn attention to this feature of the text (*op cit*, 473).

'stealing the heart of' (deceiving) Laban (31:26). Furthermore, the favouritism which Jacob displays towards Rachel's sons is scandalous. Dinah is Leah's daughter and hence regarded as expendable. But some time later, when Jacob is led to believe that Joseph is dead, his grief knows no bounds (37:34,35). It is of no small interest that in the only significant reference outside of Genesis, the prophet Hosea speaks of Jacob's rebelliousness extending from the womb to adulthood (Hos 12:2-4).

Thirdly, by looking at the verbal and thematic connections between the story of Dinah and the stories among which it is embedded, it seems probable that Shechem is portrayed as Jacob's double, as Jacob's other twin. The similarities between the portraits of the two men are remakable.

First and foremost, both are notorious 'takers'. The verb 'to take' hover about both like a moth around a candle. The word is used constantly when Rebekah and Jacob conspire to steal the blessing (27:7,9,10,13,14,15). After Isaac discovers that he has been hoodwinked, he tells Esau:

> Your brother came deceitfully, and he has *taken* away your blessing.' Esau said, 'Is he not rightly named Jacob? For he has supplanted me these two times. He *took* away my birthright; and look, now he has *taken* away my blessing (Gen 27:35,36, NRSV).

As a man who spends so much of his time expropriating what belongs to others, Jacob imagines that others must be tarred with the same brush. When Laban and Esau, each of whom he has dispossessed of priceless possessions, in turn finally catch up with him, his automatic reflex is to appease them by offering them rich takings from his own vast store of goods (31:32; 33:10,11). In this way he reveals the neurotic belief that others share his own bad habits.

Shechem is likewise, at heart, one who takes. He sees Dinah and immediately takes her (34:2). Soon afterwards he commands his father Hamor: 'Get (literally: take) me this girl to be my wife' (34:4). Hamor and Shechem are involved in delicate negotiations with hostile brothers. They want permission for Dinah's hand in marriage. So they make a grand display of largesse, giving the Israelites permission to take and take and take. The father and son team instinctively believe that the way to propitiate the Israelites is by a generous, but totally deceptive, offering of 'takings'—land, property, business oppor-tunities, daughters as marriage partners (34:9,10). Like Jacob, Shechem believes that people can be bought if the money is right. Jacob and Shechem are look-alikes; each believes it is more blessed to receive than to give, and neither credits other people with the ability to live by any higher ideal.

Secondly, both Jacob and Shechem become heavily involved in a bargaining process, bartering desperately for the object of their desire. Each seeks 'favour in the eyes of' his adversary (32:6,20; 33:10,12,15; cf 34:11). And each is willing to pay inordinately huge sums in order to achieve his goal. Jacob offers Esau an excessively large gift of livestock in the hope of securing favour in his eyes (32:14-16). Shechem goes one step further by declining even to set a limit to the dowry he is willing to pay and the bridal gift he is willing to give, in order to secure the favour of Jacob and his sons (34:11,12).

Thirdly, both believe that their lives are at risk at the hand of their adversaries. They are therefore motivated by fear of reprisal rather than a sense of guilt and remorse for what they have done. Jacob fears for his life because he has stolen Esau's birthright and blessing. Shechem fears for his life because he has raped and abducted Dinah. The two men are linked by their willingness to throw caution to the wind in their desperation to achieve their cherished ambitions and escape the consequences of their actions.

Fourthly, Jacob and Shechem are deceivers. They deceive others and are deceived in return. Jacob deceives Isaac and Esau and Laban. And though Laban tries on several occasions to turn the tables on Jacob (29:21-27; 30:35,36), they are poor attempts, and Jacob ends up way ahead at the end of his stay in Haran (30:43; 31:1,18).

For his part, Shechem tries to deceive Jacob and his sons into thinking that they will receive tremendous social and economic advantages in return for letting him marry Dinah, whereas in fact he plans to deprive the Israelites of their property and possessions. 'Will not their livestock, their property, and all their animals be ours?' (34:23) he asks his fellow Shechemites. He also deceives his fellow townsmen by pretending that he is only interested in the advantages which will accrue to them from cohabitation with the Israelites, while saying nothing about his own investment in the matter—his proposed marriage to Dinah. He further deceives his own people by wildly exaggerating the advantages they will derive from the liaison with

Israel, and by making the condition set by the Israelites—circumcision—appear to involve nothing but a momentary inconvenience (34:21-23).

While busily deceiving Jacob and his sons, Shechem is himself being deceived (verse 13). Jacob's sons make circumcision for all men of the city of Shechem the condition for Shechem's marriage to Dinah (34:13,15). But they have not the slightest intention of honouring their word; rather, they choose the precise moment when the men are most seriously affected by the surgery to attack the city and retrieve Dinah (34:25).

Fifthly, each story reaches the stage where the protagonist's situation can be described as 'safe'. After overcoming the threat to his life that Esau poses, Jacob is said to have arrived at the city of Shechem 'safely' (*shalem*, 33:18). Presumably breathing a huge sigh of relief after his perilous encounter with Jacob and his sons, Shechem reports back to his kinsmen that 'these men are friendly (*shelemim*) with us' (34:21). Maybe a better translation would be, 'these men are quite safe'.

Better Hebrew words are available for 'safely' and 'friendly', but *shalem* and *shelemim* are derived from the same root, and the author has chosen the words deliberately, in order to provide another link between the Jacob cycle and the Shechem episode. The first is used precisely at that moment when Jacob believes that the last danger to life and limb has been overcome. The second is used when Shechem believes, in his case erroneously, that he too can be assured of staying alive and obtaining his heart's desire.

Sixthly, only of Jacob and Shechem is it said in Genesis that they contemplate a deed (in the case of Jacob) or actually perform a deed (in the case of Shechem) that is simply 'not done' (29:26; 34:7). And seventhly, they are the only two in the entire book of Genesis who are accused of acting foolishly (31:28; 34:7).

Like a Shakespearean sub-plot, the story of Shechem is a scaled-down version of Jacob's story. Linkage is provided by their conduct and an array of verbal associations. Jacob and Esau may have been fraternal twins, but they bear no resemblance to one another in terms of appearance or lifestyle (25:25-27). On the other hand, the author makes Jacob and Shechem bear an uncanny resemblance to one another in terms of their worldview and their behaviour. But at a highly telling moment, Shechem's life's journey takes a totally different turn from Jacob's. Whereas Jacob receives confirmation of the blessing, is rescued from death, and is given the name of Israel (32:28-30),

Shechem dies at the hands of his avengers, and his community is devastated. Those who take Shechem's life are motivated by indignation (*'atsav*, hithpa'el, to be grieved, or distressed), and anger (*charah*, to become heated, or angry, verse 7). These are precisely the emotions which are aroused within the Lord God as a prelude to judgment (Gen 6:6,7; 18:30,32). Through Simeon and Levi the Lord stretches out his punitive hand against Shechem. His death represents a massive departure from the otherwise parallel lives of Jacob and Shechem.

After Jacob's sons have completed their reprisal raids against Shechem and rescued Dinah, the previously silent patriarch finally speaks, delivering a stinging attack on Simeon and Levi (34:30). But why should Jacob take this pair to task? Their attack on the city had been clean and direct. Temporarily crippling the men of the city by circumcision and then killing every last one of them were necessary measures if the two men were to achieve their one goal of rescuing their sister, held captive in a secure house within a fortified city. Measures that were any less drastic would have failed to achieve the desired result. They did what simply had to be done under the circumstances. Surely if anyone deserved a tongue-lashing it was the other brothers, who went on a wild orgy of pillage and plunder in city and countryside, after Dinah had already been rescued (verses 27-29). Surely their senseless acts of destruction were far more likely to cause the wrath of the Canaanites to descend on Israel's head.

So why does Jacob round on this pair? Is it a simple case of singling out the ring-leaders? Or are Jacob's harsh words symptomatic of a guilty conscience? Simeon and Levi have done what Jacob as head of the household had so patently failed to do. Their successful rescue mission has exposed his blatant dereliction of duty as Dinah's father, to protect her and care for her, and do everything in his power to rescue her from her abductors.

But that only goes part of the way towards explaining Jacob's reaction. Quite simply, Jacob attacks Simeon and Levi so vehemently because he recognises himself in Shechem, the man who falls victim to Simeon and Levi. Shechem is virtually Jacob's other twin. To put it bluntly, Jacob is paired with a rapist and a standover man. Names, dates, places, and incidents may have been changed, but in reality it is Jacob's own life's story that is being played out before his eyess. At least subconsciously he knows it. Therefore it is perfectly credible, from a psychological perspective, that he should not remonstrate with his sons en masse, but single out precisely those two who had killed Shechem. It is as if he felt in his own body the sword thrusts which Shechem received.

The eighth and final parallel between Jacob and Shechem is given in Simeon and Levi's words after they have been taken to task by their father: 'They said, "Should he treat our sister like a whore?"' (verse 31). Who has treated their sister like a whore? And to whom are they speaking? At first glance the words are a reply in defence, spoken to Jacob. Shechem has treated Dinah as a mere object of gratification by raping and abducting her, and then as a commodity to be bought with expensive gifts. But the text is deliberately ambiguous. The reader is not told to whom the brothers are speaking. It is also to be understood that they have left their father's presence and are now talking to one another about him. Surely Jacob is equally guilty of treating Dinah as a whore. He has been totally indifferent to her plight. He regards her as expendable in the interests of harmonious and mutually beneficial living arrangements among the Canaanites. 'Should he treat our sister like a whore?' Simeon and Levi ask. Let the reader understand that they have two whoremakers in mind, Shechem and Jacob. The two men are of the same ilk. The parallel lives diverged at one point and one point only. At the end of the chapter they are firmly and intimately linked together once again.

Jacob has been a spectator throughout the major part of the story, unsuspectingly watching his own life unfold in the events in which is alter ego is involved. The major and decisive difference between Jacob and Shechem is that Jacob is the blessing-bearer, whereas Shechem is not. Their moral conduct is on a par. Yet the emissaries of God—Simeon and Levi—carry out the death sentence against Shechem. The lesson which Jacob is meant to derive from the graphic object lesson which is played out before his eyes is that it is he who deserves Shechem's fate. But he fails to learn it. No prophet like Nathan appears before him to announce: 'You are the man' (2 Sam 12:7). Rather, like the adjudicator of a debate, who has missed the plot, Jacob himself takes the podium at the close of the story and delivers his verdict, for Shechem and against Simeon and Levi.

Jacob consistently fails to appreciate that the blessing is an unconditional gift of grace, with the result that he wastes it, grasping presumptuously for that which God has promised to give him freely. Rather than confessing his wrongdoings in the light of Shechem's graphic object lesson, Jacob denies the truth by turning against Simeon and Levi, whose killing of Shechem represents the punitive hand of God stretched out against Jacob himself. He has missed the point entirely, and the reader of the story alone learns that the punishment Jacob deserves for a life of rebellion is shown in all its force and fury falling upon Shechem. In other words, Genesis 34 plays a vital theological role within the Jacob cycle. In telling the story of Shechem's abhorrent conduct and ignominious end, it clearly shows how Jacob's story could have ended and should have ended, if Jacob had not been the privileged bearer of the divine blessing. The chapter acts as a black back-drop, throwing into stark relief the magnanimity with which God has dealt with Jacob and his seed. The reader is left to marvel at the brilliance of divine grace which blesses even in the face of such abject blindness.

5. Conclusions

Biblical interpreters constantly face the temptation to regard their reading of the text as the last word that needs to be spoken, rather than a small contribution to a constantly growing reservoir of readings. This self-confidence is reflected in Sternberg's contention that discerning readers need only follow the clues provided by the author and they will inevitably discover the meaning in the text.[20] Despite the delicate balance in the evaluation of characters in Genesis 34, Sternberg contends, in the final analysis Simeon and Levi's clinical rescue mission, made possible by the destruction of Israel's heathen neighbours, is clearly accorded the most positive appraisal. Shechem's uncontrollable sexual appetite and his deceptive words, almost disguised beneath his smooth exterior, prove beyond doubt that he and his people pose a radical threat to Israel's faith and national identity. From this perspective, Israel sins when it turns a blind eye to religious pluralism and syncretism. Such religious indifference inevitably leads to moral laxity, and thence to unconcern for the victim of abuse and violence. Salvation is then possible only when people are willing to perform the radical surgery that is necessary to remove the cancerous growths that erode the religious faith and moral fibre of the nation.

---

20. See also ED Hirsch, *Validity in Interpretation* (New Haven: Yale University Press, 1967).

Discerning readers themselves, Fewell and Gunn, irritated by Sternberg's confident pronouncements regarding the thrust of the text, pick up on a totally different set of clues and so read the text in a way that is diametrically opposed to Sternberg's reading. Surely strangers have the potential to become friends. At first glance they may appear threatening, but on closer acquaintance they show their true colours. To judge by Hamor and Shechem, strangers are genuinely concerned about neighbourly cooperation and cohabitation. Friends of multi-culturalism, they invite nations like Israel to discard the cloaks of xenophobia and religious intolerance, their besetting sins, and truly become the blessing to the nations that God desires. Salvation will arrive when all racial and religious barriers have been dismantled, and all people live together happily in an atmosphere of trust and good-will.

What lies behind our interpretations of texts? We know from the discipline of biblical hermeneutics how much our ideological presuppositions inform our readings. But it is invariably far easier to work out what makes the other person tick than what makes ourselves tick. In keeping with that opinion it well may be that Fretheim's assessment is to some extent informed by events in today's Israel.

The deep suffering that Dinah had to undergo could have served as a vehicle for a greater good, but the violent response deepens her suffering. Israel loses the opportunity to bring good out of suffering, and Dinah becomes even more of a victim. The temptation for the oppressed to become oppressors themselves offers an all too prevalent possibility, a turning-the-tables kind of mentality that places them precisely in the position of those who perpetrated the violence in the first place.[21]

This paper has suggested that Shechem has been depicted as Jacob's alter ego, his second twin. The death Shechem dies is the death Jacob deserves. The sin of Jacob and the sin of Shechem is the sin of everybody. However sin is understood, and presumably a range of understandings will emerge, Jesus was clear that it proceeds from the human heart (Matt 15:19), and Paul argued that no-one was exculpated by virtue of their good deeds (Rom 3:9-20), and that sin's wages was death (Rom 6:23). But God presented Jesus the Christ 'as a sacrifice of atonement by his blood' (Rom 3:25), and in him God has given all people the free and unmerited gifts of forgiveness and righteousness

---

21.   Fretheim, *op cit*, 580.

and life (Rom 5:12-19). Informed by such New Testament thinking, Genesis 34 may be read typologically, so that Jacob, the chosen child of God, receives God's favour without deserving, as a gift of pure grace. It is not possible to regard Shechem's death as a vicarious death, but something of the cost to God of human redemption is perhaps faintly prefigured.

In dispensing grace, God is scandalously prodigal. Grace should add up; it should be reserved for the deserving, not the Jacobs of the world. Failing to trust the giver, Jacob selfishly grasps for the gifts God has unconditionally promised. Lest it be said, however, that arguing for an unreformed patriarch who retains the blessing provides a persuasive argument for cheap grace, to use Bonhoeffer's term somewhat anachronistically, the cost to Jacob of his life of mistrust and deceit ought to be noted. After deceiving Isaac and Esau, he is forced to leave home. Never again does he set eyes on his mother Rebekah who loved him so dearly. He spends his life on the run, in constant fear of reprisals. His life of deceiving and being deceived leads to fear, suspicion, and profound dislocation. He is obliged to suffer from the constant anxiety caused by failing to appreciate that what God has promised will come to fruition. He experiences emotional turmoil and physical disabling on the way to his final reckoning with Esau. In the course of the Joseph cycle he is filled with anxiety, imagining that he has been bereaved of one son after the other. And he has an unruly household until the day of his death.

It may be, contrary to Brueggemann, that Genesis 34 indeed has the potential for wider 'theological exposition'. It could well be that every biblical narrative resonates with profound theological significance. Socio-political, rhetorical, and psychological readings of texts make an invaluable contribution and should never be discounted. But arguably we miss the full value of what is on offer if we fail to make further enquiry into what the text has to say about God's dealings with humanity in grace and judgment, and humanity's response in praise and service.[22]

---

22. The various interpretations given to the remarkable welcome Jacob receives from Esau upon Jacob's return from Haran bears out the point well. After threatening to kill his cheating brother next time he set eyes on him (27:41), Esau instead runs to meet him, embraces him, falls on his neck and kisses him, and the brothers weep (33:4). This is totally unexpected, especially since Esau has come out to

meet Jacob with four hundred armed men, clearly indicating hostile intent (32:6; 33:1). Some (eg Hermann Gunkel, *Genesis, übersetzt und erklärt* [Vandenhoeck und ruprecht, 1902]; John Skinner, *A Critical and Exegetical Commentary on Genesis* [Edinburgh: T&T Clark, 1912], 412) say that Esau, the good-natured nincompoop, lets himself be dazzled by Jacob's splendid gifts (32:13-15) and gracious words (33:10-11). Others (eg W Günter Plaut, *The Torah: A Modern Commentary* [New York: Union of American Hebrew Congregations, 1981], 325; Bruce Vawter, *On Genesis: A New Reading* [Garden City, New York: Doubleday, 1977]. 351) ascribe the sudden turnabout to Jacob's remorse. How could Esau not forgive his brother whom he sees approaching with a limp, bowing submissively seven times as he approaches, and clearly repentant? (32:31; 33:3) A gracious Esau is willing to let bygones be bygones. Another opinion (eg Westermann, *op cit*) is that Esau's basic good nature, his substantial material assets, and the long passage of time since he was deprived of the blessing, have allowed brotherly affection to replace his plans for revenge. But Luther (*Luther's Works,* Volume 6, *op cit,*157-58) and Calvin (*Commentaries on Genesis,* 207) stand alone in reading the text theologically. They insist that Esau changes for no other reason than that Jacob's prayer to be delivered from the hand of Esau (32:9-12) has brought into effect the transforming power of God. For a brief moment God has softened Esau's hard heart and made him compassionate and forgiving, just as wild animals are able to be tamed.

3

Paul's Adam Myth Revisited

Brendan Byrne SJ

At a significant point in his letter to the Romans, Paul suddenly and without explanation refers to 'one man' through whom a legacy of sin and death have come to the entire human race (Rom 5:12). Very soon he goes on to compare and contrast this with a legacy that another 'one man', Jesus Christ, has brought: a legacy of righteousness leading to life. Soon it becomes clear that the earlier 'one man' he is referring to is Adam, the ancestor of the entire human race according to the biblical record. In an earlier letter, 1 Corinthians, Paul had made a similar passing reference to Adam in the context of the resurrection: 'as in Adam all die, so in Christ shall all be made alive' (15:22; also v 45). The reference to Adam in the letter to Corinth is more understandable, since here at least Paul was writing to a community he had himself evangelised, where he could build on his own earlier instruction. The community in Rome, however, was not one he had founded or visited before. In their case, he could only appeal to what he believed to be commonly shared Christian belief. This suggests that Paul, at least, thought that the view of Adam he was presupposing belonged to the common patrimony of the early Jesus movement.

We do not know whether the allusion to Adam helped the Christian community in Rome to better appreciate Paul's presentation of the gospel. We certainly do know that in the shape of the doctrine of 'original sin' it was destined to make a very significant impact on subsequent Christian theology, especially in the Western tradition dominated by Augustine. It is also no secret that in its classic form the doctrine presents almost insuperable problems in the contemporary theological climate. Let me simply list what I see to be some of the most obvious.

1. The sense of an inherited legacy not only of physical limitation but of actual guilt and alienation stemming from a single ancestral figure is obnoxious to justice and a sense of individual responsibility.

2. The *theo*logical implication is equally repulsive, suggesting, as it does, that every human life begins under the 'frown' or displeasure of God.

3. The presupposition of universal human descent from a single ancestor is obnoxious to the scientific explanation of evolution or at least is vulnerable to being undermined whenever, in the course of scientific investigation and discovery, such a single origin comes into question. In any case, it seems incredible to load the first animal to arrive at what might be termed full human consciousness—whoever she or he may have been—with such responsibility.[1]

4. Highly problematic is Paul's association of (physical) death with the onset of sin. That humans die seems simply to be part of the physical makeup they share with all other living creatures. It is simply a phenomenon of existence. Why view it as a punishment—as if, had things gone otherwise at some very early stage, humans would not have died? Something which long since would have rendered our planet more crowded than it is!

5. The doctrine rests upon an interpretation of Genesis 2–3 that is insensitive to literary form and general context. It interprets the account literally and historically, as a story about 'back there', when everything suggests that it is an aetiological myth with primary reference to present and continuing human experience.

At the same time, standing as we do on the threshold of a new century and necessarily reflecting upon the one from which we have just emerged, we are acutely conscious, as never before, of the capacity of our species for evil. There is no need to rehearse the evidence for that provided by the century just past. As one recent theologian, Gabriel Daly, has said in respect to original sin,

> nothing could be clearer than our need of a doctrine
> which realistically recognises the dark side of our
> human nature with its appalling history of violence,
> injustice, cruelty, oppression, and misuse of power,
> together with the proclivity to wrong-doing which

---

1.   For an attempt to reconcile the theological doctrine with evolution see JD
      Korsmeyer, *Evolution and Eden: Balancing Original Sin and Contemporary
      Science* (New York/Mahwah, NJ: Paulist, 1998).

any human being looking into himself or herself can
so quickly discern.[2]

As an exegete primarily rather than a theologian, it is certainly not
my aim to attempt here a reformulation or rehabilitation of the
doctrine of original sin. What I propose to do is to re-examine the
Pauline texts which lie behind the doctrine and which seem to bear
essentially upon the theme of sin and salvation. Granted the historical
centrality of Paul in the Christian tradition, I would hope that,
appropriately interpreted, his writings might still have something to
contribute.

My procedure will be:

1. To survey Paul's introduction and use of the Adamic myth in his
letter to Rome. This will involve moving beyond the explicit allusions
to Adam in Romans 5:12-21 to the more positive Adamic *christology*
implicit in the hope for salvation—in regard to both human beings and
the rest of creation—asserted in Romans 8.

2. To evaluate the Adamic myth in its Pauline form and see what
elements of it may remain useful and indeed necessary in a
contemporary theology regarding sin and salvation.

My hope would be to show that the Pauline Adamic myth, shorn of
elements no longer tenable, retains its theological relevance not only
because of its sense of solidarity in human sinfulness beyond
individual acts of sinning but also because of its essential reference of
human action, for ill and for good, to the future of the wider non-
human world. In this sense, I maintain, it has something significant to
contribute to a contemporary understanding of salvation.

1. The Pauline Adamic myth

Along with virtually all recent interpreters, I am persuaded that it was
in no sense Paul's intention to provide in Romans 5:12-21 a theological
instruction upon the onset of sin and death to the human race. Paul's
concentration is upon the positive—upon the onset of righteousness
that comes with Christ and the sure hope of life thereby entailed. In
this part of Romans (Rom 5-8) Paul presents the case for hope in the

---

2. Gabriel Daly, 'II: Original Sin' in *Commentary on the Catechism of the Catholic
    Church*, edited by MJ Walsh (Collegeville, Minn.: Liturgical Press, 1994), 97-
    109, see 98.

face of the stark reality confronting the communities who believed that
Jesus was the Messiah of Israel and indeed the saviour of the world.
Despite what they believed about Jesus—in particular that he had been
raised from the dead—the times did not look particularly 'messianic'.
Same old world: same realities of violence, suffering and death still
around. Somehow or other the much-heralded transition from the old
era to the new seemed to have run aground. Was there any basis for
believing—hoping—that the new age had already dawned, that the
final conquest of sin and death was still in sight?[3]

In the particular passage under consideration Paul deploys one of
his favorite forms of argument: *a maiore ad minus*. He points to what
God has already done in the much harder negative case as an
indication of how certain it is that God will finish the job successfully
in the much easier positive case that now obtains. In other words, Paul
introduces the tradition about Adam as the instigator of a legacy and
sin in the human race,[4] as a foil over against which to assert the much
more powerful legacy of Christ, who as instrument of God's grace
brings a legacy of righteousness leading to eternal life. The recourse to
Adam is there, not for its own sake, but primarily to say something
about Christ.

The problem is that, entering at 5:12 upon what was intended to be
a sustained series of contrasts between Adam and Christ, Paul
formulated, in a long complex sentence, the negative, 'Adam' side of
the equation and then broke off without adding a complementary
positive statement about Christ. That is, Paul wrote: 'Therefore, as sin
entered the world through one man and through sin death, and so
death passed to all on this basis, namely, that all sinned—' (v 12),[5] and
then turned aside to deal—in what today would be expressed as a
footnote (vv 13-14)—with a particular though obscure problem
concerning the presence of sin in the absence of law. Only at v 15,
though not in strict form until v 18, does the full, balanced formulation
appear. While in the end it becomes clear that the primary intent is to

---

3.   On the distinctive eschatology addressed in Romans 5–8—the 'overlap' between
      the old era and the new—see JDG Dunn, *The Theology of Paul the Apostle*
      (Grand Rapids, Mich; Cambridge, UK: Eerdmans, 1998) 464; B Byrne, *Romans*
      (Sacra Pagina 6; Collegeville, Minn: Liturgical Press, 1996), 162-64.

4.   Paul—or the early Christian tradition which he is presupposing—seems to have
      inherited the 'Adam' myth (the idea that death is a legacy from the first father of
      the human race) from the Jewish matrix; on this, see Byrne, *Romans*, 174-75.

5.   For this translation, see Byrne, *Romans*, 162-64.

say something about Christ, the anacolouthon at the end of v 12 conveys the sense of a concern to explain the onset of sin and death—something that was destined to mesmerise the Christian theological tradition, at least in the West.

Of course, attempts have been made to read Romans 5:12-21, especially Romans 5:12, in a way that plays down the 'legacy from Adam' aspect. It has been suggested, for instance, that Paul is actually overthrowing or challenging an 'Adam' myth inherited from his Jewish matrix[6] and correcting it in the interests of stressing individual responsibility.[7] In the latter case Paul would simply be pointing to the factual universality of all human sinning but not to a kind of transcendent solidarity in sin. While I think there is an element of tension in Paul's argument between a legacy and individual responsibility, to eliminate all sense of the former—all influence of Adam for ill upon all—completely undercuts the argument as a whole, which is driving at asserting the universally beneficent effect of God's grace in Christ. It makes Paul's appeal to Adam so useless and so counterproductive that any reason for introducing it falls away.[8] Adam was important for Paul—important for what he wanted to say about Christ.

While the complete Augustinian doctrine of 'original sin'—especially the sense of a guilt or sinfulness transmitted through the act of procreation— is hardly to be found in Paul, and while Augustine, as he later owned, was initially misinformed about the Greek text underlying his Latin translation of 5:12d, his fundamental insight into the passage was, I believe, correct.[9] Paul appears to have

---

6.   So Egon Brandenburger, *Adam und Christus: Exegetisch-religionsgeschichtliche Untersuchungen zu Röm 5:12-21 (1 Kor 15)* (WMANT 7; Neukirchen: Neukirchener Verlag, 1962).

7.   Brandenburger, *Adam und Christus,* 70-74, 175-80; see also U Wilckens, *Der Brief an die Römer (Röm 1-5)* (EKKNT VI/I: Köln/Neukirchen-Vluyn: Benziger/Neukirchener Verlag, 1978), 316.

8.   I have critiqued this tendency at length in B Byrne, '"The Type of the One to Come" (Rom 5:14): Fate and Responsibility in Romans 5:12-21', *Australian Biblical Review* 36 (1988): 19-30.

9.   Even if Augustine was wrong in detail about 5:12d, the subsequent negative clause in 5:19a 'As through one man's disobedience, many were made sinners . . . ', confirms the main lines of his understanding: namely, that through his disobedience Adam bequeathed to all his descendants an 'original' relational alienation from God.

believed that God's gracious act of intervention into human affairs in Christ addressed the human situation transcendentally—that is, it did not simply address the sum total of factual human sinning, no matter how universal that factuality be conceived. It addressed a more fundamental human alienation from God, an alienation that is 'there' prior to every human life and its history of sin and/or virtue.

In this connection it is important to note that, while Paul may have interpreted the Genesis story in a literal way, he did not do so fundamentalistically. What I mean is that I am sure that, if you asked Paul, 'Did Adam really exist?', he would have replied, 'Of course!' So, yes, Paul did believe that Adam existed and that he was disobedient to God in the way that Genesis 3 seems to depict. But Adam for Paul was far more than a sinful individual who opened the gate and let the beast 'Sin' into the garden. Paul thought of Adam in *symbolic* terms as well—and this symbolic aspect is primary. Adam, for Paul, represents every human person struggling unsuccessfully to combat the force of sin in human life. Adam represents every human person held within the grip of that spark of rebellion against the Creator that seems to be an essential concomitant of freedom. Adam, in short, represents every human person standing over against God, pushing autonomy too far and reaping the consequences.

Here I would draw attention to the dominant image that accompanies Paul's whole depiction of Adam in Romans: that of slavery. Throughout this part of the letter Paul consistently speaks of 'sin' (*hamartia*) in the singular and in a personified way. Paul rarely uses this word in the plural. He is not in fact very interested in 'sins'—murder, theft, fornication, etc. For him these are simply the symptoms of a deeper malaise infesting the human condition: the condition of being enslaved to 'Sin' as to a monstrous slavemaster.[10]

Paul never precisely defines what he means by this radical conception of sin but in connection with human beings falling under its sway he introduces the word 'desire' (*epithymia*; cf Rom 7:7-8). Sin in this most radical sense would seem to refer to radical selfishness: the consuming desire to turn all things other than myself—God, other human beings, other creatures—to the service of my interest, regardless of their own autonomy. It is desire in this sense that functions as the force to which Adamic humanity is enslaved. Human beings may not want to follow the dictates of this master but, as slaves

---

10.   On this Pauline sense of 'sin', see Byrne, *Romans*, 175-76, 215.

compelled to do many things which left to themselves they would rather not do, they cannot resist. Enslaved to this force, *non possunt non peccare*. This is the situation Paul describes across Romans 7:14-25. It reaches a climax in the highly rhetorical concluding sequence where the 'I', torn between the righteous requirements of the law, to which in its higher parts it assents, and the dictates of Sin in its members, which it cannot resist, cries out in despair, 'Wretched one that I am! Who will deliver me from this body of death?' (7:24).

There is, of course, another factor that for Paul bulks large in this connection: namely, the law. Paul in Romans is not writing a dogmatic theology of sin and salvation but, largely in defence of his gospel and strategic mission (1:1-3, 16-17), is wrestling with the issue as to how God can be faithful as Creator to the entire world, while at the same time remaining faithful to the chosen people, Israel.[11] Granted the absolute centrality of the law (Torah) to Israel, the problem of Israel necessarily has its fine point of focus upon the Mosaic law. Hence Paul's preoccupation in this part of the letter with, on the one hand, defending the essential holiness and rightness of Israel's God-given Torah (3:31; 7:12, 16, 22; 8:4, 7), while, at the same time, insisting upon its radical impotence to do anything about the grip of sin in human lives (3:20b; 4:15; 5:20a; 7:5, 7-8; 8:3). The law has not prevented or preserved Israel from falling into the Adamic situation besetting the rest of humankind. On the contrary, not only has the law been no help, it has in fact been hijacked by Sin and ranged upon the negative rather than the positive side in the quest for salvation (7:7, 13; cf also 5:20a)—a situation Paul depicts graphically in 7:7-25.

For many years I have argued that Paul does not want us to read this passage describing captivity under the law simply in itself. Rather, we should see it as a negative foil to the positive passage that follows, early in chapter 8. Here a wholly new factor—the Spirit—enters in. Paul describes how the Spirit has become a liberating factor in human lives because of the saving intervention of God in the person and career of Jesus Christ (8:3-4). Where the law was impotent in the face of sin, the Spirit could really get into the hearts of people, setting them free from the enslaving grip of sin and empowering them not only to

---

11. I expound this issue at length in a recent article, B Byrne, 'Interpreting Romans Theologically in a Post-"New Perspective" Perspective', *Harvard Theological Review* 94/3 (2001): 227-41.

live but to actually *want* to live the values which the law, as external code, could only prescribe but not bring about.[12]

Paul, of course, associates the gift of the Spirit very closely with Christ. Just as it was the Son's costly entrance into the depths of 'sinful flesh' that released the Spirit (Rom 8:3-4), so now to experience the Spirit is to experience the continuing influence of Christ as risen Lord. The Spirit communicates to believers the 'mind of Christ' (1 Cor 2:16b): that essential attitude of self-sacrificing love that led him to give himself up for all (Gal 2:19; Rom 15:3). In this way, the Spirit impels believers to live a life radically determined by unselfish love. More accurately, through the Spirit the risen Lord continues to live out in the persons (bodies) of believers the unselfish love that characterised his life, culminating in his obedience unto death on a cross (Phil 2:6-8). In this sense Paul can write that 'the whole law is summed up (or 'fulfilled') in the command, "You shall love your neighbour as yourself"' (Gal 5:14; cf Rom 13:9).

As will be evident, such an attitude, communicated through the Spirit, represents the exact opposite to the radical selfishness, expressed in the 'desire' or power of Sin to which humanity, under the rubric of Adam, is enslaved. In Gal 5:16-26 and in a still longer sequence in Rom 8:5-13, Paul spells out this dichotomy, offering a sustained contrast between 'walking in the Spirit' and performing 'the desire of the flesh'. Living 'according to the flesh'—in the grip of 'desire'—leads to death; living according to the Spirit leads to life.

Noteworthy in each case, including the positive, is the *ethical* reference. The Spirit is not a force for life in an automatic sense. It leads to life because it communicates to believers the ethical capacity to live out the righteousness required for life. It is in this sense that 'the Spirit means life because of righteousness' (8:10c). The life of believers 'in the body', their bodily obedience under the influence of the Spirit, contributes intrinsically to the onset of salvation.[13] There is a genuine

---

12. Paul appears to see this transfer from law to Spirit—from ethical impossiblity leading to death, to ethical possibility leading to life—as the fulfilment of a divine pledge for the messianic age contained in the combined witness of two prophetic texts, Jer 31:33 and Ezek 36:26: to put 'the law' (= the Spirit) *within* the hearts of the people. On this see further B Byrne, 'The Problem of *Nomos* and the Relationship with Judaism in Romans', *Catholic Biblical Quarterly* 62 (2000): 294-309, especially 304-06

13. I have defended this view extensively in an article, 'Living Out the Righteousness of God: The Contribution of Rom 6:1–8:13 to an Understanding of Paul's Ethical

causal link between the life of believers here and now, where they offer their 'members (= their bodily life) as instruments of righteousness to God' (Rom 6:13), and the future that is still an object of hope. Salvation is still primarily the gift of God—but not a gift that will bypass contribution from the human side.[14]

I would also maintain that later in Romans 8 the Adamic myth recurs, at least implicitly, in a way that significantly bolsters this sense of human cooperation in salvation. Romans 8:18-22 is an interesting passage because it is the only place where Paul clearly sets the human path to salvation in relationship to the non-human remainder of creation—the only place, that is, where the third member of the 'God/human beings/rest of creation' 'triangle', established in the creation account of Genesis 1:1–2:3, is taken into account. I have argued—albeit in an interpretive minority—that the mysterious allusion to the 'subduer' (*hypotaxanta*) in v 20 is in fact an allusion to Adam and to the injury done to the non-human rest of creation because of its unwilling though inevitable implication in his fall.[15] The implication is necessary because, on a particular reading of Genesis 1:26-28 human beings and creation are locked together in a common fate. When the Adamic or 'sin' story runs in human life that redounds ruinously upon creation as well.

In Romans 8:18-22, however, Paul is deploying an argument for hope. The only reason he makes this allusion to the negative side is to bolster—in characteristic antithetical mode—the corresponding positive: the possibilities opened up by the new dispensation of grace established by the 'last (latter-day) Adam': Christ (1 Cor 15:45). Once again, as in Romans 5, we are dealing with myth and symbol: that is, not with something 'back there' but with something abidingly valid in

---

Presuppositions', *Catholic Biblical Quarterly* 43 (1981): 557-81, especially 578-79; *Romans*, 240-41, 244-45.

14. Interpreters from the Reformed or Protestant tradition may perhaps be perturbed by a suggestion of 'synergism' here. But the great Catholic exegete of the middle of the last century, S Lyonnet, pointed out that Paul preserves the absolute gratuity of the gift of salvation with the passive formulation ('might *be fulfilled* in us') in 8:4; see S Lyonnet, 'Gratuité de la justification et gratuité du salut', in *Études sur l'Épître aux Romains,* edited by A Vanhoye (Analecta Biblica 100; Rome: Pontifical Biblical Institute, 1989) 163-77; B Byrne, 'Living Out the Righteousness of God' 577, note 37.

15. Byrne, *Romans*, 260-61.

human life. The 'sin' story told in Adam and the 'grace' story told in Christ represent two conflicting possibilities for human living: one leading to violence, exploitation and death; the other to peace, joy and life, albeit not without involvement in the paschal mystery (cf Rom 8:17). Paul draws hope for salvation—a salvation that somehow includes the non-human created world—from the belief that the 'grace' story worked in human lives under the influence of the Spirit is more powerful than the 'sin' story told in Adam.[16]

2. Evaluating the Adamic myth

Let us now stand back and review the path through the centre of Romans that we have so swiftly travelled. I have tried to set Paul's introduction and handling of the 'Adam' myth within the wider flow of the letter where, as an instance of the dialectical cast of his thought, it functions as a negative foil to the assurance of salvation granted to believers 'in Christ'. What elements of this can form part of a contemporary theology meaningful for today? What elements can—in all responsibility—be left behind?

First of all, in connection with sin, I think we have to distinguish two aspects in Paul. I have already stressed Paul's sense of sin as a captivity from which God's action in Christ sets human beings free. This is what one might call the 'plight' aspect of sin, calling for liberation. The other aspect is sin in the more relational sense of alienation from God. In this sense sin is not just something that affects human beings; it also affects their relationship with God. Christ's 'work' in this sense was not simply concerned with setting human beings free from captivity to selfishness; it also brought about—for believers—a restoration of right relationship with God. Paul describes this restoration in a variety of ways, chief among them being 'justification'. In respect to justification the extended and complex statement making up Romans 3:21-26 has been of crucial significance.

---

16.   For a fuller exposition of this interpretation of Romans 8:18-22, see B Byrne, *Inheriting the Earth. The Pauline Basis of a Spirituality For Our Time* (Homebush, NSW: St. Paul Publications, 1990); most recently, B Byrne, 'Creation Groaning: An Earth Bible Reading of Romans 8:18-22', in *Readings from the Perspective of the Earth: The Earth Bible I* edited by Norman C Habel (Sheffield, UK: Sheffield Academic Press; Cleveland, OH: Pilgrim, 2000), 193-203; for a more detailed exegetical justification of a reading of the text along these lines, see Byrne, *Romans*, 254-62.

Here Paul proclaims how God graciously draws sinful human beings into right relationship with Godself when in faith they appropriate the benefits of Christ's sacrificial death in their regard. The 'plight' from which human beings are thereby rescued is not so much their own radical selfishness in an objective sense but the situation of alienation from God created by sin, a situation of guilt that in a juridical sense merited condemnation.

The inheriting of this juridical state of alienation from God is a key element, if not *the* key element, of the Adamic legacy according to the classic Western doctrine of original sin. It sits comfortably with and perhaps even demands a particular view of the function of Christ's death: that is, of Christ's death as making satisfaction to divine justice for the evil of sin. Though most forms of this doctrine of redemption strive to preserve a sense of the divine initiative, its primary preoccupation is not with the human situation in an objective sense but with the attitude of God.

As is well known, the 'Satisfaction' explanation of the redemptive death of Christ, which owed so much to interpretation of this same passage, Romans 3:21-26, has come under serious question in recent times.[17] Theologically, it seems to involve the oddity of God moving in Christ to alter a disposition in Godself. Exegetically, it has failed to take account of the more likely biblical background to Paul's language in Romans 3:24-25, especially what would appear to be a clear allusion to the Day of Atonement ritual in connection with the shedding of Christ's blood. Understood in the light of this allusion, the whole emphasis of the divine action would be upon changing something in human beings rather than in God, whose initiative is paramount from the start. God 'wipes away' (expiates) the human sinfulness that creates the barrier to vital relationship with God.[18]

In the light of this changed assessment of Paul's view of God's action in Christ—that is, the move away from the narrowly 'satisfaction' approach—the question arises as to whether the stress upon the relational as distinct from the situational aspect of sin ought not also be reassessed. In interpreting Paul on sin, has the Christian theological tradition, especially in the West, placed too much emphasis

---

17. For a survey see G O'Collins, *Christology: A Biblical, Historical, and Systematic Study of Jesus* (Oxford: Oxford University Press, 1995), 197-212, 279-95.
18. For fuller discussion see Byrne, *Romans*, 122-34.

on the relational—that is, on 'justification'—at the expense of the situational—and liberative? It may not be so much a matter of abandoning one in favour of the other, as of trying to reassess the balance and place more stress upon Paul's sense of God's act in Christ as directed against the captivity in which Sin, as slavemaster, holds human beings bound.

To the best of my knowledge and information the Eastern tradition, while reading a negative inheritance from Adam out of Romans 5:12-21, has never felt the necessity to postulate an inheritance of actual guilt—being content, so to speak, to see a legacy only of mortality and corruption; for this tradition culpability could result only from a freely committed personal act.[19] Is it time to assess the Western tradition, with its great stress upon justification, against this broader Christian framework? My sense is that, for all the impact it has had on the Western tradition, especially since the Reformation, 'justification' is simply an image imposed upon Paul by the symbolic universe of apocalyptic Judaism within which he operated. If we question the contemporary interpretive relevance of other aspects of that universe, why cannot we question this juridical image as well?

My suggestion, then, would be to place more stress upon the liberative, as distinct from the juridical, aspects of Paul's sense of Christ's work in respect to sin. Applied to 'original sin', this would relieve us from the necessity of holding every human life to come into being 'under God's frown', that is, as radically alienated from God prior to any moral act.

What would remain intact in regard to Paul's use of the 'Adam' myth is the sense of solidarity in human sinning that is transcendentally prior to the 'sin' history of each and every human being. No one sins entirely alone and no one sins without adding to the 'sin' burden of the entire race. Paul's appeal to the 'Adam' myth implies

---

19.   David Weaver, 'From Paul to Augustine: Romans 5:12 in Early Christian Exegesis [3 pts]', *Saint Vladimir's Theological Quarterly* 27/3 (1983): 187-206; 'The Exegesis of Romans 5:12 among the Greek Fathers and Its Implication for the Doctrine of Original Sin: the 5th-12th Centuries, pt 2', *Saint Vladimir's Theological Quarterly* 29/2 (1985): 133-59; 'The Exegesis of Romans 5:12 among the Greek Fathers and Its Implications for the Doctrine of Original Sin: the 5th-12th Centuries [3rd of 3 articles]', *Saint Vladimir's Theological Quarterly* 29/3 (1985): 23-57; Bradley L Nassif, 'Towards a "Catholic" Understanding of Augustine's View of Original Sin', *Union Seminary Quarterly Review* 39/4 (1984): 287-99.

this sense of universality and solidarity on the negative side as the presupposition for the equally universal and transcendent scope of God's gracious action in Christ.

Secondly, interpreting both the narrative in Genesis 2–3 and the appeal to Adam in Romans 5:12-21 as *myth* rather than history, we are liberated from the necessity to think of the work of Adam and that of Christ in terms of successive epochs: of an original state of bliss, from which Adam 'fell', taking all his progeny down with him, followed by an era of redemption and restoration initiated by Christ. On the contrary, Adam functions not primarily as an explanation of how the state of affairs came about but as a symbol of human beings apart from the grace of God made available in Christ. Adam and Christ would symbolise two radically opposed patterns of human living before God, before other human beings, and before the remainder of creation: one where human beings are locked into a captivity to radical selfishness, another where human beings, without loss of essential liberty, live under the inspiration of the Spirit. The outcome of the former is death, not in the sense that physical death is tied to sin—an element of Pauline thought that we can abandon—but in a more radical sense where human selfishness makes death and its concomitant forces of destruction, violence and terror far more prevalent and premature than they need be. The outcome of the other pattern is life—but, again, not in the sense of the abolition of physical death (a false expectation Paul had to clear up as early as 1 Thessalonians: cf 4:13-18; cf 1 Corinthians 15)—but in the sense that those who yield themselves to the pattern of the paschal mystery come under the scope of God's power displayed in the resurrection of Christ. In this there is hope: not in the sense of a future for the world or human beings that can clearly be glimpsed (Paul dealt with *this* in Rom 8:24-25) but in the sense of a hope that, 'unseeing' and in the face of much to the contrary, rests in the faithfulness of God.[20]

On this view, derived from Paul, redemption becomes that aspect of creation (seen as an ongoing process) where God's grace, radically and historically focused in the Christ event, victoriously overcomes human resistance to the divine offer of life and love. In every human life both Adam and Christ are born and, like Jacob and Esau, wrestle for dominance. Baptism does not remove a human life entirely from

---

20. See further, Byrne, *Romans*, 262-65.

the influence of Adam. In the present, 'overlap of the ages' time,[21] where full salvation remains outstanding, baptism triumphantly claims a particular human life for life and for love in the name of Christ's paschal victory over sin and death, a victory that has to be won over and over again as life unfolds. Whenever, on that basis, human beings live out the radical unselfishness that Christ breathes into them through the Spirit they constitute in the world a 'beachhead' of salvation.[22]

Salvation remains an object of hope and remains the gift of God. However, as I have argued, aspects of Paul's Adamic myth, and in particular its implications on the positive side in respect to the 'Last Adam', suggest that salvation is not something purely other-worldly, discontinuous with the present state of affairs; nor is it something gained or lost by human beings on a purely individual basis apart from the fate of the world. Paul's Adamic myth insists upon a transcendental human solidarity in respect to both sin and grace, the threat to salvation and its attainment. Beyond this inter-human solidarity, it recaptures and reaffirms the foundational vision of Genesis 1:26-28 where relationship to and responsibility for the rest of creation enters essentially into human relationship with the Creator.

In making such reflections upon the Adamic myth I am, of course, aware of the difficulties theological affirmations concerning the future of the world encounter in respect to contemporary scientific cosmology. These difficulties I shall have to leave to others. My aim in this paper has been to indicate areas where I believe Paul's vision and its implications may still have some contribution to make.

---

21. See note 3 above.
22. There are, of course, ecclesiological issues here concerning the position of members of the Christian Church as explicit community of faith and that of the rest of the human family, which I cannot pursue here.

4

Art, Sin and Salvation: The Aesthetics of Salvation[1]

Wes Campbell

1. Introduction

A theological consideration of 'art' in the context of 'sin and salvation' is less surprising now in our newly visual age than in previous centuries. The role of art in Christian theology, however, is still contended.

My primary observation is this: as people of Christian faith and theologians we are here because of *salvation*. Christian proclamation, in a variety of ways, narrates the 'art' of God's story of saving the world.[2] Thus, *art* is not an optional add-on—a peripheral item to the main system. Art is the means of the telling. *Sin* is thus a consequence of salvation: knowledge of sin follows the awareness of God's saving. Sin and salvation are therefore not theological equals. If we did not know of salvation, there would be no *sin* (Hauerwas).[3] The task of Christian

---

1. A powerpoint presentation was developed alongside this paper, in order to demonstrate visually the themes addressed. That presentation included paintings by others and myself. Previously published in *Interface* 5/1, March 2002: 17-29.

2. For one exploration of that emphasis: George A Lindbeck, *The Nature of Doctrine: Religion and Theology in a Postliberal Age* (Philadelphia: Westminster Press, 1984).

3. Stanley Hauerwas makes this point in a variety of ways. Stanley Hauerwas, *The Peaceable Kingdom: A Primer in Christian Ethics* (London: SCM, 1984), 46ff; also: '"Salvation Even in Sin": Learning to Speak Truthfully about Ourselves', *Sanctify Them in the Truth: Holiness Exemplified* (Edinburgh: T&T Clark (1998), 61-74; and *Unleashing the Scripture: Freeing the Bible from Captivity to America* (Nashville: Abingdon Press, 1993), 111-116; also Stanley M Hauerwas, *Wilderness Wanderings: Probing Twentieth Century Theology and Philosophy* (Colorado: Wesview Press, 1997), 44-45; Stanley Hauerwas and William H Willimon, *Resident Aliens* (Nashville: Abingdon Press, 1989), 28ff. For another

proclamation is to recount the story of God's saving which uncovers sin.

Art, then, in its fundamental form, is the means of acting. The question of human speaking, singing, music making, painting, sculpting belongs within that frame. The question for the church is how that human activity as 'art' proclaims God's salvation.

The intention of this paper is to hold together the substance of Christian claims concerning salvation with that of 'art'.

2. Personal location

I take up this task as a Protestant Minister of the Word (formerly Methodist), aware of the implicit prohibition of image in the proclamation of the gospel, with its scant regard for the Eucharist. I also approach this task as a systematic theologian whose pre-occupation, especially prompted by German theology of the past two centuries, has been that of Christian faith's location in 'history', particularly the account of the 'death of God'; and, furthermore, as a 'lay' observer of visual (painted, Western) art and a self-taught painter in oils.

I am acutely aware that a Protestant, who is also an Australian, brings baggage to this theme. Landscape, liturgical location and the artwork peculiar to Australia all belong to this. As a Methodist child I was raised in a church with little ornamentation and was warned against Roman Catholic 'idolatry', and the figure of the crucifix that demonstrated lack of faith in the resurrection of Christ. At the same time, thanks to the *Women's Weekly*, I saw prints of Drysdale and Dobell and Hans Heysen that matched the heat and dust and aridity of the Australia I walked in. (However, on an unusual visit to the Western Australian Art Gallery, my father steered me away from the section where, as I later discovered, nudes were on display.) As a secondary school student in country Western Australia I suffered a curriculum heavily oriented towards maths and sciences, amongst contemporaries with little feeling for either literature or faith, certainly not of the conservative type which was my home. Theological and university studies opened up the world of the mind and metaphor and imagination, yet was curiously silent about aesthetics and visual art,

---

account of the same point see: James Alison, *The Joy of Being Wrong: Original Sin through Easter Eyes* (New York: Crossroad Publishing,1998), especially chapter 6: 'Original Sin Known In Its Ecclesial Overcoming'.

apart from occasional illustrative glances toward Rembrandt, Gruenewald's study of crucifixion and, of course, Mozart. (Bach was, I admit,
with Bob Dylan more to my taste.) It was by chance that I encountered
icons from the Orthodox tradition, and thereby glimpsed a world of
liturgy and theology that was at once alien, yet highly suggestive.
More recently, and in an analogous fashion, I have become aware of
the artwork of Indigenous Australia.

I have undertaken this self-description because, as both theological
and cultural studies in our contemporary setting insist, everyone
speaks from a particular location. The experience and expression
universal is unavailable to any human speaker. In this case I speak not
only as a Protestant but also as a Protestant of the Uniting Church, in
Australia. I am therefore aware that I am in some ways an
eavesdropper in the Lutheran and Roman Catholic dialogue on sin and
salvation, concerning the disputed 'justification', just as I am when it
comes to appreciating how *art* will assist in this theme. I have inherited
a 'Methodist' propensity for mining resources wherever I find them,
much as a magpie will do when a thing that glistens catches the eye.

In this discussion, then, I will attempt to speak as a theologian who
is also an Australian, aware that Catholic and Orthodox voices speak
with a different accent.

3. Aesthetics: a source of contention

There is a resurgence of Protestant interest in art as a means of self-
expression. 'Centres for spirituality' are found in many places and a
chief feature is their use of visual materials. The current cultural and
pedagogical mood, which centres on self-expression, will resist
investigation of the aesthetic quality and the theological character of
such work. One reason—I speculate here—would be the Liberal
Protestant legacy (allied with Romanticism) that locates the experience
of the 'divine' in the self, and hence intuitive self-expression as a truer
expression than prescribed or doctrinal forms of faith or 'spirituality'.
A second reason would be a 'postmodern' aesthetic that rejects any
'canon' by which creative work is assessed or proscribed, given that
subjectivity is the defining character of all experience.

The resurgence of Protestant interest in artistic expression is
certainly a rejection of the Puritan spirit that removed visual
representation from both liturgical and personal expressions of faith.

In this, Protestants are looking sideways to Catholic and Orthodox practice, along with the variety of contemporary expressions of art. They are also taking a backward look into the long history of art-making in Christian and other religious traditions. Moreover, they are observing the practice of Christian artists in recently missionised cultures, as they depict biblical themes in the artistic styles available in that culture.[4]

The term 'aesthetics' is now being employed in Christian theology. Hans Urs von Balthazar, as a Catholic theologian, has taken aesthetics as the lead category in his systematic theology, *The Glory of the Lord: A Theological Aesthetics*.[5] John Dillenberger (in the tradition of Paul Tillich, *A Theology of Culture*)[6] applies himself to aesthetics in *A Theology of Artistic Sensibilities: The Visual Art and the Church*,[7] and with Jane Dillenberger in *Perceptions of the Spirit in Twentieth Century American Art*.[8] There is indeed an explosion of theological interest in art and creativity, as recent publishing lists show. It is not surprising, therefore, that Mark C Taylor, a proponent of a/theology that locates itself firmly within postmodernity, also seeks in *Disfiguring: Art, Architecture, Religion*, an 'A/theoesthetics' which breaks up former theological and aesthetic understanding.

The apparent rapprochement of theology and aesthetics is not simply given. Indeed, Taylor reminds us that some theologians have rejected a 'theoesthetics'. Kierkegaard, for one, refused the identification of art and religion and, against Schleiermacher and Hegel's 'system', subordinated aesthetics to faith in the Infinite.[9]

---

4. See for example *The Bible through Asian Eyes,* edited by Masao Takenaka and Ron O'Grady (Auckland: Asian Christian Art Association, Pace Publishing, 1991).

5. Hans Urs von Balthasar, *The Glory of the Lord: A Theological Aesthetics,* translated by Erasmo Leiva-Merikakis, edited by Joseph Fessio SJ and John Riches (New York: Crossroads/Ignatius Press, 1983).

6. Paul Tillich, *A Theology of Culture,* edited by Robert C Kimball (New York: Oxford University Press, 1964).

7. *A Theology of Artistic Sensibilities: The Visual Art and the Church* New York: Crossroad, 1986).

8. *Perceptions of the Spirit in Twentieth Century American Art* (Indianapolis, Ind: Indianapolis Museum of Art, 1977).

9. Mark C Taylor, *Disfiguring: Art, Architecture, Religion* (Chicago: University of Chicago Press, 1992), 310-2.

All the more startling, therefore, is the exploration of beauty, as the beauty of God in Jesus Christ, by that well-known successor to Kierkegaard, Karl Barth.[10] It is clear that such beauty cannot be represented without the crucifixion: 'If the beauty of Christ is sought in a glorious Christ who is not the crucified, the search will always be in vain . . . No other face . . . speaks at the same time of the human suffering of the true God and the divine glory of the true man.'[11]

There is therefore a tension in this subject. Barth also detects limits on the capacity of art to represent this subject matter.

> No human art should try to represent—in their unity—the suffering God and triumphant man, the beauty of God that is the beauty of Jesus Christ. If at this point we have one urgent request to all Christian artists, however well-intentioned, gifted or even possessed of genius, it is that they should give up this unholy undertaking—for the sake of God's beauty. This picture, the one true picture, both in object and representation, cannot be copied, for the express reason that it speaks for itself, even its beauty.[12]

Eberhard Jüngel, with characteristic thoroughness, explores the relationship of aesthetics to Christian theology.[13] Jüngel charts the problematic relationship 'since at least the nineteenth century, when aesthetics or the work of art seemed to take the place of religion and theology'.[14] In his exploration of aesthetics, Jüngel traces the relationship between the beautiful and truth,[15] beginning with Kant and other Enlightenment figures, such as Schiller. Arguing that light

---

10. *Church Dogmatics* Volume II1, *The Doctrine of God* (Edinburgh: T&T Clark, 1957/1964), 665ff.

11. *Ibid*, 665.

12. *Ibid*, 666.

13. '"Even the beautiful must die"—Beauty in the Light of Truth. Theological Observations on the Aesthetic Relation', *Theological Essays II*, edited with an introduction by JB Webster translated by Arnold Neufeldt-Fast and JB Webster (Edinburgh: T&T Clark, 2000), 59-82.

14. *Ibid*, 59.

15. *Ibid*, 62.

constitutes the character of beauty and truth, Jüngel explores the theological dimension of the death of Jesus Christ, as one whose beauty is hidden, only to be revealed in the glory of Easter light.[16] After such careful and appreciative analysis, Jüngel concludes:

> Thus if a theological observation regarding the aesthetic relation is allowed, if indeed there should still be or be allowed to be such a thing at all, then it should be a double observation: that in fact only what makes a claim to be *truth* deserves to be called *beautiful,* and that only where *truth* establishes itself in a work can one speak of a *work of art.* But beauty and art are both welcome and dangerous competitors with the Christian *kerygma,* for in the beautiful appearance they anticipate that which faith has to declare, without any beautiful appearance and indeed in contrast to it: namely, the hour of truth.[17]

Jüngel's words illustrate a tension, if not a situation of alienation, between the aesthetic and Christian theology. Behind this lies a double history. In its recent form it is the challenge of modernity's light of reason in opposition to the church's claims of the light of revelation. In artistic form that opposition may be witnessed as the shift from, for example, Rembrandt's fascination with light against the dark as a *theological* confession, compared with Monet's attention to the momentary play of natural light on his subject in *plein air.*

In that brief discussion, it is clear that there is a 'non-theological' challenge to any faith claim concerning aesthetics. There is, equally, an 'inner-theological' reserve.

3.1 Theological prohibition of image

That theological reserve has often been expressed as the active advocacy of the aural in opposition to the visual. That advocacy may be briefly typified as the prohibition of all visual images (based on commandments prohibiting idolatry: Exod 20:4, 23; 34:17; Lev 19:4; 26:1; Deut 4:15; 5:8), leading to the iconoclastic controversies and councils of the eighth to the tenth centuries and the Puritan

16. *Ibid*, 80.
17. *Ibid*, 81.

Reformation's destruction of images. We leave aside, for the moment, discussion of the permission provided in biblical texts for art-making, including the instructions for the two tablets of stone (Deut 10:1), the detailed instructions for and implementation of the construction of the Ark of the Covenant (Exod 36–40) and Solomon's temple (I Kgs 5–7), and the theme of the space required in such constructions,[18] between the seraphim and in the 'Holy of Holies' (1 Kgs 8) and the cloud of the glory of the Lord that settles upon the tent of meeting and fills the tabernacle—and, later, the 'holy place' in the temple—and then is taken up to permit the next stage of the journey (Exod 40:34-38).

3.2 What is the substantial issue at stake in this matter?

The theme here is not simply 'the relationship of aesthetics to Christian faith'. That way of framing the matter suggests that the term 'aesthetic' is a neutral concept or, more deviously, is a matter of fact that simply exists. But the tension and debate already briefly introduced makes clear that the 'aesthetic' must be contended. At stake here is a 'Christian aesthetic'.

It might be protested immediately that such a formulation is 'sectarian' because it makes aesthetics adjectival, and therefore not that which is simply *true*. In theological discussion, therefore, a term like *aesthetics* would be employed as if it were self-evident. In modernity, philosophy and theology developed the habit of treating concepts (including 'reason', 'art', 'history', 'world', 'nature', 'science') as if they were either neutral or universal. Often they were employed ideologically and polemically against Christian faith. A European 'eschatological' claim to be complete also challenges a Christian eschatological expectation that waits for that which is not yet realised.

On the other hand, a protest against the term 'Christian' aesthetic would come from theology that has not registered the surrounding pluralism of 'faiths' and ideologies and continues to speak as if the church and Christian theology continued in splendid isolation in Christendom or, on the other hand, from theology (like that by Mark C Taylor) that in seeking an accommodation with the contemporary *Zeitgeist* requires Christian faith to give up the scandal of particularity of Jesus Christ crucified and risen.

---

18. See: Rowan Williams, 'Between the Cherubim: The Empty Tomb and the Empty Throne', *On Christian Theology* (Massachusetts: Blackwell, 2000), 183-196.

Contending for a 'Christian aesthetic' means recognising that
Christian faith makes a claim for truth and beauty in the midst of other
claims, and is engaged now with the memory of Christendom and
modernity, both of whom spoke in universals. The representation of a
Christian aesthetic springs from the particularity of Jesus Christ
crucified and risen, and is expressed in hope of a final reign of peace in
a world of suffering brokenness.

When representing the subject matter of Christian faith, we have as
a background twenty centuries of art in all its style and theological
variety. Now, as we face the task of representation, we view with some
consternation the multi-storied paintings with heavenly and demonic
beings visible. Much as John Drury[19] is able to articulate the sense of
these paintings, engaging the theological discomfort of heaven's
engaging earth, we live in a time when the biblical cosmos has
dissolved, as Hans Frei[20] has so clearly described. Not only has science
and philosophy combined to dismantle that cosmos, but modernist art
has also contributed to the process. In that modernist movement the
attempt has been made to remove all narrative and, beyond that, all
theory. The claim is that the art will be present as object. (I leave aside
for the moment Tom Wolfe's polemic, *The Painted Word*,[21] in which he
argues that this claim is a sham, for modernist art above all requires a
theory and is the preserve of a small band of profiteers who define the
current trend in art.)

The contention for a Christian aesthetic, then, is not carried out in a
vacuum. This is a task precisely engaged in giving expression to
Christian faith in a post-Christendom world; that is, when the biblical
narrative is largely silent, and is present even in the church in a
fragmentary form. The challenge in representing light, beauty and
truth *theologically* requires that this be a representation of the God
known in faith through Jesus Christ. That is to say, in the Jewish figure
who was crucified and, more, is confessed as the ground of hope for
the end of dark suffering in a final resurrection. Here is an interplay
between that which is *visible* and that which can only be known as
hidden.

---

19. *Painting the Word: Christian Pictures and Their Meanings* (London, New Haven
    and Longson: Yale University Press, in association with National Gallery
    Publications Ltd (1999).
20. *The Eclipse of the Biblical Narrative: A Study in Eighteenth and Nineteenth
    Century Hermeneutics* (New Haven and London: Yale University Press, 1974).
21. Farrar, Straus and Giroux (New York, 1975).

4. Imaging sin and salvation: the cross as the 'beauty of God'

The following sections consist of a number of propositions.

- Sin and salvation are focused in the cross of Jesus Christ: the cross as the cost of sin; the cross as the means of salvation of the world.

- Image is presented as an issue by Jesus Christ. He is the image of God; the light of the glory of God shines from his face. The cross presents a double image: *in the 'light' of sin*—the broken image, human suffering and darkness; *in the 'light' of resurrection*—the image of human glory (an icon of Jesus Christ reigning supreme).

- Art as the means of presenting both sin and salvation involves a history of suspicion and prohibition: iconoclasm has a long history; and was refined in the Puritan removal of images in the name of the Word.

- Jüngel[22] identifies the challenge of 'art' to theology: an ideological challenge which arises as the product of and opponent to Christian theology. Thus 'beauty' and art as visual are suspect—a Lutheran suspicion?

- Can the cross be beautiful? There are traditions that attempt to portray the victory of the cross: icons of orthodoxy, the Renaissance cross as a placid moment. Other traditions show the horror of suffering: medieval (cf Gruenewald) identification of the suffering Christ with the sufferers; the agony of the tortured (Latin America).

- The recovery of the God-abandoned suffering in Auschwitz, Hiroshima (to say nothing of the trenches of the First World War), which—as markers of the ongoing suffering of human violence—focuses the cross of Jesus. There is no beauty in suffering.

- Does art transform? Or does it uncover? Art is a matter of both plastic quality and representation. Beauty may be a matter of plastic quality. Beauty may be in representation. That identifies the quandary: *how can the crucifixion, even through the prism of resurrection, be beautiful*? A vision of the end without tears?

---

22.   *op cit.*

5. Revelation in an age of 'eclipse'

Can art assist in an age when God is experienced as absent or eclipsed? Can it function as proclamation? Why can it not function as *public* proclamation of the salvation of the world?

It would be necessary, then, to keep the double task clear: to *image* the glory of God seen in the face of Jesus Christ, who is the light and glory of the world; and to *uncover sin* as darkness and destruction which denies that salvation.

It will be helpful, then to recall Barth's employing of 'hiddenness': the glory of resurrection light is not yet seen on the cross.

As the Word of God is given in flesh and in things of this world, things visible can also provide an intimation of things not seen.

6. 'Plasticity' demanded

There are 'permissions', if not commands, for 'plasticity'[23] in the proclaiming of salvation in Jesus Christ. These may be found in the fundamental event: The Word made flesh in Jesus Christ. In a wider sense permission is found in the 'prophetic actions'—cf Jeremiah's naked posturings, pot breaking, potter's wheel.[24]

Two fundamental permissions—if not dominical commands—are the sacraments of baptism and the Lord's supper (Eucharist). Water, bread and wine are integral to the action of the Holy Spirit in forming and feeding the people of faith as the body of Christ. A Catholic and Orthodox account may want to tell of other sacraments as similar permissions.

Liturgical action and space are further forms where the story of salvation is re/presented visually, aurally and viscerally.[25] The

---

23.   *Plastic* is understood here as that which is *material*, *tangible*, and has *form*.

24.   Eg: Jeremiah 13, 16, 18, 19, 27.

25.   '*Visceral*' takes up the *bodily character* of faith's existence; exactly as biblical emotion is experienced in the gut or bowels. According to F Wilbur Gingrich, *The Shorter Lexicon of the Greek New* Testament (Chicago and London: University of Chicago Press, 1965), in Koiné Greek: *to splagchnon* (noun): 'lit. inward parts, entrails; fig, of the seat of the emotions, in our usage *heart*'. *splagchnizomai* (verb): 'have pity, feel sympathy'. Also, in an older reference, *The Analytical Greek Lexicon* (New York: Samuel Bagster and Sons, year unavailable): (noun): 'the chief intestines, viscera, the entrails, the affections of the heart, the tender affections'; (verb): 'to be moved with pity or compassion', as Jesus in *The Gospel according to Mark* 6:34.

church's account of the human condition and God's action requires the narrative which is enacted in liturgy in spaces constructed and decorated to enhance the telling.

Icons, painted *polytychs*, stained glass windows, the shape of the liturgical space, candles, coloured banners and cloths contribute to the narration of salvation. The spoken word informs and elaborates that visual setting; the visual elaborates and expands the spoken telling.

The encounter with Australian Indigenous art is instructive: it demonstrates an art form (visual music, dance) that 'stories' country. There is a clue here for the Australian (Protestant) church: against the de/narrating of art and the silencing of the biblical story from 'the world' (Robert W Jenson).[26] We may reclaim the task of re/storying salvation in a multimedia fashion.

There are hints for the exploring of the conjunction of the story of salvation in Jesus Christ and our own location: icons in the Orthodox tradition clearly tell the story of salvation in styles that reflect a variety of ethnic locations. Australian artists have taught us to 'see' the landscape (Philip Adams),[27] and the violence of our society. That is, visual art 'trains' the eye to re/cognise what is being viewed, just as the ear and eye are also trained.

The narrating of salvation places our diversity of geographies and ethnicities into the one story of Jesus Christ. His humanity is our saving; his suffering is the uncovering of the destruction of humanity and the rest of creation through the dividing of sin that, until the encounter with this one Jesus Christ, is deemed normal and necessary.

The beauty of Jesus Christ is his body that is the means of unifying and healing human brokenness. This is a story of glimpses and intimations, in water, bread and wine, and the community that

---

26. Robert W Jenson, 'How the World Lost Its Story', *First Things*, October (1993). Jensen explains that in 'Can We Have a Story?' March 2000: 16-17: 'Modernity's project . . . was the attempt to maintain the Bible's grasp of reality while dispensing with the Bible's God. The longer reading of Scripture in the West taught us—including those who did not notably obey Scripture—to perceive reality Scripture's way, as a history that makes a whole because it has a conclusion and so a plot. The modern West tried to inhabit this world while believing no Teller of the story.'

27. As observed in 'Sign your own scenery', in *The Weekend Australian*, Saturday 26 May 2001.

confesses 'Lord we believe; help our unbelief'.[28] The telling of the story of salvation is the church's task.

For the telling of salvation, visual, aural and visceral imagery is not only required but also demanded.

7. Conclusion

This paper has explored the nature of the 'art of salvation' in which Christian proclamation, in a variety of ways, narrates the 'art' of God's saving of the world. *Art* is not an optional add-on but is the means of the telling. *Sin* is a consequence of salvation, following the awareness of God's saving. Sin and salvation are not theological equals. If we did not know of salvation, there would be no *sin*. The task of Christian proclamation is thus to recount the story of God's saving which uncovers sin in order to heal it.

Art, then, in its fundamental form is the means of acting. Human speaking, singing, music making, painting and sculpting belong within that frame. The question for the church is *how* that human activity as 'art' proclaims God's salvation. As Christians, then, we have no option but to engage in art-making. The question is whether it is a faithful telling.

---

28.   *The Gospel According to Mark*, 9:24: following the transfiguration of Jesus, the cry of the father seeking his son's release from demonic possession.

5

Sin and Death: Theological Issues for Pastoral Practice

Rosalie Hudson

1. Introduction

When a minister or priest stands before the open grave or before that final disappearance from view of the coffin before cremation, he or she stands at the edge of the deepest abyss that we can contemplate, 'the most shattering spot in the world'.[1] Likewise, when a pastoral carer attends a person who is dying, there is confrontation with death's finality—the end of all relationships. What gaping reality is this? What does this mean for our own mortality? Is death to be regarded merely as a phase of life, a slipping through another doorway, or is it the 'most shattering spot in the world'? What does it mean to ask these questions in the light of the Christian's 'sure and certain hope' in the one who has conquered death?

My interest in this subject began when, as a community hospice nurse, I was confronted not only by challenging clinical issues, but by questions of death's meaning. In the context of bereavement care of families, I also attended many funerals. There is probably no task more difficult for clergy than to offer appropriate words of comfort in the face of death. What I perceived on many occasions, however, was a disjunction between the liturgy and the eulogy, an incongruence between the priest as liturgist and the priest as pastor, which led me to question what it means in practice to proclaim that Jesus Christ is the resurrection and the life.[2] Or, to ask more personally, what has the death of Jesus Christ to do with my death? Is sin involved here, in that

---

1. Eric Schick, in *The Minister's Prayer Book*, edited by John Doberstein (Philadelphia: Muhlenberg Press, 1959), 362.
2. For more detail on this discussion see Rosalie Hudson, 'Ministers and Funerals: Priests or Pacifiers?', *Trinity Occasional Papers*, Vol 3, No 2 (1989): 21-30.

we refuse to accept death's limit, to acknowledge its cosmic as well as its individual import? Do we believe that in the humanity of Jesus Christ, in his death and descent to hell, in his being raised from the abyss, death's sting is removed and the wages finally paid? If so, what are the implications for pastoral practice?

In exploring the relationship between the death of Jesus Christ and our death, a comparison will be drawn between the individualised, heroic death of Socrates and the ignominious, godforsaken death of Jesus Christ. This theme is woven through the discussion, to show the pastoral implications that may ensue from a Platonic, rather than a Christian view of death. Reflection on two particular funerals will serve as examples, offering a contrast in the way pastoral practice reflects belief. In the first scenario questions are raised about our defiance of death's limit coming to expression in the ideology of heroism, together with a perception of death as 'journey'. The second scenario leads into a discussion on the church's worship as the place where sin and death are acknowledged and hope proclaimed. Some distinctions will then be drawn between 'palliative' and 'pastoral' care; in the former, false comfort may obscure the truth while in the latter the truth of the Word is held in unity. The conclusion to be drawn from these various comparisons is that the locus of pastoral care lies not in the cultural propensity for privatised religion, nor in the pervasive Platonic view of death, but in the church's kerygmatic community.

2. Mr Snow's unexpected journey

Mr Snow had been diagnosed with motor neurone disease. A particularly rapid form of the disease was to shorten his life to six weeks from diagnosis to death. Recently retired and anticipating travelling round Australia with his wife, Mr Snow, aged sixty, found himself with progressive paralysis of muscles—first in his lower limbs, then his arms, then his swallowing reflex and last, his respiratory muscles. His mind remained actively alert. Against hospital advice, he made the decision to return home to die, where his wife, together with the community nurse, would assist him in the necessary routine of each day's living.

The funeral oration highlighted his 'gentle acquiescence and his heroic patience in the face of such a cruel disease'. The priest continued: 'He equipped himself admirably for this last journey of his life, his soul was at peace'. If these words were to be believed, one may assume Mr Snow merely uttered a deep sigh of resignation towards the inevitable. The reality, witnessed by the family, was expressed in Mr Snow's terror, disbelief, panic, anger, resentment, hostility and a vehement crying out against God.'Why does God do this to me? I've lived a good life, never harmed anyone, given forty years of my life to hard work in preparation for an enjoyable retirement. Why, why, why!' Mr Snow's last hours were a physical struggle, an emotional, spiritual and psychological resistance to this death he knew was imminent but which he fought with his last breath. He died cursing both God and his family.

This illustration raises many of the vexed issues regarding the clergy's role in conducting funerals, particularly when the deceased person was not known to them. It may have been impossible in this situation for the priest to offer pastoral care prior to the death, or to provide follow-up bereavement care. The family may also have been resistive to such visits. A discussion at the 'funeral wake', however, centred on the anguish and incredulity the priest's words had aroused in Mr Snow's family. In dying, Mr Snow was the same man he was in living; for the most part a calm and caring conscientious employee, husband, father; aroused at times to indignation and anger. What the mourners heard was a description that denied his outrage, cursing and rejection of others, while praising his heroic acceptance of his fate. I do not suggest the funeral is the place for listing all the deceased person's negative characteristics; but what the family heard was a distortion of reality containing glaring inaccuracies. What the family experienced was not true comfort and hope, but words that heightened their own sense of inadequacy and guilt, articulated by the daughter: 'I had no way of getting near him. At the end, all I heard were his curses. I didn't see any patience, much less heroism. And I didn't see any sign of a soul at peace. Have I missed something? How should I remember him?'[3]

The priest referred to Mr Snow's 'journey' and his 'heroism'. 'Journey' used as a metaphor for death often connotes a pathway or passage to and through death as though the route were merely through another doorway. However, when physiological symptoms appear with their inevitably alienating character (such as unattractive

---

3.   For a heartfelt, first-hand response to presumptions about the state of a deceased person's soul, see CS Lewis, A *Grief Observed* (London: Faber and Faber, 1961), 23.

sights, sounds and smells), when emotional anguish is evident, when the family appears exhausted or the dying process seems inordinately prolonged, carers may be prompted to hasten this journey by giving the patient permission to die. With this pastoral practice Matthew Fox would concur: 'By becoming skilled in our many acts of letting-gos [*sic*], we are preparing for a gentle death, a relaxed entry into another realm, another transparent and divine kingdom and queendom.'[4] It is being argued in this discussion that death is neither transparent, universally gentle, nor a means of humans attaining divinity.

When death is regarded as a gentle journey, Jesus Christ may simply become a friendly companion, one example among many, or simply irrelevant. When death is perceived as a mere phenomenon or a natural part of life's pattern, death's enmity and mystery are underplayed, the relationship between sin and judgment, salvation and reconciliation made redundant. On this metaphorical broad highway no direction is needed; no Saviour to prepare the way.

> Words like sin and guilt and conscience and judgment are exchanged for others, and the religious language game in which they hold their meaning is exchanged for some pyscho-logical language game which plays by its own rules.[5]

In this process the pastor becomes a mere travel agent for the ultimate journey. And so, the radical nature of death is distorted and its cosmic proportions denied. Death is not an idea or abstraction or even a personal destination, but a pervasive, universal power affecting the whole of creation. Thus, whenever vacuous poems are permitted to creep into the funeral liturgy (such as those describing death as merely another stage of life or slipping quietly into the next room) we allow

---

4.   Matthew Fox, *Original Blessing: A Primer in Creation Spirituality* (Santa Fe, New Mexico: Bear & Company, 1983), 165. See also Rosemary Radford Ruether, *Sexism and God-talk: Toward a Feminist Theology* (Boston: Beacon Press, 1983), 257-58 where acceptance of death is described as merely 'the final relinquishment of individuated ego into the great matrix of being'. In contradistinction to Fox's 'spiritual journey' the Eastern Church describes the eschatological passage of the Kingdom of God as that transformation known as baptism whereby we enter a passage from the old into the new.

5.   Carl Braaten, *Justification: The Article by Which the Church Stands or Falls* (Minneapolis: Fortress Press, 1990), 167-168.

the demonic to usurp the truth. 'Demonic' is used here in Stringfellow's terms. 'Demonic does not mean evil; the word rather refers to death, to fallenness.'[6] In other words, being cut off from true life, separated from life, alienated from God, rejecting God, wanting to be like God, we take control of death.

Sin is more than an idiosyncratic tendency towards human pride. It is a replacing of the true God with some other idol, such as the worship of death or the denial of death. Therefore to give undue emphasis to the manner of dying or the moment of death, or alternatively to underplay death's reality, is to deny the cosmic presence and power of death in the world. Of course, death is the terminal experience of life, the moment when the last breath leaves our body. However, death is not some other-worldly unfortunate fatality to befall someone else. Death is an imminent, this-worldly reality impinging on the whole of existence. As Peters says, 'We are different from the other animals to the extent that we are conscious of our mortality . . . The problem is that we deny it. In fact, we go to great lengths to create systematic illusions that hide the stark realization.'[7] Similarly, for Neuhaus:

> We are born to die. Not that death is the purpose of our being born, but we are born toward death, and in each of our lives the work of dying is already underway . . . all our protest notwithstanding, the mortality rate holds steady at 100 percent.[8]

---

6.   William Stringfellow, *Free in Obedience* (New York: Seabury Press, 1967), 62.

7.   Ted Peters, *Sin: Radical Evil in Soul and Society* (Grand Rapids: Eerdmanns), 52-54. Commenting on Ernest Becker's *Escape from Evil* (New York: Macmillan, 1975), Peters says: 'He now maintained that evil results from some-thing much more basic to human nature, namely, our awareness of our own mortality and our response to it . . . Becker says we create the illusion that we can attain immortality . . . By relocating the root of evil from alienating social structures to the fundamental human condition, the later Becker came as close as a nonreligious social scientist could in advocating a doctrine of original sin. For a comprehensive discussion on death, denial and heroism see Ernest Becker, *The Denial of Death* (New York: The Free Press, 1973). Hans Schwarz, *Evil: A Historical and Theological Perspective* (Minneapolis: Fortress Press), xii.

8.   Richard Neuhaus, 'Born towards dying', *First Things*, Vol 100 (February, 2000): 15-22.

Of death denial, Schwarz says, 'Evil is neither a primeval decree nor an inescapable fate, but has its origin in a power that always denies or negates'.[9] This denial and negation of death's limit results in a desire for immortality. Immortal longing comes in many guises, particularly in the ideology of heroism, expressed in such contemporary descriptions as 'losing the battle with cancer', 'unable to fight any longer', 'succumbing to an untimely death', and is particularly exemplified in the account of Mr Snow's funeral. The desire for immortality is also alive and well in our preference for the Platonic heroism shown in the death of Socrates, rather than the weak and powerless death of Jesus Christ.[10] At work here is the body/soul dualism that presupposes the soul's imperviousness to death for the sake of the soul's perfection, rather than the death of total abandonment endured by Jesus Christ, for our sake.[11]

---

9.   Hans Schwarz, *Evil: A Historical and Theological Perspective* (Minneapolis: Fortress Press), xii.

10.   Fergus Kerr, *Theology after Wittgenstein* (New York: Basil Blackwell, 1986), 185, describes the desire for immortality as the 'fatal flaw of finitude' in which we disregard our creatureliness and desire to be as gods in order to do away with mortality, failure, ambiguity, mistakes, doubt and ignorance, deluding ourselves that we are immortal, omniscient and omnipresent, refusing to accept the conditions of our humanity. The metaphysical temptation is that we are above the vagaries of history and creatureliness and finitude. For Kerr, this is megalomania and the utmost hubris. Rather than creating harmony and community, it is alienating and divisive of people from each other, from the world and from nature.

11.   Oscar Cullmann also describes the contrast between a Platonic understanding and a Christian understanding of death (*Immortality of the Soul or Resurrection of the Dead?* [London: Epworth, 1958]). In his commentary on Cullmann's work, Alan Lewis agrees that human beings have no inate capacity to survive death; we have no immortal soul. 'Are we essentially immortal because, despite the corruption of our bodies, our souls are indestructible? Or is God alone immortal, and his creatures mortal but offered the *gift* of sharing in God's eternity through his once-for-all act in raising Christ from the dead?' (Alan Lewis, *Between Cross and Ressurection: A Theology of Holy Saturday* [Grand Rapids: Eerdmans, 2001, 59, note 26.) See also Jürgen Moltmann, *Is There Life After death?* (Milwaukee: Marquette University Press), 15: 'If we are called by name, our whole life becomes immortal in the relationship of God to us. We remain immortal and permanent—even as mortal and transient creatures—in the immortal and permanent relationship of God to us . . . When we die, the book is finished, but it will not be destroyed. We remain for eternity in the memory of God and are thereby immortal.'

Jüngel describes the Platonic teaching in which the body is an unfortunate aberration to be dispensed with at death so the soul may be freed.[12] Some of the distinctive differences between a Platonic understanding of death and a Christian understanding of death will now be identified, in order to set the scene for a discussion on sin as death's limit.

3. The death of Socrates and the death of Jesus Christ

Comparing the death of Socrates to the death of Jesus, the following contrasts emerge.[13] Socrates' attitude towards his imminent death was positive. In the hours preceding his death he debates, discourses, jokes with his disciples, teaching them serenely about immortality and the appropriate silence of stoicism. Jesus trembles, begging his disciples not to leave him. His death is preceded by loud cries and tears.[14] 'My soul is very sorrowful, even to death (Mk 14:34 RSV). Or, in the NRSV, 'I am deeply grieved.' Whereas Socrates' soul was to soar heavenward, Jesus, in his full humanity, descended to the place of the dead. For Socrates, burial was irrelevant. 'How shall we bury you?' asks Crito. 'As you please, he answered: only you must catch me first . . . I shall not remain with you after I have drunk the poison, but I shall go away to the happiness of the blessed.'[15] Jesus' preaching pointed to the seed which must die in order to be raised to new life, the temple that had to be destroyed in order to be rebuilt, the necessity for him to be buried, to leave the disciples in order to be with them again. 'A little while,

---

12. Eberhard Jüngel, *Death: The Riddle and the Mystery* (Edinburgh: St Andrew Press, 1975), 42.

13. These comparisons are based on some of the material in Chapter 3 of Jüngel, *ibid*.

14. For a full account of Socrates' careful preparation for his death see Plato, *Phaedo* (Indianapolis: Bobbs-Merrill Educational, 1951), 72. Bonhoeffer draws the distinction between suffering that brings honour and suffering that brings tragic rejection. 'Jesus Christ must suffer and be rejected . . . There is a distinction here between suffering and rejection. Had he only suffered, Jesus might still have been applauded as the Messiah. All the sympathy and admiration of the world might have been focussed on his passion. It could have been viewed as a tragedy with its own intrinsic value, dignity and honour. But in the passion Jesus is a rejected Messiah. His rejection robs the passion of its halo of glory. It must be a passion without honour' (Dietrich Bonhoeffer, *The Cost of Discipleship* [London: SCM Press, 1959, 76]).

15. Plato, Phaedo, *op cit*, 71.

and you will no longer see me, and again in a little while you will see me'(Jn 16:16). 'It is for your advantage that I go away' (Jn 16:7). Death for Jesus Christ was no flighty game of hide and seek, 'catch me if you can'. The gospels record the significance of Jesus'death as final and decisive—burial in the tomb. There was no short cut to another realm, no reprieve whereby his body died but his soul lived on. 'Jesus . . . prepares for death not with exhilaration that his soul shall soon escape a tomb, but with dread that his body shall soon be placed in one.'[16] For Socrates, death was a runaway victory where the reward would be a continued quest for knowledge, a climb to the highest rung of the ladder and a perfect example to be emulated. While there was weeping at his death, Socrates' disciples knew he had departed to achieve a higher life. For Jesus' disciples there was despair, disappointment and disillusionment. 'But we had thought that he was the one to save Israel'(Lk 24:21). Jesus' death is no example of heroism for us to follow, as it was for Socrates' disciples. Rather, it is his absolute identification with the 'relationlessness'[17] and utter isolation of human death that gives us the victory over death.

Further comparison between the death of Jesus and the death of Socrates is noted in the 'swansong',[18] whereby Socrates' triumphant last sweet moments are sharply contrasted with Jesus'cry of

---

16. Alan Lewis, *Between Cross & Resurrection, op cit,* 418. Lewis continues: 'And yet, and yet: the Christian good news of victory over death is not about survival. The very function of Easter Saturday is to prevent the rubbing out of Friday and its grievous memories by the instant and overwhelming exuberance of Sunday. Easter Saturday says that Jesus was gone and finished, subjected to death's power for a season. So Christ himself did not—despite centuries of popular theological and homiletical deceit—survive the grave! He succumbed to death and was swallowed by the grave—his Sabbath rest in the sepulchre a dramatized insistence that his termination was realistic and complete, a proper subject of grief and valediction. This was departure—painful, ugly, uncurtailed; no docetic illusion, no serene transcendence of the spirit highfloating over purely physical distress, no momentary, insignificant hiccup in Christ's unstoppable surge to glory. God's victory over death, as the Christian gospel tells it, is not a matter of smooth, ensured survival but a new existence after nonsurvival—a quite different reality, for us as well as God' (428).

17. Jüngel, *Death, op cit,* 78.

18. The positive nature of death is exemplified by the swansong, described by Jüngel as Socrates' loud sweet note full of joy because he is dying, to Apollo, the god of song and his lord. Here, says Jüngel, Socrates' swansong even surpasses the swans' song (*ibid,* 51).

dereliction. Socrates' 'sweet poison' was Jesus' 'bitter cup'. For Socrates, individualised fulfilment was the aim. Jesus' death, by contrast, is not merely the death of an individual human being for self-fulfilment but God crucified for the salvation of the world. This death has Trinitarian significance, not for the sake of the three persons of the Godhead, but for the sake of our humanity. 'For us and for our salvation . . . ' This death has cosmic and eschatological import. 'The earth shook, and the rocks were split.' The hour of darkness signified a cataclysmic event, the fulfilment of which will be known 'in the last day'. For Socrates, death is a personal achievement. In Jesus Christ, death becomes a part of God's purpose for creation—a gracious limit imposed, paradoxically, for our freedom.

4. Sin and death's limit

It has been suggested in the discussion thus far that a preference for Platonic dualism as it relates to death is reflected in some pastoral practice. If the death of Jesus Christ is so identified then pastoral practice will reflect only the positive aspects of death and dying; judgment will be ignored and heroism glorified. If, on the other hand, death is seen to be God's judgment on sin, then it has transforming, cosmic implications for every death and a pastoral word is not dependent on our interpretive gloss. In a death-denying culture where youth and beauty are the consummate goals of existence, discussion about sin and judgment has no place. Such discussion is considered an unwelcome, inappropriate and unnecessary intrusion into the positive pastoral encounter. We may readily dismiss the notion of death as God's judgment on sin, for we do not become sinless and in the end we all die, so it would seem death itself has not been conquered. As Küng says, 'What constitutes the most mysterious aspect of the mystery of sin is not that the sinner deserves to die, which is rather self-evident, but rather that the sinner, in the average situation, continues to exist'.[19] In the face of sin's persistence and death's ever-present reality,

---

19. Hans Küng, *Justification* (London: Burns & Oates, 1964), 147. Here Küng emphasises the fact that doubt persists in the face of the unequivocal statements in Scripture about sin, death and judgment. 'Is this not a case of dramatization? Are these expressions not unnecessarily forced?' Bonhoeffer raises similar questions with his interpretation of the serpent's question in the Garden of Eden as the 'first religious question in the world . . . "Did God say?", that plainly is the godless

what is to be believed about Jesus Christ conquering both sin and death?

When sin and death are regarded as mere phenomena we look for explanations and problem-solving techniques in order to manage and control each challenging situation. In this sense, the death of Socrates has more appeal. In the death of Jesus Christ we see the death of death as judgment on the sinfulness of sin. We reject God's merciful judgment on death as borne by Christ in our place when we seek to fulfil our desire to be our own judges and saviours.[20] We see death's limit either as promise in terms of grace or as enemy in our wish to be God. All these questions are called into question by God's action in the death and resurrection of Jesus Christ.

Is the limit good? Barth says unequivocally that the limit of finitude is neither a curse nor an affliction.[21] Rather than a threat to be overcome, our finitude is a gracious promise. It is not our natural inclination to accept that our span of life is limited. We gain this understanding, through faith, as we partake in Christ's humanity. 'Our existence with its possibilities is to be explained in the light of his existence, not vice versa.'[22] Against our desire for limitless time, for immortality, Barth says:

> Man as he really is, as God created him, stands questioning before these frowning walls of rock which enclose him in the narrow gorge of being, and

---

question. "Did God say," that he is love, that he wishes to forgive our sins, that we need only believe him, that we need no works, that Christ has died and been raised for us . . . did he really say it to me?' (Dietrich Bonhoeffer, *Creation and Fall* [New York: Macmillan Publishing Company, 67]).

20. Warren Clarnette, 'The Cross and the Hope of a Righteous World', *The Auburn Report on Church and Society,* Vol 13, No. 2 (2001): 5-8. In other words, we confuse the issue when we regard sin as a moral rather than ontological category. As Zizioulas states: 'Sin, therefore, entered as *idolatry,* ie as an ekstasis of communion with the created world alone. In this way, what sin did was of deep ontological significance: it made the limitation of creaturehood show itself in the existential contrast between being and nothingness.' (John Zizioulas, 'Human Capacity and Human Incapacity: A Theological Exploration of Personhood', *Scottish Journal of Theology,* Vol 28, 1975: 401-448).

21. Karl Barth, *Church Dogmatics,* III/4 (Edinburgh: T&T Clark, 1963), 567. For a concise treatment of Karl Barth's Christological metaphysics see Fergus Kerr, *Immortal Longings: Versions of Transcending Humanity* (London: SPCK, 1997).

22. Fergus Kerr, *ibid,* 26.

seem to fling at him the twofold taunt: Once you were not! And: One day you will be no more![23]

The limit is not abstractly or artificially imposed, but freely willed by the God who comes to us in Jesus Christ to be our neighbour, our 'other'. Contrary to the cultural and bio-medical persuasion that death is a troublesome aberration to be overcome by science, Barth argues that God cares for us by giving us an allotted span instead of unending time, in order that a singular unrepeatable unique bond is established. Thus, it is wrong to rebel against this limitation, or merely to resign ourselves angrily or anxiously to its inevitability. The limit imposed by death is the gracious limit of our being as creatures, freed from the need to justify ourselves as gods.[24] To understand our existence 'in Christ' is not to strive for divinity, rather it is to be freed for our full humanity, which includes our mortality. For Kerr:

> Instead of merely enduring our limitation with a sigh, we should take it seriously, affirm it, welcome it, praise God for it, that we are what we are precisely in our limitation by him . . . Thus we best understand our relationship to God, as God's commanding and our recognizing his command, in terms of limitation—God's limiting and our being limited. The only freedom there is for human beings lies precisely in our finitude.[25]

---

23.   Karl Barth, *Church Dogmatics,* III/2 (Edinburgh: T&T Clark, 1960), 557.

24.   For a more comprehensive elucidation of death as limit, see Thielicke, H *The Evangelical Faith,* Volume III (Grand Rapids: Eerdmans), 392-5. Here Thielicke says that 'death represents a limit, the fact that life has a goal and we have to leave it'. Thielicke's second thesis is that we, as creatures, notoriously desire to be without limits. 'It comes on man the day that he eats the forbidden fruit which lies beyond the limit. The barrier of finitude is lowered against the one who wants to be without limits' (392).

25.   Kerr, *Immortal Longings, op cit,* 38. Similarly, Lewis says it is good that we ultimately come to nothing in termination and decay. Death's limit flies in the face of our 'cherished myths of immortality', but in this very limit our hope is grounded. 'We face suffering, distress, and death with courage, faith, and trust, not by maintaining serenity of psyche or buoyancy of soul within, but precisely by casting ourselves in all the times of emptiness, aridity, and worldlessness—as

How then, are we to consider death's stark finality, while at the same time offering words of hope in pastoral care? It seems that in Mr Snow's story there were things too hard to say about death, but ignoring the existential realities resulted in hope-less pastoral care. It is apparent that Platonic dualism is at work in many funeral liturgies and pastoral practices; what is believed about death dictates the integrity of both worship and pastoral care. Is the death of Jesus Christ a matter for purely private reflection? Is it a matter of concern only within the Godhead and therefore irrelevant to the pastoral encounter? Or do we find, in the death of Jesus Christ, the pre-eminent truth about solidarity in suffering, the only hope-full word?

Turning to the Eastern Church we find a marked emphasis on Christ's solidarity with suffering and death; not only on the day of crucifixion and resurrection, but on the second day of Easter, on Holy Saturday when our destiny is enacted. 'Indeed, soteriologically Holy Saturday may be the most significant of the three days.'[26] Of Jesus' death as a total event, with truly amazing implications for pastoral care, von Balthasar says, with emphasis:

> It is a situation, which signifies in the first place the
> abandonment of all activity and so a passivity, a state
> in which, perhaps, the vital activity now brought to
> its end is mysteriously summed up . . . In the same
> way that, upon earth, he was in solidarity with the

---

well as those still more spiritually dangerous times of optimism or elation—upon the gift of grace outside us and around us. God promises to do what we cannot do, and go where we need not go, to enter the dark valley ahead of us and defeat on our behalf the frightening foe.' (Lewis, *Between Cross and Resurrection, op cit,* 430-431). On the subject of immortality, Zizioulas says, 'Man was not created immortal, but by having his personhood he was made capable of communion with the immortal God. Death came to him not as a punishment in a juridical sense but as an existential consequence of the break of this communion; it came at the moment that man became introverted, and limited the ecstatic movement of his personhood to the created world' (Zizioulas, 'Human Capacity and Human Incapacity'; *op cit*, 424).

26.   Vigen Guroian, 'O Death, Where Is Your Sting', in *Sin, Death and the Devil,* edited by Carl Braaten and Robert Jenson (Grand Rapids: Eerdmans), 118-131.

living, so, in the tomb he is in solidarity with the
dead.[27]

What other solidarity do we have to offer, if not the firm promise
that the one who has experienced it all graciously condescends to stand
with us in our death? Not merely in sympathy or even with profound
empathy, but bearing death's limit for our salvation, 'Christ's descent
into Hades is a triumph over the desolation and the loneliness, the
isolation and the despair, that Satan, sin, and death have inflicted upon
every human being'.[28] Here we begin to understand what the death of
Jesus Christ means for our death. For if it does not involve the
alienation and despair experienced by Mr Snow, then how is the truth
of the gospel proclaimed in pastoral practice? It is in this area, I
believe, that the disjunction occurs between the liturgy and the eulogy;
when the words of the liturgy are 'surpassed' by the well-meaning
pastoral words of the priest. In an attempt to say more, or to say better,
what has already been said, the mystery of death is purportedly
explained away. By contrast, pastoral care may speak well in silence.
Lewis understood from personal experience the horror of death's
immanence and the inadequacy of language in relation to death's
silence:

> Death means speechlessness. Not only does the
> aloneness of the dead terminate conversation, but
> also conversely, a loss of communicative power

---

27. Hans Urs von Balthasar, *Mysterium Paschale* (Edinburgh: T&T Clark, 1990),
    148-9. Similarly, Lewis says of God's solidarity with us in death, 'God's unity
    with the dead and buried Jesus is what ultimately marks the cross as judgment on
    our sin, unmasking the violence, idolatry and foolishness with which humanity
    seeks the destruction of its Maker' (Alan Lewis, 'The Burial of God: Rupture and
    Resumption as the Story of Salvation', *Scottish Journal of Theology*, Vol 40,
    1987: 335-362). Further, Lewis says of the Easter story: 'The tomb once occupied
    is empty, according to our three-day story; though it is, we have been arguing
    throughout, equally important, and just as central to the story, that the empty tomb
    was previously occupied, and that the only one risen from the grave is its
    still-wounded occupant. There is no other way to the Sunday of his joy and
    victory, and ours, than through his and our Sabbath of sorrow and defeat' (Lewis,
    Between Cross and Resurrection, op cit, 426).
28. Guroian, *op cit*, 129-130.

signals the collapse of personal being, and a
suppression of the human voice amounts to and
often precedes the extinguishing of life itself. In the
face of death even the language of the living peters
out into inconsequence and incapacity. The
platitudes of consolation and formulaic obsequies
indicate the rupture of language, as death's invasion
at once relativises the value of mere words and
maximises the pain of their inadequacy.[29]

This does not mean we have no words to offer at the time of death.
It does indicate, however, that care is required to ensure these words
do not contradict the words of Scripture in the church's liturgy. It is
also a reminder that pastoral words are not intended to defy or deny
the experience of dying and the reality of death. Furthermore, this does
not mean all our words need to be right, pure or holy; for many a
parable of God's truth is enacted in a faltering, hesitant and even
clumsy pastoral encounter. What is at issue is what we believe about
death, and the integrity of word and deed.

For Lewis, it is the way we treat the story that is determinative.
Resurrection is no mere interpretation hastily superimposed on the
crucifixion, completely missing the chapter of Holy Saturday. 'Death is
given space and time to be itself, to be termination, unabbreviated in
its malignancy and infernal horror.'[30] Failure to recognise the
termination of the second day or Holy Saturday is not merely to leave
out a significant chapter of the story, thereby weakening the plot; such
failure takes no account of the horrors of death.

Then not only one day of history but all of them,
including those of Exodus and Auschwitz, have lost
their *created* integrity and are rendered out of bounds
to memory and faith.[31]

The narrative order is decisive; in the retelling of the story we should
not forget the unravelling, the discovery of the story as it unfolds. We

---

29.   Lewis, 'The Burial of God: Rupture and Resumption as the Story of Salvation',
      op cit, 339.

30.   *Ibid.*

31.   *Ibid*, 345.

cannot remember the happy ending until we have looked back on the cataclysmic horror of the day of Christ's descent to hell. Lewis's compelling use of the terms 'rupture' and 'resumption' invite us into the

> . . . no man's land disjoining cross and resurrection . . . Story recapitulates, as in the first instance no other discourse could, both the numbing shock of history's rupture in the death of Christ, and the festive surprise of his resumption in his raising.'[32]

For Stringfellow, the last word is the same as the first word:

> Death is not the last word. Nor is the last word some nebulous, fanciful, fake promise of an after life . . . The last word is not death, nor life after death, but the last word is the same as the first word, and *that* word is Jesus Christ. He has, holds, and exercises power even over death in this world. And His promise is that a man may be set free from bondage to death in this life here and now. [33]

The point has been made that contemporary cultural influences persuade us to gloss over our finitude in favour of immortality in its many and various guises. The implications are now to be explored of the effect on pastoral practice, when palliation is confused with pastoral truth.

---

32.   *Ibid.*

33.   William Stringfellow, *Instead of Death* (New York: Seabury Press, 1963).

5. Spiritual care: palliative or pastoral [34]

In the clinical context palliation means to cover, to protect, to care for a person in such a way that uncomfortable symptoms are covered with appropriate therapeutic measures. When in the pastoral context, however, every attempt is made to cover pain and anguish or the terrible moment of death, then pastoral care may be confused with palliation. When death's starkness is covered over, a different pall hangs over the person, the pall not so much of secrecy and denial but a pall of false comfort that camouflages death's alienation. On the other hand, it is only when the gracious covering of God's mercy and judgment is revealed in its personal, historical significance that the truth of every pastoral relationship is made known and the comfort of the gospel's promises experienced. Amidst the stark realities of illness, suffering and death the church dares to proclaim a sure and certain hope. Braaten states:

> The answer we have is something of an embarrassment. Our only answer in face of the facts is the apostolic one: The kingdom is hiddenly present in the person of the Messiah Jesus, and the Word of this event can only be received through faith in the power of the Spirit. All efforts to doctor up this bald proposition are cosmetic in nature.[35]

Thus the comfort of pastoral care derives from a particular source. 'Only doctors are allowed to give opiates to people who are suffering or dying and pastors have no business to go poaching on their preserves.'[36] Speaking of the crisis of Protestantism in an increasingly frivolous and empty world of humanism, Carroll points to a lack of seriousness in the face of death. 'Dread is interpreted as a disease of

---

34. For implications pertaining to spiritual care of older persons see Rosalie Hudson, 'Death and Dying: Too Much to Bear?' *Zadok Perspectives,* Vol 50 (October 1995): 6-10, and Rosalie Hudson, 'Death and Dying in a Nursing Home: Personhood, Palliation and Pastoral Care', *St Mark's Review,* Vol 182 (Winter, 2000): 6-12.

35. Braaten, *Justification, op cit,* 178.

36. Ernst Käsemann, *Jesus Means Freedom* (Philadelphia: Fortress Press, 1972), 19. See also Helmut Thielicke *Living with Death* (Grand Rapids: Eerdmans, 1983), 132.

the body. People don't call the priest any more lest the patient die of fright.'[37] This lack of seriousness in respect of death may issue in an artificial jollying of the person who is experiencing profound anguish. Against this pastoral propensity, Bonhoeffer counters:

> The goal of spiritual care should never be a change of mental condition. The mission itself is the decisive element, not the goal. All false hope and every false comfort must be eliminated. I do not provide *decisive* help for anyone if I turn a sad person into a cheerful one, a timid person into a courageous one . . . God is our help and comfort. Christ and his victory over health and sickness, luck and misfortune, birth and death must be proclaimed. The help he brings is forgiveness and new life out of death.[38]

This is not to say that psychological and emotional wellbeing are unimportant. Braaten, in a critical analysis of pastoral care and counselling, describes theology as

> the fine art of drawing the proper distinction between the kerygma and the situation, between theology and psychology, between pastoral care as *Seelsorge* and the medical and psycho-therapeutic functions in the healing process.[39]

He encourages open dialogue with secular processes, for 'in the actuality of lived experience they overlap'. Criticising what he sees as a misplaced emphasis on techniques in CPE (Clinical Pastoral Education) he maintains the transcendent aspect may be concealed. 'No act of counseling can take the place of transmitting the message through kerygmatic and didactic modes of communication.'[40] Braaten

37. John Carroll, *Humanism: The Wreck of Western Culture* (London: Fontana Press), 161.

38. Dietrich Bonhoeffer, *Spiritual Care* (Philadelphia: Fortress Press, 1985), 30.

39. Braaten, *Justification*, *op cit*, 162-163.

40. *Ibid*, 146.

argues for a proper dialectic so that pastoral care and theology are not artificially separated, but appropriately distinguished.

The discussion now turns to the story of Malcolm and the place of the church's liturgy in communicating the kerygmatic response to death.

6. Malcolm's baptism into death

When Malcolm died from cancer on his eighth birthday, his funeral drew many hundreds of people, including his schoolmates, from the close Roman Catholic community. The priest who presided at Requiem Mass had been present, with me, at Malcolm's death. I had observed on many occasions his quiet and gentle pastoral presence and I wondered what he would have to say at the funeral. When Malcolm died, prayers were said, but I heard no attempt at false comfort, no explanations, no desire to play down the fact of death, or to rationalise the family's grief. In answer to the many callers asking if the little boy had 'passed away' yet, the priest replied with quiet confidence, 'Yes, Malcolm has died.' At the funeral, the question was raised concerning the harsh reality of a rapidly growing cancer that could spread so quickly and kill such a young child. No attempt was made to answer the unanswerable. Rather, a recognition that we were all there to witness to the resurrection power of Jesus Christ who had poured out his love and grace on this child at baptism, confirmed his growth in grace at his confirmation and first communion, and was now no less present and active in his gracious care of the child in death. It struck me that the eucharistic prayer of the Mass, the anamnesis of Christ's death, was not incongruent with the death of this child and indeed offered the only hope in a tragic, sorrow-filled event. With Christ, Malcolm had passed through the waters of baptism from death to life. That eschatological passage was rehearsed at his death. The stark reality of this individual child's death also found its place within the communion of saints, proclaimed with confidence by the worshipping congregation.

The priest in this pastoral situation offered a confident presence through unobtrusive acts of physical closeness rather than by words of explanation and placation. He made no extraordinary claims to cover death's mystery; neither did he raise unrealistic expectations concerning Malcolm's soul. The ministry of the priest as Christ's representative differs in truth and authority from the false comfort and assumptions of the pacifier. The point of departure for the priest is:

how is the gospel, the good news of Christ's life, death and resurrection, brought to people in the face of death? The point of departure for the pacifier is: how can I remove this pain and ease this intolerable suffering? The difference is that the priest relies solely on Christ while the pacifier comes with a parcel of peace and comfort to prescribe, often with pious platitudes and gap fillers, or with pastoral techniques to practice. In the latter, the personality of the pacifier is paramount, in the former the priest merely bears the Word.

In bearing the Word, the priest narrates the cosmic nature of death, as well as the deeply personal. Thus, the church's worship rehearses both the eschatological and cosmological story: eschatological in the sense that as present reality we enjoy what is yet to be fulfilled, a new heaven and a new earth; cosmological in the sense that Christ's body is broken for the world so that good and evil, joy and suffering are taken into the totality of Christ's redemptive action—the overcoming of corruption, sin and death. All this is narrated in the eucharistic story, as Williams says:

> The Eucharist proclaims that the rupture in time,
> which is death, has been healed, that the severance of
> the faithful through death has been overcome. Hence
> St Ignatius can refer to the Eucharist as the medicine
> of immortality . . . The death that is yet to come does
> not define us, but is rather our last trial along the
> road to the heavenly banquet.[41]

As in Malcolm's death, pastoral care takes place within the fellowship of the church where the Word is proclaimed and the sacraments administered; where both pastor and person in need are brought under the discipline and grace of the gospel. On this foundation pastoral care finds its meaning and its goal. Here the warmth of our compassion, the sensitivity of our listening, the integrity of our solidarity with those who are suffering take their place as penultimate signs. Within the company of the faithful we are nourished and encouraged to witness to those ultimate realities that

---

41.   AN Williams, 'The Eucharist as Sacrament of Union', in *Sin, Death and the Devil, op cit,* 45-75.

transform the whole of our existence. Even though in our sinful pride and brokenness we are less than faithful, Lewis reminds us that

> at least one essential truth about us is preserved and illuminated, not hidden or destroyed: the truth that humanity is *connected*. We are who we are, in righteousness, and fail to be who we are, in sin, *together* not apart.[42]

When this truth is proclaimed in the context of death the church's mission is lived out. When death occurs, the liturgy of the funeral is the place where the narrative reality of God's promise is retold with confidence, together with pastoral care which rehearses in practice the same story. Similarly, when the saints are remembered, we are enveloped into a larger story:

> But on All Saints Day, as at funerals, we confront death. And even agnostic clerics find it difficult to make of death a very persuasive metaphorical opportunity. It recalls us, if we are honest, either to orthodoxy or to an empty silence. One can understand those whose rationalist dogma requires them, in the face of death, to refuse faith's consolations. One can only pity those whose only available option is desperately to try to change the subject.[43]

Reference has been made to the 'narrative order' of the gospel. Jüngel directs our task of thinking about God to the definition of God's being as love, as the God who is human in divinity in order to unite death with life for the sake of life. The language for telling of this love is story, language in which '*happened* history advances as *happening* history'.[44] Rehearsing God's story is an urgent necessity in the post-narrative, technological world of postmodernity, where God as the author of the world's story is replaced with the inviolable sup-

---

42.   Lewis, *Between Cross and Resurrection, op cit*, 421.

43.   J Nuechterlein, 'For All the Saints', *First Things*, Vol 57 (November 1995): 6-7.

44.   Eberhard Jüngel, *God as the Mystery of the World* (Grand Rapids: Eerdmans, 1983), 306.

remacy of our individual experiences.[45] In the narrative of God, Jesus became the 'loneliest of all men' so that fellowship with God is restored for all. In this relationship, we are told the mystery of our own loneliness; that through life and death we enter fellowship with God, not turning inwards in a form of private friendship but turning outwards in freedom towards our neighbour.

7. Conclusion

Confusion about the nature of worship and its place in the context of death comes to expression in a disjunction between the eulogy and the liturgy, the preaching and the panegyric. Further confusion arises when pastoral practice is divorced from theological belief. As creatures of our culture we are encouraged to celebrate life, to concentrate only on the positive. 'There's to be nothing negative in this funeral, and I want no tears.' In our desire to celebrate life we may too readily deny death's reality.

In the face of the world's seductive invitation to immortality through the cult of youth, through the medicalisation of death, through the promise of cloning, the church has another message: 'It is the church's mission to tell all who will listen, God included, that the God of Israel has raised his servant Jesus from the dead, and to unpack the soteriological and doxological import of that fact.'[46]

Death may be accepted anthropologically as merely a part of life, biologically as the natural ending of a specimen destined for decay, psychologically a 'letting go', spiritually a transition to another realm, physiologically a welcome release or ideologically a sacrifice for a higher cause. More decisively, however, 'to Christian theology it remains the worst enemy of man, the most unacceptable of all things'.[47] It is not a matter of 'letting go' but of being grasped by God's

---

45. For a full development of this theme of story and postmodernity see Robert Jenson, 'How the World Lost Its Story', *First Things,* Vol 36 (October 1993): 19-24.

46. *Ibid.*

47. Lewis, 'Rupture and Resumption as the Story of Salvation' *op cit,* 422. See also, Lewis, *Between Cross and Resurrection, op cit,* 417, where he speaks of the truth of death's anarchy and terror within a culture that is anxious to master nature and defeat death. 'Suppressed, then, yet all the more alive, is the biblical truth that whatever kind of friend mortality may be to humankind, death is also the last

all-encompassing love, particularised and made accessible through Jesus Christ's human experience of death and his being raised by the power of the Spirit.

Life is affirmed, not through our autonomous decision to choose life over death, but because, in Jesus Christ, death and sin have been disarmed. In freedom we are called into this story, not in order to circumvent death or to become divine, but in order to become more truly human.

---

enemy of our Creator and ourselves, the summation of everything irrational, fiendish, and malevolent in our existence . . . death is a demonic foe'.

6

The Genesis and Genetics of Sin

Ted Peters

With the advance of research in molecular biology and the increasing influence of sociobiology, also known as evolutionary psychology, we ask: will science soon provide a more adequate explanation for sin than theologians have traditionally been able to muster? Will genetics explain the genesis of human failure better than the biblical account of Adam and Eve? Will evolutionary theory replace hamartiology? Will theological seminaries send their students to genetics labs for pastoral training?

Robert Wright gives voice to the challenge. 'The roots of evil can be seen in natural selection, and are expressed (along with much that is good) in human nature. The enemy of justice and decency does indeed lie in our genes.'[1]

In what follows I will lift up two areas of discourse for comparative reflection: how the field of theology understands human sinfulness, and how contemporary scholars extrapolating from genetics and evolution offer a competing explanation. Perhaps, to avoid begging the question, we should suspend judgment as to whether these two alternative approaches to human behaviour actually do compete. They may at first seem to be rivals; but perhaps under closer examination it might turn out they are complementary or at least compatible.

One of the questions we will not ask here is: does genetic determinism obviate human free will? This is a fascinating question, and certainly relevant to our topic. Augustine speaks for the West when he connects sin with free will. 'Sin is nothing but the evil assent of free will, when we incline to those things which justice forbids and from which we are free to abstain. [Sin] does not lie in the things

---

1. Robert Wright, *The Moral Animal* (New York: Pantheon, 1994), 151.

themselves, but in their illegitimate use.'[2] In contrast to Augustine, contemporary sociobiologists cast considerable doubt on the very existence of the free will we take for granted on a daily basis. The concept of free will is said to be an illusion, what sociobiologists assess to be a useful cultural fiction employed by the genes to perpetuate themselves. 'So the notion of free will lives on', writes Robert Wright. 'But it shows signs of shrinking. Every time a behaviour is found to rest on chemistry, someone tries to remove it from the realm of volition.'[3] Fascinating though the question of free will may be, the question that directs this study is different: do genetic explanations for human behaviour exhaustively replace the Christian understanding of sin?

To pursue the answer to this question, I would like to remind us of the distinction between the *state of sin* and an *act of sin*, a distinction proffered by the neo-orthodox theologians at mid-twentieth century. Then I would like to turn to selected examples of human behaviour that have appeared on traditional lists of sins—lust, gluttony, greed, hatred of the enemy—which some have tried to explain on the basis of genetic determinism. Bracketing out for a moment debates over whether these really count as sins, I will note the surface similarities between genetic determinism and the theological concept of inherited sin. This·will be followed by a discussion internal to theology regarding the concepts of original sin and inherited sin to see if they match exhaustively what is being advocated by genetic explanations. My conclusion will be that these two do not match, at least not completely. What is decisive is that the concept of original sin in Christian theology is inextricably connected to its sister concept, God's grace. By *original sin* we refer to the unity of the entire human race in estrangement from God and subject to decay and death; whereas by *God's grace* we refer to the gift of redemption and eternal life God has wrought through the work of Jesus Christ. Each of us human beings live in this double definition, under both sin and grace, whether we recognise it or not. Even if genetic explanations turn out to be illuminative for some aspects of human behaviour, as scientific explan-

---

2. Augustine, *On the Literal Interpretation of Genesis*, Chapter 1, in *Saint Augustine On Genesis*, translated by Roland J Teske, SJ (Washington: Catholic University of America Press, 1991), 146.

3. Wright, *Moral Animal, op cit*, 352.

ations they fall short of supporting the theological claim that sinners are saved.

1. Sin as situation vs sin as action

The neo-orthodox and existentialist theologians were accustomed to distinguishing between 'Sin' in the singular with a capital 'S' from 'sins,' lower case and plural. The first refers to our situation of estrangement, the state of sin, into which we are born and within which we must live our lives. Paul Tillich described this as 'the state of estrangement from that to which one belongs—God, one's self, one's world.' He distinguished this from 'sins' understood as 'deviations from moral laws'. The latter are special acts that are considered sinful; and these are expressions of Sin as estrangement. 'It is not disobedience to a law which makes an act sinful', writes Tillich, 'but the fact that it is an expression of man's estrangement from God, from men, from himself. Therefore, Paul calls everything sin which does not result from faith, from the unity with God.'[4]

One of the difficulties with describing human sin in terms of situation or state is the risk of suggesting inactivity, of suggesting that sin is a static structure of being. It is an easy error to connect sin with finitude, with physical limitations, with creatureliness. Yet, according to the Christian tradition, God loves us as creatures. God loves us in our finitude; and in the incarnation God in Godself takes on the conditions of finitude, thereby blessing it. Even with our finite limitations, God can judge us to be 'very good'. Augustine put it this way: 'All the things which God made are very good; natural things are not evil.'[5]

Sin gives the misleading appearance of deriving from finitude because sinful actions seem to rely on the denial of finite limits. Finitude per se is not evil; so sin consists in a delusional denial of finitude. Reinhold Niebuhr makes this point forcefully. 'Sin is thus the unwillingness of man to acknowledge his creatureliness and depen-

---

4. Paul Tillich, *Systematic Theology*, Vol 2 (Chicago: University of Chicago, 1951-1963), 46-47. See Karl Barth, *Church Dogmatics* III/3 (Edinburgh: T&T Clark, 1936-1962), 310.

5. Augustine, *On the Literal Interpretation of Genesis*, 146. Karl Barth puts it this way: 'Finitude, then, is not intrinsically negative and evil.' *Church Dogmatics, op cit*, III/2, 631.

dence upon God and his effort to make his own life independent and secure. It is the vain imagination by which man hides his conditioned, contingent and dependent character of his existence and seeks to give it the appearance of unconditioned reality.'[6] Sin consists of a non-acceptance of our finitude, of treating ourselves as infinite in value. Such infinite value belongs only to God, of course; so treating oneself as infinite is the act whereby estrangement from God is actualised.

Awareness of finitude elicits anxiety, the fear of non-being.[7] Sin's delusion is that it can comfort us by sublimating anxiety into the will to power; and with power we fool ourselves into thinking we belong to infinite being. In the transition from past to future, our will to power influences if not determines our actions. Langdon Gilkey warns us that, due to human sin, an open future combines menace with possibility.

> The future is open because of our ontological situation of contingency, of temporality and of freedom; it is out of this that the temptation to sin arises. For those in power the anxiety of that openness is resolved by hanging onto the past; for those who seek power, that openness is secured by closing and dominating the future. Sin is neither merely the result of structures of the past nor is it

---

6. Reinhold Niebuhr, *The Nature and Destiny of Man,* Vol 1 (New York: Charles Scribner's Sons, 1941), 138.

7. André LaCoque starts with a phenomenology of anxiety and then works backward to explain myths of the fall such as the Adam and Eve story. 'The human being, as *homo religiosus*, is a creature that worries. His worrying is both his burden and his distinction . . . As soon as this ape could stand on his feet, his glance could lift itself toward the stars, that is, to a sphere higher—not only spatially—than that of the satisfaction of his bodily needs and functions. In this way man discovered the universe and, concomitantly, the existential problem of his place in the cosmos . . . In short, from being anxious, man became unhappy, stricken with guilt feelings about an initial accident that is repeated endlessly throughout human existence and can be called "sin".' André LaCoque, 'Sin and Guilt', *The Encyclopedia of Religion*, edited by Mircea Eliade (New York: Macmillan, 1987), Vols 13 & 14, 325.

merely the obstinacy of conservative forces. It can infect the creators of the new as well.[8]

Marjorie Hewitt Suchocki both criticises and complements this neo-orthodox analysis of sin. Her criticism is that we should not begin our analysis of sin with anxiety; rather, we should look to violence as the cause of anxiety. Anxiety results from prior experience with violence, not from awareness of finite limits. 'Violence rather than finitude per se is the presenting cause of anxiety . . . My thesis is that original sin is created . . . by a propensity toward violence [related to survival].'[9] Suchocki is considering here as background evolutionary biology and the violence resulting from the survival of the fittest. She is also positing a relational theology, according to which violence against creation is simultaneously violence against God. On this point, she actually complements the neo-orthodox understanding of sin, wherein violence within creation expresses estrangement from the divine.

Living in a state of sin is not something we originally choose. Once born and conscious, we wake up to find ourselves in a situation filled with anxiety and violence. As Martin Heidegger would say, we find ourselves 'thrown' into existence; and it is a sinful existence at that. In this sense, to our experience the state of sin is original sin; it precedes us and we cannot help but live in it. It is our inescapable inheritance.

2. Mean genes?

What does it mean to live in a state of sin? Could it mean that we live with a physical propensity toward ungodliness? Could it mean that we are born with a natural predilection toward immoral behaviour? Could it mean that we enter this life with a genetic predisposition toward self-expression that contradicts our spiritual goals and ethical values?

A relevant conversation partner here is what I have elsewhere called the 'gene myth' with its cardinal principle, 'it's all in the

---

8. Langdon Gilkey, *Reaping the Whirlwind* (New York: Seabury, Crossroad, 1976), 258.

9. Marjorie Hewitt Suchocki, *The Fall to Violence: Original Sin in Relational Theology* (New York: Continuum, 1994), 42. See: Mary Elise Lowe, 'Woman Oriented Hamartiologies: A Survey of the Shift from Powerlessness to Right Relationship,' *Dialog*, 39:2 (Summer 2000): 119-139.

genes'.[10] The gene myth's cultural currency is enjoying a bull market these days, due largely to growing investments in sociobiology, otherwise known as evolutionary psychology. Here the cardinal corollary principles are the 'selfish gene' and 'reproductive fitness' or 'reproductive advantage'. I refer to this as a myth because sociobology extends its explanatory claims well beyond the limits of what can be empirically known in the fields of molecular biology or evolutionary biology.[11] Sociobology explains everything in human culture according to one simple scheme: the drive for reproductive advantage by the selfish gene.

The theory of *The Selfish Gene* has become coin of the realm. The doctrine of reproductive fitness is so frequently assumed that it goes unquestioned. The phrase, 'selfish gene' coined by Richard Dawkins, attempts to provide a biological account of selfishness and altruism in human culture.[12] This superficially compelling theory is that genes are by nature selfish—ruthlessly selfish!—and that genes are the drivers directing natural and human history.[13] The organism is but DNA's way of making more DNA. Human beings as individuals and as a species serve the genes as vehicles for their replicating process and the achievement of their ultimate objective, survival long enough to reproduce. We human beings are but small coins in a genetic stock market wherein each gene seeks to profit beyond all competitors.

---

10. Ted Peters, *Playing God? Genetic Determinism and Human Freedom* (London: Routledge, 1997), Chapter 2.

11. I suggest here that molecular biologists who engage in hands-on laboratory experimentation with genetics seem to be less deterministic than sociobiologists who are developing a cultural ideology based upon Neo-Darwinian evolutionary theory. 'Genetic information does not dictate everything about us', says geneticist Walter Gilbert. 'A Vision of the Grail', in *The Code of Codes: Scientific and Social Issues in the Human Genome Project*, edited by Daniel J Kevles and Leroy Hood (Cambridge: Harvard University Press, 1992), 96.

12. Richard Dawkins, *The Selfish Gene* (New York: Oxford University Press, 1976, 1989).

13. 'Genes are selfish. They only think about themselves. For an individual gene, the human body is just a temporary vessel to be used briefly and discarded on the march through time. The gene has only one mission—to endure—and the only way it can continue to exist is if its host multiplies and passes on the genetic information to the next generation. The cold, calculated process of evolution is mercilessly unkind to genes that don't contribute to reproduction, cleansing these genes from the species, causing them to die out quickly.' Dean Hamer and Peter Copeland, *The Science of Desire* (New York: Simon and Schuster, 1994), 180.

Every aspect of our social lives—our loving and hating, our fighting and cooperating, our giving and stealing, our greed and generosity—are but transactions within the broader evolutionary economy. What we experience in our daily life as human selfishness has an underlying biological explanation. We are selfish because the genes are selfish.

Sociobiologists, curiously enough, argue that even when we are altruistic to the extent of self-sacrifice our behaviour is still explainable by the selfishness of the gene. Why? Because what appears to be genuine altruism is, when genetically understood, only an apparent or pseudo altruism. The selfish gene allegedly uses altruism in the form of cooperation—reciprocal altruism or inclusive fitness—to perpetuate its own survival through the hereditary process.

Sociobiologists like to emphasise that altruism is tied to kinship. We as individuals are willing to sacrifice ourselves for a brother or sister or someone to whom we feel loyal; and the strength of feeling of loyalty is in direct proportion to the number of genes we hold in common. Loyalty helps insure the survival of someone belonging to our own group, our own family, our own race, our own nation; and in this way loyalty insures the survival of our own genes. This explains how territorialism, xenophobia, and war are expressions of altruism. This explains why we consider a soldier dying bravely in battle as one who sacrificed for others, the others being those belonging to our own nation or group and not our enemies. What theologians take to be the highest human virtue—namely, self-sacrificial love on behalf of another—is, according to sociobiologists, blind sacrifice in service to the perpetuation of privileged genes. Altruism, just like selfishness, can be reduced to biological determinants.

Our concern here is sin, not altruism, especially if altruism is only a disguised form of selfishness. A brief clarification is in order here: selfishness, according to sociobiological theory, is not tied to a specific gene located on a specific chromosome that codes for selfishness. The concept of the selfish gene here is based upon a general principle, namely, DNA replicates itself. The observation that DNA replicates itself is lifted up by the sociobiologists into the realm of principle, telos, entelechy, emperor of nature and culture. The blind ongoing process of DNA replication is the dictator of what sociobiologists refer to as genetic selfishness.

3. Lust

Can we explain what we have come to think of as human sinfulness via genetic determinism?[14] Our medieval forebears liked the number seven and bequeathed us with septinaries of sinful behaviours that seemed to violate divine law and disrupt communal tranquillity. Most lists included pride, envy, lust, gluttony, avarice or greed, anger or wrath, and sloth. Here we will look briefly at lust, gluttony, greed, plus a sin Jesus particularly concerned himself with, fear of the stranger or hatred of the enemy.

Beginning with lust, the Christian tradition has long concerned itself with desire or concupiscence as a force that potentially leads to obsession. As a physical force, it clouds the mind. As a material force it tempts us away from higher values of the spirit. As a social force, it leads to infidelity and family disruption. Could it be genetic? It certainly appears so.

In their new book, *Mean Genes*, Terry Burnham and Jay Phelan tell us that infidelity lies in the genes. Whether in the animal world or human world, our biologies drive us to prepare to have as many children as possible in order to insure the passing on of our genes. Evolution has not constructed our bodies for monogamy; rather, evolution has sought to maximise our sexual exploitation in order to use us for reproductive purposes. 'Most animals never form marriage-like bonds. Love 'em and leave 'em one-night stands are the norm. Monogamy among mammals, in particular, is rare . . . Faithful or not in life, human bodies are designed for infidelity.'[15]

In human beings about ninety-nine per cent of sperm when ejaculated are not themselves fertile; rather, they have the function of seeking out and destroying the sperm other men have left in the womb. Some anti-sperm actually seek out other men's sperm and

---

14. Most sociobiologists wish to avoid a 'right-wing doctrine of genetic determinism', preferring instead to emphasise the interaction between genes and environment. See: Wright, *Moral Animal*, 348. Even if this is a two-part determinism, it remains determinism; and the cardinal principle that DNA functions as a puppet in every environment remains intact. My own counter has been to argue for a three-part determinism: genes, environment, and self. I believe the human self is an emergent property and cannot be reduced completely to its genetic or environmental substrate. *Playing God?* 165-168.

15. Terry Burnham and Jay Phelan, *Mean Genes: From Sex to Money to Food: Taming Our Primal Instincts* (Cambridge MA: Perseus Publishing, 2000), 174-175.

block their access to the uterus. Interpreted, this means that in our evolutionary history women mated with numerous men, and those whose progeny survived must have had the victorious warrior sperm. 'The prevalence and universality of human infidelity have deep biological roots . . . Unfaithful women are seeking better genes for their babies and / or better partners. Unfaithful men are seeking additional fertility and / or better partners.'[16] Robert Wright puts it this way:

> Natural selection has wielded its influence largely via the emotional spigots that turn on and off such feelings as tentative attraction, fierce passion, and swoon-inducing infatuation. A woman does not typically size up a man and think: 'He seems like a worthy contributor to my genetic legacy.' She just sizes him up and feels attracted to him—or doesn't. All the 'thinking' has been done—unconsciously, metaphorically—by natural selection. Genes leading to attractions that wound up being good for her ancestors' genetic legacies have flourished, and those leading to less productive attractions have not.[17]

Are lust and infidelity genetic? Men have eyes for reproductively attractive women; and 'human females are not devoutly monogamous by nature', says Wright, who clearly holds that lust and infidelity are in the genes.[18]

Not everyone attempting to connect genes with behaviour operates with such a simplistic model. Molecular biologist John Medina has reviewed the classic seven deadly sins in light of emerging genetic knowledge and brain research. When it comes to our emotional experience of lust, much happens physically at a level below consciousness, to be sure; but all this activity is not reducible to gene activity. Hormonal, glandular, neuronal activity is operative. Yes, much of this activity happens *to us*, so to speak, rather than activity we *will* into existence. Biology does have its influence, to be sure. Nevertheless, it's not all in the genes, according to Medina. He argues: 'There

---

16. *Ibid*, 177-178.
17. Wright, *The Moral Animal, op cit*, 37.
18. *Ibid*, 89.

is no gene for promiscuity.'[19] Although Medina here helps reduce the spectre of genetic determinism, he still misses part of the point. The sociobiologist would counter that our biological propensity toward infidelity is due to the general principle of reproductive fitness, not a specific gene.

Medina could counter this counter by arguing that what we experience as sexual arousal—lust—is not reducible to genetic activity. By studying the physiology of sexual arousal, Medina observes levels of complexity that involve incalculable extra-genetic physical factors and even cultural factors.

> There is no one true gene involved in sexual arousal . . . The feelings of sexual desire are best understood as an emergent property of at least four interlocking physiological systems, at least eleven different regions of the brain, more than thirty distinct bio-chemical mechanisms and literally hundreds of specific genes supporting these various processes.[20]

If sexual lust is an emergent property, then it's not all in the genes.

Nevertheless, the theologian should not seek comfort in severing off some portion of human moral or immoral activity from our biology. No doubt due to hormonal activation lust has a significant physiological component, even if it cannot be exhaustively reduced to what is physical.[21]

4. Gluttony

So many of us feel tempted to eat too much. Although we in the modern world seldom refer to the sin of gluttony, we know the

---

19. John Medina, *The Genetic Inferno: Inside the Seven Deadly Sins* (Cambridge UK: Cambridge University Press, 2000), 6.

20. *Ibid*, 26.

21. Philosophical theologian Holmes Rolston accepts genes as deterministic. 'Human *concupiscence* or *cupiditas* (selfish desire) has long been recognized and lamented, *eros* (self-love) produces vices as readily as virtues, and the need for moral reformation is no new claim. What might be new is that, now in biological science, the cause has, for the first time, been found in genetic determinants.' Holmes Rolston III, *Genes, Genesis, and God* (Cambridge UK: Cambridge University Press, 1999), 226.

difficulty of dieting and reducing. This too has an explanation deriving from the gene myth, an aetiological explanation. Back in prehistory, so the genetic explanation goes, our primordial ancestors were hunter-gatherers living in a hostile natural environment. Drought and famine were common. Our ancestors met these challenges by overeating in time of plenty and then enduring time of scarcity. Their genes allegedly adapted to the cycles of plenty and scarcity by building up fat and then burning it. Because of the rise of modern civilisation and our ever-present food availability, we no longer have scarcity to contend with. Our thrifty genes, adapted for a bygone age, now get us into trouble by driving us to overeat in anticipation of a scarcity that never comes. 'Our genes have built us to love food and hate exercise; accordingly, the root of our weight problem is that our wild genes now live in a tame world.'[22]

Such an argument is an elementary extrapolation of common sense. 'Every creature on the planet has to solve a similar and continual energy crisis, finding enough fuel to live to another day', writes Medina. 'Since organisms with no appetite by definition starve to death, creating an appetite is a beneficial thing to do.'[23]

5. Greed

'Greed is good', says Gordon Gekko in the movie *Wall Street*. 'Greed captures the essence of the evolutionary spirit and has marked the upward surge of mankind.' What makes greed greed—or what theologians associate with concupiscence, covetousness, avarice, envy, and such—is its insatiability. More than meeting needs and attaining satiety, greed like gluttony pursues consumption beyond biological or even psychological fulfilment. Greed is what propels us toward what we think will provide happiness; yet, once the object of greed is attained, we set new unreachable goals that makes happiness ever elusive.

Could this tragedy be genetic? Well, yes, according to sociobiological thinking. 'Happiness is a tool that our genes use to induce us toward behaviours that benefit them', write Burnham and Phelan.[24] Evolution is a competitive game in which victory comes not from

---

22. Burnham and Phelan, *Mean Genes*, 52.

23. Medina, *Genetic Inferno*, 106.

24. Burnham and Phelan, *Mean Genes*, 112.

achieving some attainable goal but rather by outscoring the opposition. We are descendents from the peoples who 'had the most children, not from those with "enough" children'.[25]

Medina indirectly counters, 'The problem is that *no one has ever found a gene for avarice in human beings.* No one has ever found a region in the human brain exclusively devoted to greed for that matter.'[26] According to Medina, what we know as greed or avarice is a subjective category, a distinctively human phenomenon not reducible to genetic or neuronal biology. Certainly anxiety and fear, which are associated with gene expression and neuronal activity, are also associated with the insatiable desire to obtain and consume; yet no causative connection between biology and greed can be scientifically established. 'A subjective category constructed by humans does not always reflect a biological function constructed by nature.'[27]

5. Xenophobia

Combining the drive for reproductive fitness with evolutionary competitiveness, we can understand why Alfred Lord Tennyson would describe nature as blood 'red in tooth and claw'. Any Darwinian interpretation of the human species must include this brutal propensity toward violence. It seems to explain war. Further, it seems to explain war in the form of clan revenge and tribal rivalry and racial prejudice. Sociobiology attributes social divisions to genetics. Persons who share a greater number of genes will band together to commit violence against those outside the genetic fold. Families fight against families, clans against clans, tribes against tribes, races against races. Xenophobia, fear of foreigners, is reproductively adaptive. EO Wilson explains human violence in terms of genetic determinism:

> Human beings are strongly predisposed to respond
> with unreasoning hatred to external threats and to
> escalate their hostility sufficiently to overwhelm the
> source of the threat by a respectably wide margin of
> safety. Our brains do appear to be programmed to
> the following extent: we are inclined to partition
> other people into friends and aliens . . . We tend to

---

25. *Ibid*, 118.
26. Medina, *Genetic Inferno*, 110, author's italics.
27. *Ibid*, 327.

fear deeply the actions of strangers and to solve conflict by aggression. These learning rules are most likely to have evolved during the past hundreds of thousands of years of human evolution and, thus, to have conferred a biological advantage on those who conformed to them with the greatest fidelity.[28]

Instead of loving one's enemy as Jesus teaches, our selfish genes teach us to decimate the enemy. In Darwinian and Spencerian terms, reproductive fitness is said to be the product of evolutionary development that constitutes a 'biological advantage' for those who conform with the greatest fidelity.[29]

If we are genetically programmed to fear strangers and decimate our enemies, should we ask our genes to provide the values and ethics to live by? Do we receive moral validation from nature to limit doing good to those who do good to us, and for hating our enemy? If our genes are selfish, should we be selfish as well? Can we base the *ought* of our ethics on what *is* true about nature?[30] Molecular biologist Dean Hamer would say, no. 'Biology is amoral. It offers no help distin-

---

28. Edward O Wilson, *On Human Nature* (New York: Bantam, 1978), 122-123.

29. Wilson says this descriptively, of course, not prescriptively. Just because we can describe a pattern of human behavior developed through our evolution, this does not mean we should prescribe that behavior or make it a moral standard. Arthur Caplan reminds us not to confuse conclusions drawn from 'the evolution of human ethics' with commitment to 'the ethics of evolution'. 'Ethics, Evolution, and the Milk of Human Kindness,' *The Sociobiology Debate*, edited by Arthur L Caplan (New York: Harper & Row, 1978), 313.

30. Is Neo-Darwinian biology merely descriptive, or is it also prescriptive? Should we develop an ethic of Social Darwinism based on the selfish gene? Those who oppose Social Darwinism include in their arguments opposition to the naturalistic fallacy. This fallacy is committed when we assume that what exists in nature is good, and that what exists in nature sets the standard for human morality. It is a fallacy to base the *ought* on the *is*. 'It is important to emphasize this point', writes William Irons, who is an advocate of Human Behavior Ecology, 'because people frequently assume that any attempt to address morality in evolutionary terms must include some argument to the effect that it is somehow morally good to do the things that we evolved to do. This is emphatically not what I argue . . .' 'How Did Morality Evolve?' *Zygon*, 26:1 (March 1991): 51.

guishing between right and wrong. Only people, guided by their values and beliefs, can decide what is moral and what is not.'[31]

So, where do we find ourselves? On the one hand, genes are said to be deterministic. Yet, on the other hand, when it comes to moral living, some of us wish to transcend our genes, perhaps even disobey our genes. Can we do it?

6. Can we outsmart our genes?

Can the human race catapult itself culturally so as to fly above and away from its biological base? Can the future escape the determinism of its evolutionary past? No, says E O Wilson.

> Can the cultural evolution of higher ethical values gain a direction and momentum of its own and completely replace genetic evolution? I think not. The genes hold culture on a leash. The leash is very long, but inevitably values will be constrained in accordance with their effects on the human gene pool.[32]

Yes, say others. 'Understanding the often unconscious nature of genetic control is the first step toward understanding that—in many realms, not just sex—we're all puppets', writes Robert Wright, 'and our best hope for even partial liberation is to try to decipher the logic of the puppeteer.'[33] Wright assumes that if we understand the puppeteer then we will have what it takes to liberate ourselves from genetic determinism.

Similarly, Burnham and Phelan in *Mean Genes* contend that we can transcend our genetic heritage. We should 'fight' against our 'mean genes'.[34] How can we win? We fight our genes by *understanding* them

---

31. Hamer and Copeland, *Science of Desire*, 214.
32. Wilson, *On Human Nature*, 175. When responding to critics, Wilson goes on to say that 'human nature can adapt to more encompassing forms of altruism and social justice. Genetic biases can be trespassed, passions averted or redirected, and ethics altered; and the human genius for making contracts can continue to be applied to achieve healthier and freer societies. Yet the mind is not infinitely malleable.' 'For Sociobiology,' *The Sociobiology Debate*, 267.
33. Wright, *Moral Animal*, 37.
34. Burnham and Phelan, *Mean Genes*, 195.

according to Darwinian evolutionary theory, making a *decision* to act according to our will, and taking *control* of our lives. Burnham and Phelan see our genes as providing temptations and our fighting them as overcoming temptations.

> Our temptations are powerful and persistent, but we are not destined to succumb. Ancient and selfish, our mean genes influence us every day in almost every way. But because we can predict their influence, self-knowledge plus discipline can provide a winning strategy in the battle to lead satisfying and moral lives.[35]

At work here is a curious assumption. Even though we have a doctrine of strong genetic determinism, the assumption is that the human self is not exhaustively determined by the genes. Even though the genes 'influence us every day in almost every way', somewhere there exists a self independent of genetic influence. It is this self who predicts genetic influence and provides a winning strategy. It is this self who, despite genetic determinism, can lead a satisfying and moral life. Now, we might ask: where does that self come from? Wilson and Dawkins seem to get along without such a non-reducible self; but Burnham, Phelan and Medina indirectly affirm such a self.

Medina repudiates forcefully reductionism. He addresses misperceptions about the relation of genes to behaviour:

> I don't know how many times I've thrown down a newspaper after reading things like, 'scientists have isolated the genes responsible for adultery' or an article describing the 'DNA behind the desire to eat chocolate', or that there are actually chromosomes responsible for the predilection to vote Republican. The attitude that, 'If you have the gene, then you have the tendency' occurs with such frequency that

---

35. *Ibid*, 252. The scientific, or better, technological, approach to solving human problems according to the *understanding-decision-control* (udc) formula I developed when analysing futurology. See: Ted Peters, *Futures—Human and Divine* (Louisville: Westminster/John Knox, 1977).

> many of us who wear lab coats have quit reading the
> popular press. From a researcher's perspective, most
> of these headlines carry no more scientific integrity
> than an ointment made from a hanged man's skull
> garden.[36]

What we see here is that the jury is still out on the question: is human behaviour, including sinful behaviour, exhaustively reducible to genetic determinism? It is my own preliminary judgment: probably not. Regardless of what verdict the scientific jury returns with, we still should heed what Audrey Chapman says, 'To conclude that there is not yet definitive genetic evidence for a correlation between specific genes and antisocial or aggressive behaviour behaviour does not, of course, say anything about the existence or non-existence of sin'.[37]

7. Is sin a bio-inheritance?

If we simply grant without further argument the basic claims of sociobiology regarding the selfish gene, we end up with an anthropology according to which each of us inherits biologically a propensity for destructive behaviour. Curiously, theologians of the modern period have nearly abandoned the notion of bio-inherited sinfulness. Friedrich Schleiermacher tries to sever the tie between Adam and Eve's first sin and our bio-inheritance. While affirming the universality of human sinfulness, Schleiermacher rejects as essential the belief that the first pair of human beings altered human nature and then passed on this corruption biologically through subsequent generations.[38]

The longer Christian tradition, however, has presumed that we inherit the originating sin of Adam and Eve through our birth into the one human family. This one human family shares a disease, sin. The Augsburg Confession of 1530 puts it this way:

> Since the fall of Adam all men who are born
> according to the course of nature are conceived and
> born in sin. That is, all men are full of evil lust and

---

36. Medina, *Genetic Inferno*, 2-3.

37. Audrey R Chapman, *Unprecedented Choices: Religious Ethics at the Frontiers of Genetic Science* (Minneapolis: Fortress, 1999), 193.

38. Fredrich Schleiermacher, *The Christian Faith* (Edinburgh: T&T Clark, 1928, 1960), 291.

inclinations from their mother's wombs and are unable by nature to have true fear of God and true faith in God. Moreover, this inborn sickness and hereditary sin (*Erbsünde*) is truly sin and condemns to the eternal wrath of God all those who are not born again through Baptism and the Holy Spirit.[39]

John Calvin speaks for much of Western Christianity when he writes,

Original sin, therefore, seems to be a hereditary depravity and corruption of our nature, diffused into all parts of the soul, which makes us first liable to God's wrath, then also brings forth in us those works which scripture calls 'works of the flesh' (Gal 5:19).[40]

Even though the predisposition to sin is inherited, it is also clear in Calvin that this predisposition does not belong to our nature. Sin is a corruption of our nature. If we could say there is consonance between what sociobiologists mean by the selfishness of our genes and what Calvin means by original sin, a difference would remain, namely, the

---

39. Augsburg Confession, Article II, in *The Book of Concord*, edited by Theodore G Tappert (Minneapolis: Fortress Press, 1959), 29. Now, we might ask, are we sinful by nature? The answer may be less than fully clear here in the Augsburg Confession. We get greater clarity regarding the relationship of nature to sin in the Formula of Concord: '. . . there is a distinction between man's nature and original sin, not only in the beginning when God created man pure and holy and without sin, but also as we now have our nature after the Fall.' *Ibid*, 466. Philip Hefner comments, 'The mainstream of the tradition wishes to avoid two extremes in thinking about this sin: on the one hand, a cool view of sin as defect, overlooking the ferocity of sinful intention; on the other hand, a view of sin as total depravity that demolishes the God-given original goodness that pertains to humans. I cite the Lutheran versions of the doctrine because they seem, when taken as a whole, to represent the main tradition without the extremes—the *Augsburg Confession* articulating the inherent ferocity of the sin, the *Formula of Concord* insisting upon human created goodness.' *The Human Factor* (Minneapolis: Fortress, 1993), 127.

40. John Calvin, *Institutes of the Christian Religion*, Vol XX of *The Library of Christian Classics*, translated by FL Battles (Louisville: Westminster/John Knox Press, 1960), 251.

first is considered natural and the second not. Original sin may be inherited sin, but it is added to an otherwise originally good nature. As we mentioned earlier, Christians affirm the goodness of creation coming originally from the hand of a good creator. No matter how pervasive be human sin in our world today, it represents an infection by an alien virus of an otherwise healthy creation. Original sin is something like a disease that is passed on congenitally.

How, then, can we conceptualise an original good nature when we are born into sin? Traditionally, the Genesis account of Adam and Eve provided a narrative way to overcome this apparent logical contradiction. By using a historical framework, ancient theologians could place first in time what we read in Genesis Chapter one: the creation is 'very good'. Then, second, they could follow this with the fall and the corruption of a previously good creation. Temporal sequence overcame the apparent contradiction.

However, with the appearance of evolutionary theory in the nineteenth century and its widespread acceptance in the theological community—the battle over scientific and biblical creationism notwithstanding—this temporal approach lost considerable credibility. Reliance upon deep time and the picture of evolving nature left no room for a datable historical Garden of Eden and a perfect paradise from which all other life forms devolved. Even though the fact that we inherit a propensity for selfish behaviour seems obvious to anyone looking, theologians lost a handle on the original or first sin.

Philip Hefner, a theologian for whom sociobiology plays an important constructive role, says,

> I rejected the 'first sin' interpretation of the story of Adam and Eve and the serpent, with its etiological approach. Consequently, I reject also a concept of original sinlessness and the fall . . . [Yet we are] predisposed to feeling guilty because of the broad range of evolutionarily originated information that it carries within it . . . Furthermore, this character can and does engender real evil, what the tradition calls *actual* sin.[41]

---

41. Philip Hefner, *The Human Factor* (Minneapolis: Fortress, 1993), 240.

What we see here is acceptance of the fact that we are born with a propensity for sinful actions; but the term 'original sin' should not apply if it refers to an alleged historical event in the lives of Adam and Eve. Instead of Adam and Eve, it is evolution that has provided us with the sinful disposition we inherit.

For the most part, to my reading, contemporary theologians find the concept of original sin vital; yet they do not intend by it reference to a historical Adam and Eve. Rather, the term *original sin* simply acknowledges that all members of the human race are born into the same fundamental condition, the same interlocking relationships between self, other, and God.

Curiously, Karl Barth defends the doctrine of original sin but opposes the metaphor of biological inheritance saying, '"Hereditary sin" has a hopelessly naturalistic, deterministic and even fatalistic ring'.[42] Upon reviewing the Adam and Eve story, Barth suggests that the actual sin that they committed was quite trivial. We today are capable of much worse. We are also free.

> This does not mean that he [Adam] has bequeathed it to us as his heirs so that we have to be as he was. He has not poisoned us or passed on a disease. What we do after him is not done according to an example which irresistibly overthrows us, or in an imitation of his act which is ordained for all his successors. No one has to be Adam. We are so freely and on our own responsibility.[43]

Perhaps Barth could be corrected by genetic science or by sociobiology regarding an inherited predisposition toward sinful behaviour; but his assumption that sin is universal would go unchallenged. Persons are made up of DNA everywhere.

We can see that if Barth were alive today and participating in this discussion, what would energise him most would be the challenge of genetic determinism to human freedom. The point here, of course, is that even though Barth avoids the metaphor of inherited disease, he certainly recognises the universal scope of human sin. All of us find

---

42. Barth, *Church Dogmatics*, IV/1:501.
43. *Ibid*, IV/1:509.

ourselves 'in Adam', and hence in sin. The story of Adam is the truth about us.

8. We are Adam and Eve

This brings us to the doorstep of what is most important to Christian theology regarding the concept of original sin, namely, its universality and its significance for our relationship to God. What is most important here is not human behaviour, nor even our inborn predisposition to behave sinfully. Rather, first on the list of importance is acknowledgment that the condition or state in which we currently find the human race is one of estrangement, of alienation from the mind and heart of our divine creator and redeemer. A careful retracing of Augustine's biblical exegesis will help illuminate my observation here. The ancient Bishop of Hippo wrestled with interpreting biblical texts such as the following:

> Sin came into the world through one man, and death came through sin, and so death spread to all because all have sinned . . . For if the many died through the one man's trespass, much more surely have the grace of God and the free gift in the grace of the one man, Jesus Christ, abounded for the many. And the free gift is not like the effect of the one man's sin. For the judgment following one trespass brought condemnation, but the free gift following many trespasses brings justification (Rom 5:12; 15b-16)

> For since death came through a human being, the resurrection of the dead has also come through a human being; for as all die in Adam, so all will be made alive in Christ (1 Cor 15:21-22)

What does Augustine read here? What attracts his eyes are the phrases 'in Adam' and 'in Christ'. And, within these phrases, he focuses on the little word, 'in'. He wonders just how we could be thought of as 'in' Adam and 'in' Christ at the same time.

It is not enough to say that those of us who sin today merely imitate the sin that Adam committed many years ago, says Augustine. It is not enough to say that each of us behaves *like* Adam. Adam's act and our acts are somehow tied together. We participate in Adam somehow, and Adam participates in us. The prepositional phrase, '*in* Adam', is key here. Augustine's initial concern is Christ and the work of salvation. The saving power of the gospel is that Christ enters into us and we into him. Christians do not merely imitate Christ. By the power of the Holy Spirit, the resurrected Christ himself enters the inner life of the person of faith, and 'his grace works within us our illumination and justification'.[44] Apparently by reverse logic, in order to keep true to the Pauline juxtaposition, Augustine asserts that our relation to Adam must parallel our relation to Christ in similar respect.

What is decisive for understanding the doctrine of original sin, at least as we have received it from Augustine, is its role in describing the human condition. As human beings, we enjoy a double ontology. We find ourselves both *in Adam* and *in Christ*, in death and in life, in sin and in grace. The Lutheran Reformation siphoned off some of the meaning here to describe a saint as *simul justus et peccator*, simultaneously justified yet sinful. Whether we accept or even acknowledge God's gracious disposition toward us through Jesus Christ, we sinners are still doubly defined by our diseased and our healed relationship to God.

Augustine is driven by intellectual curiosity, by energy to invest in figuring out puzzles. So, he ponders a puzzle: how is it that Adam's sin of yesterday is *in* our sin today? Could the answer be through biological inheritance? So, Augustine puts forth the idea of a congenital disease as an explanation for the unity of the human race as sinful. Sin passes to all of us by natural descent, not merely by imitation. Augustine distinguishes each of our actual sins from original sin, to be

---

44. Augustine, *On the Merits and Remission of Sins, and On the Baptism of Infants* (*De Peccatorum Meritis et Remissione, et de Baptismo Parvulorum*), I:10. Jaroslav Pelikan believes Augustine may have made an error in exegesis here, being misled by the Latin translation he was using. The key clause in Romans 5:12 should have read, 'because all have sinned' as we see in the current NRSV version, but the text on which Augustine was relying read, 'in whom all have sinned.' *The Christian Tradition: A History of the Development of Doctrine*, Vol 1 (Chicago: University of Chicago Press, 1971-1989), 299. I believe it is Pelikan, not Augustine, who makes the error. The problem with Pelikan's reading here is twofold. First, 'in Adam' also appears in 1 Cor 15:22, so Augustine is not dependent upon only one ambiguous text. Second, and more importantly, Augustine's interpretation depends on more than merely the prepositional phrase; it depends on Paul's juxtaposition of Adam with Christ.

sure; but he also affirms that our being born into an already fallen human race means that we inherit the originating sin of our primordial parents.

In proffering the procreative theory he does not intend to argue for some sort of biological determinism that erases our moral responsibility. Rather, his intent is to affirm a wholeness principle wherein we can see that the whole of the human race is bound together in sin just as the whole human race is destined to enjoy the benefits of Christ's saving work.

> And from this we gather that we have derived from Adam, in whom all have sinned, not all our actual sins, but only original sin; whereas from Christ, in whom we are all justified, we obtain the remission not merely of that original sin, but of the rest of our sins also, which we have added.[45]

My point here is that the weight of Augustine's explication of the symbol of sin does not rest on the biological mechanism of transmission; rather, it rests on the need to affirm unity in Christ and correspondingly unity in sin.

Returning to the modern neo-orthodox, Reinhold Niebuhr argues like Barth against using the metaphor of inheritance, referring to it as a 'literalistic error'. What Augustine had wanted to affirm was the idea of mystical identity, observed Niebuhr, the sense of human solidarity in sin.[46] This insight stands. Niebuhr proceeds to argue for the viability of the Christian insight; yet he recognises that it is both realistic and absurd at the same time. Why? Because human sin is universal but not necessary.

> Here is the absurdity in a nutshell. Original sin, which is by definition an inherited corruption, or at least an inevitable one, is nevertheless not to be regarded as belonging to his essential nature and therefore is not outside the realm of his responsibility. Sin is natural for man in the sense that

---

45. Augustine, 'On the Merits and Remissions of Sins', I:16.
46. Niebuhr, *Nature and Destiny of Man*, 1:260-261.

it is universal but not in the sense that it is
necessary.[47]

What Niebuhr is saying is that sin is not built into nature; yet it is
inevitable. Sin is predictable, not in any given instance but as an
overall prediction regarding the human future. Sin is a universal
contingent, and the truth of the matter can be confirmed by simply
observing what human beings do over a period of time.[48] Niebuhr
was fond of quoting the *London Times Literary Supplement*, 'The doctrine
of original sin is the only empirically verifiable doctrine of the
Christian faith'.[49]

The use of the term 'empirically verifiable' connotes something
scientific; yet the neo-orthodox theologians seem to immunise
themselves prematurely against science. Gerhard Forde, in a fashion
similar to Barth and Niebuhr, alerts us to an apparent danger of
thinking of sin as hereditary. That original sin exists is obvious, of
course; but, he says, the idea of hereditary sin is

> best avoided in an age that thinks of heredity in
> terms of genes and DNA. Such talk might lead us to
> think that genetic engineering could discover and
> remove original sin. In any case it makes the mistake
> of offering a biological answer to a theological
> question.[50]

I would ask: if a biological answer might be possible, why not pursue
it?

---

47. *Ibid*, 1:242.

48. The term 'universal contingent' is employed by Robert John Russell to draw out
the implications of Niebuhr's notion of 'inevitable but not necessary'. See
Russell's 'The Thermodynamics of Natural Evil', *CTNS Bulletin,* 10:2 (Spring
1990): 20-25.

49. Niebuhr, *Man's Nature and His Communities,* 24. Karl Barth's observation was
similar. 'Is the doctrine of original sin merely one doctrine among many? Is it not
rather . . . the doctrine which emerges from all honest study of history?' *The
Epistle to the Romans* (New York and Oxford: Oxford University Press, 1933,
1977), 85-86.

50. Gerhard O Forde, *Theology is for Proclamation* (Minneapolis: Fortress Press,
1990), 53.

9. Conclusion

Now, nearly a half-century since the neo-orthodox school taught us some of the most profound lessons about human nature and human sin, we find ourselves in a curious situation. Christian theologians are affirming the notion of original sin but are reluctant to affirm its biological transmissibility, whereas natural scientists are debating the possibility that human predispositions toward what hitherto has been known as sinful behaviour is genetically inherited. Are these two telephone callers dialling one another and both receiving busy signals?

7

The Emergence of Guilt and 'Sin' in Human Evolution: A Theological Reflection

Mark Worthing

1. Introduction

Dialogue between theology and the natural sciences has always involved the challenge to find genuine common ground. The phenomenon of sin is a fruitful area of dialogue that is often overlooked because of lack of common terminology and misconceptions on both sides. Those working from the perspective of the natural sciences tend to view sin as an exclusively theological topic and find the sin language of theologians inaccessible. The evolutionary biologist resists quite understandably the attempt to impose moral valuations upon natural processes. Theologians, on the other hand, may fear that a linking of sin with evolutionary understandings of human origins will weaken the biblical conception of sin. Emil Brunner reflected the concerns of many theologians when he concluded that 'the development of Natural Science and the Theory of Evolution has not contributed anything to the understanding of sin, but has rather led people astray: leading them to regard sin as atavism—that is, going back to the pre-human stage of development'.[1] With such views persisting within each field of enquiry it is little surprise that the concept of sin, with some notable exceptions,[2] has often not been a

---

1.   Emil Brunner, *The Christian Doctrine of Creation and Redemption*, translated by Olive Wyon (Philadelphia: Westminster Press, 1952), 117.

2.   On the theological side one might mention, among others, the contributions of Karl Rahner, 'The Sin of Adam', *Theological Investigations* Vol 11 (New York: Crossroad, 1961-1972); 'Theological Reflections on Monogenism', *Theological Investigations* Volume 1, and other articles; Gerd Theissen, *Biblical Faith: An Evolutionary Approach* (London: SCM, 1984); and Philip Hefner, *The Human Factor: Evolution, Culture and Religion* (Minneapolis: Fortress, 1993).

significant point of dialogue between theology and the natural sciences. Developments within both evolutionary science and theology, however, suggest new possibilities for dialogue on the nature and origins of human sin.

A recent trend in scientific anthropology has been to study the evolutionary histories of distinctive aspects of the human being. The evolution of consciousness and language have received particular attention, mostly originating out of the fields of ethology and comparative psychology.[3] Rather than looking at the human being as a whole and asking how we became so different from other members of the animal kingdom—individual qualities that we value as distinctively human are examined. For instance, just how did communication and eventually language evolve? Are there any commonalities with what we find among animals? The same questions are being asked with regard to consciousness. The question is not so much when and how humans become conscious of themselves but rather how consciousness as such developed. What needs did consciousness and language meet and what functions did they serve that would give a species in possession of them some evolutionary advantage?

2. Theological and naturalistic understandings of 'sin'

Along with such qualities as consciousness and language, theologians usually contend that what we call 'sin' is characteristic of the human being. The tendency of all human beings to be centred upon self and to act at times in decisively non-altruistic ways is a universal phenomenon among our species.[4] But from whence does sinfulness, or the sense of sinfulness, come? At what point or stage in our evolutionary history do humans become sinful? What the current approach in comparative anthropology suggests is that we may be asking the wrong questions—or at least asking them in the wrong way. The more pertinent and interesting questions must attempt to isolate and examine sin in its own right. How and why might sin, or a consciousness of sinfulness, arise within any species? Are there related

---

3.   For instance Marc Hauser, *The Evolution of Communication* (Boston: MIT Press, 1996), Euan MacPhail, *The Evolution of Consciousness*, and Robert Axeland. *The Evolution of Cooperation* (New York: Basic Books, 1984).

4.   Cf Wolfhart Pannenberg, *Anthropology in Theological Perspective*, translated by Matthew O'Connell (Philadelphia: Westminster Press, 1985), 119ff.

phenomena among non-human species? And what evolutionary advantage does a consciousness of sin give to humanity?

These are the questions that are most interesting to theologians. But are they scientifically meaningful? Can we directly address the question of the evolutionary function of a consciousness of sin, or is sin too theologically laden a concept to be addressed in this manner? To answer these questions we must first consider what we mean by 'sin' in the context of the evolutionary history of life on our planet? We must ask whether our evolutionary inheritance, for instance the genetically programmed tendency toward territorialism, can be called sin in the theological sense. Among ethologists who have worked with this concept there is a danger of reducing the understanding of sin to aggression. What is sometimes not clear, however, in such discussions is why aggression among non-human species is seen to be morally neutral, and in the case of humans, is viewed as a moral imperfection or as an unfortunate residue of our evolutionary past.

Wolfgang Wickler, in his book *Sind wir Sünder?*, addresses this issue when he argues that 'instinctive behaviour is morally neutral. What is not neutral is the decision of reason or of conscience which at the end of the day every person must necessarily follow.' He cites the Apostle Paul in support of this distinction when, speaking to the Romans about the question of eating clean and unclean food he says that 'Those who have doubts are condemned if they eat, because they do not act from conviction' (Rom 14:23). Wickler interprets this to mean that for the Apostle, 'it is clearly of no consequence whether the actual act, viewed objectively, is right or wrong'.[5] While one might question the particular exegesis of this text, Wickler's point is clear. Sin does not refer to objective acts—otherwise we would need to condemn many of the instinctive actions of other species as sinful—but has ultimately to do with the distinctively human application of conscience to these acts.

Theologians have made similar distinctions. Karl Rahner, who reflected more on the nature of sin in light of human evolution than perhaps any other theologian of his era, suggests that we must distinguish between disorder that arises from 'sin' and disorder that arises

5.   Wolfgang Wickler, *Sind wir Sünder? Naturgesetze der Ehe* (Munich: Droemer Knaur, 1969), 22.

from being a limited and finite human being. Denis Edwards, in the tradition of Rahner, puts it this way:

> Human beings are a fallible symbiosis of genes and culture, who experience drives and impulses from the genetic side of their inheritance as well as from the cultural side, and these drives and impulses can be disordered and mutually opposed. This experience is intrinsic to being an evolutionary human but it is not sin.[6]

But if this is not sin, then what, according to the theological tradition, is sin? A number of answers to this question have been put forward.

Karl Barth spoke of evil as *Das Nichtige* (nothingness, or that which is not). Neither God nor humanity is the author of this nothingness. In its concrete form we recognise this nothingness as human sin. Yet we do not know of this nothingness directly from our experience of sin because sin can be properly known not as an aberration but as disobedience to God. Nothingness therefore includes sin but it is also more than sin. Nothingness goes beyond the moral sphere and constitutes a comprehensive totality.[7]

For Rudolf Bultmann sin was also unreality. Yet a different kind of unreality than that conceptualised by Barth. For Bultmann, the unreality of sin was understood not on the basis of a Platonic ontology of being but from the perspective of existentialism so that sin, ultimately, is the failure to reach one's own destiny.[8]

Paul Tillich preferred the terms 'estrangement' or 'alienation' to 'sin' since these show to whom humanity belongs. In this sense, sin is profoundly a theological concept that can only be conceptualised in terms of our relationship to God.[9]

---

6.   Denis Edwards, *The God of Evolution: A Trinitarian Theology* (New York: Paulist Press, 1999), 65.

7.   Cf Geoffrey Bromiley, *Introduction to the Theology of Karl Barth* (Grand Rapids: Erdmans, 1979 148ff.

8.   Cf Rudolf Bultmann, 'Die Krisis des Glaubens', in: *Glauben und Verstehen*, Vol 2 (Tübingen: JCB Mohr, 1993), 11f.

9.   Cf Paul Tillich, *Systematic Theology*, Vol 2 (Chicago: University of Chicago Press, 1957), 44ff.

Wolfhart Pannenberg, whose understanding of sin is also in part informed by his own dialogue with the natural sciences, suggests that at heart sin is human self-centredness. He contends that at the point where the human ego comes into contrast with the openness to the world the ego comes to be closed off toward God and thereby also toward its own human destiny. This state of being closed off is the essence of sin.[10] This ego-centredness is universal and is present in all persons before they commit a single actual sin. Rejecting the schools of sociological interpretation of sin, Pannenberg contends that human beings 'do not first become sinners through their own actions and by imitating the bad example of others; they are already sinners before any action of theirs'.[11] Pannenberg affirms therefore original sin but does not accept a doctrine of monogenism. Adam is the prototype, embodiment, mythical ancestor, the pure human being, but not the direct historical ancestor of all humans. He rejects both the traducian and imputation theories of the transmission of original or universal sin. None of these theories explains adequately the co-responsibility of Adam's descendants for the sin of their ancestor. Original sin is the structure that lies behind and precedes all human decisions. It is not transmitted or imputed but is radically universal because it is rooted within the very structure of human behaviour.

Finally, and perhaps most insightful for the present discussion, is Karl Rahner's understanding of sin as the experience of human freedom. The beginning of humanity for Rahner is characterised by an original freedom which was given in humanity and which was not yet co-determined through a human decision of freedom.[12] Original sin and grace, to the extent that each precedes the personal decision of the human person, do not stand in chronological relationship to one another but form together the dialectical situation of humanity to the extent that we are determined not only from the beginning (original sin) but also from Christ as our end and goal.[13]

But what precisely does Rahner understand by original sin? Original sin, in Rahner's thought, has a merely analogical character in

---

10. Cf Pannenberg, *What Is Man?* translated by O Priebe (Philadelphia: Fortress Press, 1970), 68.

11. Pannenberg, *Anthropology in Theological Perspective*, 119f.

12. Rahner, 'The Sin of Adam', in *Theological Investigations* Vol 11, 260f.

13. *Ibid*, 258f.

comparison to the guilt that comes from individual sins. According to Rahner,

> that state of analogous guilt which is called original
> sin is not a projection of the personal state of guilt 'of
> Adam' to us, but is constituted by the absence of the
> holy Pneuma . . . the absence of which corres-
> pondingly, prior to any personal decision, constitutes
> an analogous state of guilt, seeing that this deficiency
> consists not merely in the fact that the holy Pneuma
> is not present, but implies a deficiency which is the
> opposite of the situation which *ought* to exist.[14]

Yet because this situation does not constitute real, actual sin, it can only be understood analogously as original sin.

For Rahner, human freedom in the world means that individuals exercise their freedom in a situation which they find prior to themselves and which is imposed upon them. For the individual it means that they actualise themselves as 'a free subject in a situation which itself is always determined by history and by other persons . . . Consequently, the guilt of others is a permanent factor in the situation and realm of the individual's freedom.'[15] Rahner connects this idea to the doctrine of original sin by pointing out that such a 'universal, permanent and ineradicable co-determination of the situation of every individual's freedom by guilt . . . is conceivable only if this ineradicable co-determination of the situation of freedom by guilt is also *original*', that is, is already imbedded in the origin of human history. This implies an 'original sin' that is neither transmitted nor transmittable to successive generations. Original sin, in Rahner's view, is much more 'the stamp of guilt of others' which our own freedom bears and cannot eradicate since it has been present ever since the beginning of the history of our freedom. Thus original sin is viewed by Rahner prim-arily as a context of guilt which co-determines the freedom of each individual person and which is embedded in universal human history at its very point of origin.[16]

---

14. *Ibid*, 257.
15. *Foundations of Christian Faith: An Introduction to the Idea of Christianity*, translated by Wm Dych (New York: Seabury Press, 1978), 107.
16. *Ibid*, 110f.

But these definitions, helpful as they are, are designed to meet the needs of questions very different to those addressed in this paper. If we wish to enter into genuine dialogue with scientific anthropologies we need to begin with a pre-theological understanding of sin. Indeed, we may need to make a provisional shift away from sin language altogether—retuning to it only for the purposes of drawing specifically theological conclusions. We must work from a definition that is intelligible from the standpoint of the natural sciences.

But the attempt to find a pre-theological understanding of sin, particularly one that may not even embrace sin language, should not lead to the conclusion that the phenomenon of sin can be reduced mechanically and naturalistically to any particular class or category of actions when we isolate the question of the evolution of sin from the broader question of what is the human being. For instance, if a lion mortally wounds a rival male seeking to displace him from his role within the pride we might label that instinct or survival but not sin. Yet if a human male mortally wounds another male whom he discovers making overtures to his partner, we call this a sin and are generally appalled by his actions. So what is the difference?

Most would agree with Hendrikus Berkof that 'Animals cannot sin. The frightful possibility of sin arises only with . . . [humans] as the culmination of the evolutionary development.'[17] But why is this the case? One could argue the concepts of guilt and shame best describe the distinction between these two situations. Perhaps the question we really ought to examine is not the evolution of sin, as some sort of quantifiable category of action, but rather the evolution of guilt. While this solution to the difficulty has weaknesses—for instance sin and guilt are not theologically to be equated—it may well provide a way forward for the dicussion. Guilt is a concept less dependent on particular theological assumptions than sin. Yet theologically, the linkage is unavoidable. The category of 'sin' within human civilisation—indeed, even the concept of morality itself—is quite inexplicable apart from this peculiar and powerful feeling of regret or remorse that we know as guilt.

And our human experience of guilt is peculiar precisely because the very kind of non-altruistic (selfish) acts that now cause us to feel

---

17. Hendrikus Berkof, *Christian Faith: An Introduction to the Study of Faith* (Grand Rapids: Eerdmans, 1971), 206.

shame toward ourselves and disapproval toward others appear to be the very same sort of acts that led to the survival of our ancestors and their success in perpetuating their own genetic characteristics within the species. So at what point and for what reasons do such actions, rewarded generally by the evolutionary process, become guilt-producing and even worthy of the label 'sin' in modern humans? And are there rudimentary examples of guilt or shame in other species that may suggest a continuum between humans and other species, such as we appear to find with consciousness and communication? Only when these questions have been addressed may we return to the theological understandings of sin and assess their usefulness within the context of evolutionary anthropology.

3. Evolutionary speculations

Some time ago I was watching a television documentary on evolution when the words of one of the scientists being interviewed struck me. With great confidence he declared: 'Evolution knows nothing of morality—it has no notion of sin.' Admittedly this is an oft-stated opinion in some circles. Yet it is also a most ironic kind of statement for it is precisely the evolutionary process that has produced those qualities that we call morality, guilt and sin. It is not just the idea of sin that evolves but the thing itself has arisen as a result of selective processes that favour those qualities that bring survival advantages to a particular species. In other words—in the context of natural selection—guilt (and even a consciousness of sin) is good for us! But how does guilt arise? What mechanisms are involved in favouring its selection? And why does it evolve? Traditional understandings of evolution suggest that it must have evolved because it gives some advantage—that in some way it is good for us as a species. But how is guilt good for us? And finally, when does it appear? At what stage in the development of modern *Homo sapiens* does guilt arise? Can the appearance of guilt (and with it eventually the idea of sin) be identified with the true origins of modern humans—along with such factors as consciousness of self and the development of language? To ask these questions is already to assume that guilt is not simply an atavistic residue of animal instincts that now need to be held in check. Guilt arises from instinctive behaviour as something in continuity with previous patterns of behaviour, but occurs also as something essentially new. Guilt is not a remnant or residue of a previous stage of development but is itself a development that needs to be understood in a comparable manner to all other developments in the evolutionary history of humanity.

Approximately six thuosand years ago recorded history began, arising out of the great civilisations of Mesopotamia and Egypt. In the Neolithic period *Homo sapiens* built towns, developed agriculture, practised medicine, travelled, and demonstrated mastery of arts such as dying, weaving, making jewelry, etc. Few today would doubt that they were any less intelligent than ourselves. From 40,000 to 30,000 BCE modern *Homo sapiens*, migrating out of Africa, and Neanderthals, migrating out of ice age Europe, existed side by side in the Middle East. Around the same time this general migration of *Homo sapiens* also led to their arrival in Australia. By 20,000 BCE Neanderthals were extinct. Though their culture and skills appear to have been as highly developed as that of *Homo sapiens* they were out-competed in the struggle for resources. Did our own ancestors slaughter them? Were they more susceptible to disease? Were they less adapted to a changing environment? Or, as there is now some evidence to suggest, were they simply absorbed through inter-breeding by the more numerous and genetically dominant *Homo sapiens*?

But long before this fateful struggle between subspecies their common ancestor, *Homo erectus*, walked the earth from as long ago as 2.5 million BCE to 200,000 BCE. What little evidence has been found of *Homo erectus* suggests the ability to use and make tools, the propensity to travel or migrate, the existence of burial rites, the knowledge of red ochre as a dye, and even the likely use of rafts and boats. Again, this all suggests a level of sophistication once thought impossible. It also suggests that language also must have existed. Yet other branches of the primate family never developed beyond basic communication forms, rudimentary social structures, and the use of discovered and sometimes adapted tools.

This is the basic story of human origins as most know it. It assumes a long but steady linear development of hominids that finally leads, almost inevitably, to *Homo sapiens*. But this view of hominid evolution has in recent years been amended by a more complex picture of human origins. Instead of a slow but steady linear development, we have now come to realise that 'the history of the hominid family has been one of repeated evolutionary trial and error: of new hominid species spawned, competing, and becoming extinct . . . In the past, coexistence and competition among hominid species have quite likely been . . . typical.'[18]

So when in this long and complex history of our species did guilt arise? When did our ancestors first develop a sense of guilt? Was this a necessary corollary of consciousness of self? Did the appearance of guilt and even of the idea of sin contribute to the development of other human traits? Could a sense of guilt that extended even to what might be considered a consciousness of sin have also evolved in hominid species now extinct? And perhaps most intriguingly from a theological perspective, what was the relationship between the appearance of guilt and the development of religion?

3.1 Some proposals

(1) With regard to the mechanism of natural selection, how do altruism and self-sacrifice—encouraged by that quality we call conscience —benefit the survival of the species in seeming contradiction to the assumptions of selfish gene theories?[19] One suggestion is that a sense of guilt and the non-altruistic actions that are thereby minimised do not promote the survival of the species in the usual sort of way. Instead, the evolution of guilt serves only indirectly to secure the survival of the individual and the species. The sense of sin and the feeling of guilt serve in the first instance to promote and secure the survival of civilisation and only secondarily of the species.

(2) In evolutionary terms there is no such thing as pure altruism. It has been said that evil and sin are not problems for evolutionary theory—the true problem is the existence of altruistic behaviour.[20] Philip Hefner puts the problem of altruism succinctly when he writes that 'even though the genetic programs that drive human behaviour seem insufficient to account for trans-kin altruism, that altruism has nevertheless become a distinguishing characteristic of the human

---

18. Ian Tattersall, 'Rethinking Human Evolution', in *Archeology* (July/August 1999): 25.

19. The now famous concept of the selfish gene, which carries with it the misleading connotation of will and choice, was popularised but not originated by Richard Dawkins in his book, *The Selfish Gene* (Oxford: Oxford University Press, 1989).

20. Cf, for instance, Ralph Wendell Burhoe, 'Religion's Role in Human Evolution: The Missing Link between Ape-Man's Selfish Genes and Civilized Altruism', in *Zygon* Vol 14 (June 1979): 135ff.

species over the millennia'.[21] If altruism has arisen, then according to the strict dictates of evolutionary selection, it must give some advantage. Yet altruism, which characterises human civilisation, has so far eluded explanation in purely biological or genetic terms. Another suggestion is that altruistic behaviour fosters the survival of civilisation itself, which in turn leads also to the survival of the 'civilised' species. The human experience of guilt guards against dangerous levels of non-altruistic behaviour.

Though the mechanisms are complex, if altruistic actions ultimately further the survival of the species, then they are not only no longer inexplicable, they are also not purely altruistic. The complexity of the human species means that our survival is not linked merely to the impulse of the individual to act in ways that will most likely ensure the passing on of their own genetic material. The classic example of pure altruism often put forward is that of Mother Theresa. Clearly her own life choices ensured that her genetic material would not be passed on. Yet those same choices ensured the passing on of ideas and values ultimately of far more value to humanity and our continued survival. If the survival and advancement of *Homo sapiens* as a species is at least as much linked to the survival of human civilisation as to the perpetuation of advantageous physical traits and qualities, then apparent altruism no longer appears as an evolutionary anomaly.

(3) A sense of guilt in rudimentary form is not lacking in other members of the animal kingdom. Though, like arguments about animal consciousness, this point is almost impossible to demonstrate conclusively, anecdotal evidence suggests not only a basic awareness of self in some animals but also a basic sense of guilt and wrong action. Could these qualities be similar to those that manifested themselves in our earliest ancestors and eventually evolved along with language and awareness of self to produce *Homo sapiens*? Perhaps the development of feelings of guilt even played a necessary role in the process of speciation that saw our ancestors branch away from other primates some 4.5 million years ago. In other words, in the case of humans, initial speciation may have had as much if not more to do with the

---

21.   Philip Hefner, *The Human Factor: Evolution, Culture and Religion* (Minneapolis: Fortress Press, 1993), 195.

appearance of psychological qualities such as consciousness of self and a sense of guilt than with physical traits such as walking upright.[22]

Homo sapiens and other animals exist on an evolutionary continuum of consciousness and intelligence that suggests a difference of degree rather than one of kind existing in the area of morality and guilt. The questions for our understanding of human evolution are also profound. There exists not only the problem of consciousness and what evolutionary benefit it may confer, but also the problem that the long assumed hierarchy of intelligence and perhaps even consciousness among non-human species may well not exist. There are also important questions arising concerning human nature and behaviour. Continuity between humans and animals not only suggests that ideas such as consciousness and emotion may to some measure be applied to animals but that animal instinct and behaviour would also shed light on human action.[23] Indeed, this has long been recognised as a valid avenue of research by thinkers such as Konrad Lorenz and Wolfgang Wickler.[24]

The theological implications of the emerging continuity between animals and humans did not escape David Hume, who was one of the earliest and most radical proponents of animal intelligence and consciousness. Hume wrote in 'On the Immortality of the Soul' that 'animals undoubtedly feel, think, love, hate, will and even reason, though in a more imperfect manner than . . . [humans]: are their souls also immaterial and immortal?'[25] As Stephen Walker explained, 'if one has concluded that the mental capacities of animals differs from . . . [ours] in only quantitative ways, one of the grounds for drawing moral . . . distinctions between . . . [humans] and beasts is removed and it

---

22.   It is thought that walking upright freed human ancestors for a greater use of their hands which in turn had a direct and dramatic impact on brain size as so many more tasks could now be accomplished that required thought.

23.   For a fuller discussion see my paper on 'Human and Animal Intelligence: A Difference of Degree or Kind?' in *God, Life, Intelligence and the Universe*, edited by T Kelly and H Regan (Adelaide: ATF, 2002), 85-109.

24.   Cf Konrad Lorenz, *On Aggression*, translated by M Latzke (London: Methuen, 1966), *and Civilised Man's Eight Deadly Sins*, translated by M Wilson (New York: Harcourt Brace Jovanovich, 1974); and Wolfgang Wickler, *The Biology of the Ten Commandments*, translated D Smith (New York: McGraw-Hill, 1972) and *Sind wir Sünder? Naturgesetze der Ehe* (Munich: Droemer Knaur, 1969).

25.   David Hume, 'On the Immortality of the Soul' in *Essays*, 424.

becomes less obvious that immortality should be reserved for the human species'.[26]

Lesley Rogers, an Australian ethologist at the University of New England has summarised the matter well. She writes:

> If there is a discontinuity between *Homo sapiens* and other living species, it does not lie in the exclusive possession of any one of these traits [viz, tool using, language, culture, social complexity, high intelligence and consciousness]. Other animals use tools but we use more of them and more complex ones. Other animals have complex communication systems that share aspects of human language . . . The kind of consciousness that *Homo sapiens* has may be special, but we are not likely to be alone as the only species that is aware of itself . . . No single feature on its own makes us special.[27]

Similarly, one might suspect that humans are also not the only species to experience guilt and shame. Yet the role that these feelings play within the human species and the extent of their development raise us to a unique level of evolutionary attainment.

4. Theological reflections

But what might all this mean from the perspective of theology? Clearly, theology can never be happy with a purely naturalistic understanding of sin or of human origins. One avenue of approach is to raise the question of the connection between the experience of guilt and sin and the experience of the divine.

Is it inconceivable that the sense guilt and sin may well be a primal experience of God? Is this sense, the idea of sin becomes a reflection of the transcendent experience of the divine. We might well suggest that it is precisely through our sense of guilt and failing that we become aware of transcendent reality. Or, alternately and more profoundly,

---

26. Stephen Walker, *Animal Thought* (London: Routledge and Kegan Paul, 1983), 29f.

27. Lesley Joy Rogers, *Minds of Their Own: Thinking and Awareness in Animals* (Sydney: Allen and Unwin, 1997), 163f.

perhaps it is our sense of this transcendent reality that first awakens in us a sense of sinfulness. In other words, could it be a God-initiated encounter that awakens in us the first feelings of guilt—of falling short—that play a decisive role in the advent of modern humans? In either case, the potential link between the origins of guilt and religion would seem clear.

It should also be observed that the biblical story, in light of the evolutionary story, does not become unintelligible. Far from being repudiated, the foundational truths of the biblical accounts of creation and fall—when liberated from literalist interpretations for which they were never intended—speak with remarkable relevance to the situation of the evolution of guilt.

The link between the origins of guilt, sin and religion are portrayed in the story of the fall, in which the first act of religion is not calling upon the name of Yahweh (this is the first act of worship) but rather the eating of the forbidden fruit motivated by a desire to be like God. The biblical portrayal of sin as a universal phenomenon of non-altruistic centredness upon self (eg, the account of Cain and Abel) also corresponds well to modern understandings of the universal character of guilt and sin as well as its essential nature. The same is true of the implicit connection between freedom and the origins of human sin. Even the account of the fall, often thought to be incompatible with the story of human evolution, contains fundamental truths that become even more intelligible in light of advances in knowledge about our origins. Indeed, the example of the biblical concept of the fall serves well to illustrate that biblical religion need not assume an incompatibility with evolutionary anthropology. To the contrary, the biblical story of the fall may also be seen as embodying the story of the evolution of sin.

5. The fall and the evolution of sin

Evolutionary theory has long been associated with an overriding theme of progress. The idea of evolutionary progress, however, has not lacked scientific challenges. The Second Law of Thermodynamics and entropy—both concepts from the realm of physics—have long presented certain conceptual difficulties for the evolutionary view of the development of life which appears to move in precisely the opposite direction, namely that of increasing complexity. Also, some modern biologists, such as Stephen J Gould, have challenged this concept, asking where the inevitable progress is to be found, for instance, in the long history of extinctions.[28] Nevertheless, the problem of evolutionary progress over against the de-evolutionary nature of the fall remains one of the most striking apparent difficulties posed by modern science for the Christian doctrine of the fall. Indeed, the term evolution itself conveys the sense of progress. Life forms, through the mechanism of natural selection, first clearly described by Charles Darwin, are constantly developing into increasingly advanced, better-adapted, and more complex forms. How then are we to understand the fall, which appears to suggest that as a species we have devolved from the highest state we have ever known as a species into a lesser state of pain, selfish actions, senseless crimes, and death?

The fall account, however, need not be seen as contrary to the evolutionary idea of progress. The so-called Irenaean interpretation of the fall reminds us that this need not be the case. Irenaeus, the second-century bishop of Lyon, taught that God did not make humans originally perfect. He wrote: 'God had power at the beginning to grant perfection to man; but as the latter was only recently created, he could not possibly have received it, or even if he had received it, could he have contained it, or containing it, could he have retained it.' Hence from the beginning God created humans good but not perfect, so that the human race had to progress through, as it were, an infancy. As Irenaeus explained, 'it was necessary that . . . [the human being] should in the first instance be created; and having been created, should receive growth, should be strengthened, should abound; and having abounded, should recover [from the disease of sin]; and having recovered should be glorified'.[29] For Irenaeus, humanity is on a long forward journey toward final union with God and glorification. In this context the fall into sin has been interpreted as a fall upward—an important developmental stage in the maturing of humanity.[30]

---

28. Cf Stephen J Gould, *Eight Little Piggies. Reflections in Natural History* (New York: WW Norton, 1993), 307ff.

29. Irenaeus, *Against Heresies*, Book iv, xxxviii, in: *Ante-Nicene Fathers*, Vol 1.

30. This theme of a fall upward was picked up very clearly by Friedrich Schiller who declared that although the fall indeed brought moral evil into creation this only occurred in order 'to enable the moral good within creation. Therefore without doubt it is the happiest and greatest event in human history. From this moment onward [human] . . . freedom is inscribed . . .' Cited in Hans Schwarz, *Our Cosmic Journey*, 177.

Process theologian John Cobb and biologist and process thinker Charles Birch note the apparent congruence of the concept of a fall upward with evolutionary theory when they contend: 'The symbol of the fall and specifically a fall upward can be properly used to describe particular occurrences in the evolutionary process. It identifies the occurrence of a new level of order and freedom bought at the price of suffering.' In this vein, they suggest that both the appearance of animal life, which brought with it the first suffering, and the appearance of human beings were significant falls upward in our evolutionary history.[31] While the process view is not to be identified with that of Irenaeus it does reinforce the notion that a 'fall' does not necessarily need to be seen as an entirely backward or de-evolutionary step.

The so-called Irenaean model of a fall upward dovetails very well with our knowledge of the very real pains and difficulties that accompany a major evolutionary leap. The implications of emergent evolutionary models in which new developments within a species and even entire new species emerge rather quickly on the scene, but not without accompanying upheaval, merit further reflection with regard to the Irenaean model. Yet we must be careful not to reduce the fall to a mere birth pang or an unpleasant by-product of an evolutionary leap. Biblically and theologically, the fall is something fundamentally more profound than this. In the Irenaean model the fall is indeed not something to be viewed as altogether negative—yet something very real and very significant has been lost. Hence Hans Schwarz's observation that 'it is difficult to assert, on strictly biological grounds, that an evolutionary development toward a higher stage is necessarily better'.[32]

While not all will be happy with such an interpretation of the fall, the possibility of such an understanding illustrates the point that the biblical theology of the fall and the scientific theory of human evolution are not necessarily incompatible accounts of the story of humanity. In theological language, the 'fall' is the account of the awareness of sin coming into the story of humanity. Evolutionary an-

31. Charles Birch and John Cobb, Jr, *The Liberation of Life* (Cambridge: Cambridge University Press, 1981), 117ff. Cf Also John Cobb, Jr and David Griffen, *Process Theology: An Introduction*, Chapter 5 where they observe that the emergence of new structures of existence is always progress but that this progress comes at a great price.

32. Hans Schwarz, *Responsible Faith: Christian Theology in the Light of 20th Century Questions* (Minneapolis: Augsburg Press, 1986), 142.

thropology also has a story to tell about the emergence and positive role of guilt and perhaps even the concept of sin. The fact that an early theological model exists for viewing the 'fall' or the awareness of sin as having also a positive developmental side demonstrates that the two stories need not be contradictory but could well be seen as two versions of the same story of guilt and sin within human evolutionary history.

6. Concluding thoughts

If God brought forth modern humans through the process of evolution then it would seem clear that at some point (likely prior to the old stone age) our ancestors killed over mating rights and fought to the death over access to food sources, first with bare hands and feet, then increasingly with clubs and other weapons—yet without sin. This was an original state of righteousness far indeed removed from that which most of us were taught in Sunday School. From this original state of righteousness the appearance of conscience, guilt and sin can only be seen (in the tradition of Irenaeus) as a fall upward—a coming of age for *Homo sapiens*.

The emergence of guilt and subsequent awareness of what theologians call sin is itself a positive development in the history of human evolution. It elevates us as a species to a new level of development. For the first time our survival is not simply linked to being the strongest, fastest, most ruthless, etc—but rather in our ability to consider the implications of our actions on ourselves and others. And it is here, too, we would contend that consciousness of self, guilt, freedom, and an awareness of the divine all converge not only to bring sin onto the stage of the human—but also for the first time the possibility of salvation.

8

Sin, Salvation, and Scientific Cosmology: Is Christian Eschatology Credible Today?

Robert J Russell

1. Introduction

One can pose at least four generic question regarding sin: what constitutes sin (eg, disobedience to God), what is the origin of sin (eg, the fall), what are the consequences of sin (eg, death), and what is God's means for overcoming it (eg, the birth, ministry, death and resurrection of Jesus, the parousia and the new creation). The first, second and third can be reconstructed 'relatively' easily in light of the natural sciences, as scholars in 'theology and science' have shown in diverse ways, though profound questions still remain: what is the relation between disobedience to God and our relation to the environment, what are the evolutionary preconditions for the occurrence of sin in homo sapiens, what are the biological consequences of sin given the ubiquity of death in the evolution of life, etc. The fourth, however, raises staggering conceptual problems when the resurrection of Jesus, the parousia and the new creation are considered in light of contemporary science —problems which have hardly been addressed in the literature.[1]

These problems are really quite evident if one starts with the most popular response to the first three questions: The 'kenotic' response

---

1.   For an initial venture see Robert John Russell, 'Bodily Resurrection, Eschatology and Scientific Cosmology: The Mutual Interaction of Christian Theology and Science', in *Resurrection: Theological and Scientific Assessments*, edited by Ted Peters, Robert John Russell and Michael Welker (Grand Rapids: Eerdmans, 2002); Robert John Russell, 'Eschatology and Physical Cosmology: A Preliminary Reflection', in *The Far Future: Eschatology from a Cosmic Perspective*, edited by George FR Ellis (Philadelphia: Templeton Foundation Press, 2002); *The End of the World and the Ends of God: Science and Theology on Eschatology*, edited by John Polkinghome and Michael Welker (Harrisburg: Trinity Press International, 2000).

begins with disease, suffering, death and extinction in nature, recognises that these are more or less inevitable in an open and dynamic universe in which God allows complexity to be 'self-creating', views suffering in nature through the lens of the cross thus rendering nature 'cruciform', and adopts a 'crucified God' approach which addresses the joint questions: is nature to be redeemed (yes!), and how do we deal with theodicy/natural evil (God suffers with us). But this theological 'vector' from suffering in nature to a 'crucified God' form of redemption requires a doctrine of the resurrection of Jesus for its completion (lest the suffering of God never end!), and this in turn raises an absolutely crucial question and unavoidable, although it is in fact seldom acknowledged: what is the eschatological significance of the resurrection of Jesus, and how is it to be intelligible in light of scientific cosmology? I will call this the problem of 'eschatology and cosmology'.

The problem of 'eschatology and cosmology' is intensified to the breaking point if we take the resurrection of Jesus to entail 'bodily resurrection', since this view of the resurrection is coupled with an eschatology which entails the transformation of the present creation into a new 'heaven and earth'. On the other hand, scientific cosmology knows of no such transformation; instead the ultimate future of the universe is either 'freeze or fry'. Of course the twentieth century has seen enormous and protracted debates over what I will call the 'subjective/existential' and 'objective/bodily' interpretations of the resurrection of Jesus.[2] Clearly the subjective interpretation succeeds in minimising the problem raised by science by avoiding what many biblical scholars argue is the original New Testament message of the bodily resurrection of Jesus.[3] Accordingly in this paper I will assume the objective interpretation as a kind of 'worst case' scenario, the one which makes Christianity the most vulnerable to its atheistic critics and motivates the subjectivistic option so strongly. This interpretation is, of

---

2.   A pivotal example is Bultmann vs Barth; a contemporary example is the Jesus Seminar vs scholars such as Gerald O'Collins. For details, see Russell, 'Eschatology and Physical Cosmology: A Preliminary Reflection', and Russell, 'Bodily Resurrection, Eschatology and Scientific Cosmology: The Mutual Interaction of Christian Theology and Science'.

3.   It is apparent that the subjective interpretation of the resurrection of Jesus is motivated, at least in part, precisely by the challenge of science; its roots lie in Schleiermacher who, in turn, was responding to the challenge of early modem science and Enlightenment philosophy.

course, highly debatable, but my point is that if it happens to be correct it raises serious, and perhaps unsolvable, conflicts and contradictions with science.

Therefore it is worth pursuing, since it represents a 'test case' of the highest order which is particularly germain to those of us who urge that 'theology and science' should be in a posture of 'creative mutual interaction' and not in one of 'conflict'. The purpose of this paper is to begin to address these conflicts. This paper will be entirely in the style of 'research in progress' and is meant as an open-ended conversation with others interested in the problem.

2. Conceptual challenge: eschatology, big bang cosmology and the 'freeze or fry' scenarios '

> (I)f it were shown that the universe is indeed headed for an all-enveloping death, then this might seem to constitute a state of affairs so negative that it might be held to falsify Christian faith and abolish Christian hope.[4]

To consider the universe from a scientific perspective, we must turn to physics and its theory of gravity, and thus to big bang cosmology.[5]

---

4.   John Macquarie, *Principles of Christian Theology*, second edition (New York: Charles Scribner's Sons, 1977 (1966)), Chapter 15, especially 351-62.

5.   This material is drawn from my survey article, 'Theology and Science: Current Issues and Future Directions', Parts II B, E. It can be found through the CTNS website homepage. For a non-technical introduction, see James Trefil and Robert M Hazen, *The Sciences: An Integrated Approach*, second edition/updated edition (New York: John Wiley &Sons, Inc., 2000), Chapter 15; Donald Goldsmith, *Einstein's Greatest Blunder? The CosmologicalConstant and Other Fudge Factors in the Physics of the Universe* (Cambridge, Massachusetts: Harvard University Press, 1995), Chapters. 1-9; James S Trefil, *The Moment of Creation: Big Bang Physics from before the First Millisecond to the Present Universe* (New York: MacMillan Publishing Company, 1983), Chapters. 1-9; Willem B Drees, *Beyond the Big Bang: Quantum Cosmologies and God* (La Salle: Open Court, 1990), Appendix 1; George F Ellis and William R Stoeger SJ, 'Introduction to General Relativity and Cosmology', in *Quantum Cosmology and the Laws of Nature: Scientific Perspectives on Divine Action*, edited by Robert J Russell; Nancey C Murphy and Chris J Isham, *Scientific Perspectives on Divine Action Series* (Vatican City State; Berkeley, Calif: Vatican Observatory Publications; Center for Theology and the Natural Sciences, 1993), 33-48; William R Stoeger

There are two big bang scenarios for the far future of the universe: 'freeze or fry'. If the universe is open or flat, it will expand forever and continue to cool from its present temperature (about $2.7°K$), asymptotically approaching absolute zero. If it is closed, it will expand to a maximum size in another one to five hundred billion years, then recollapse to arbitrarily small size and unendingly higher temperatures somewhat like a mirror image of its past expansion. Throughout the 20th century, intense observational efforts went into determining which model applies. Today, scientists believe that it is unlikely that the universe is closed; instead is most likely flat or marginally open, and it will expand and cool forever.[6]

What about the future of life in the universe? It turns out that the overall picture is bleak, regardless of whether it is open or closed (ie, freeze or fry).[7] In five billion years, the sun will become a red giant, engulfing the orbit of the earth and Mars and eventually wind up as a white dwarf. In 40–50 billion years, star formation will have ended in our galaxy. In 10^{12} years, all massive stars will have become neutron

---

SJ, 'Key Developments in Physics Challenging Philosophy and Theology', in *Religion and Science: History, Method, Dialogue*, edited by W Mark Richardson and Wesley J Wildman (New York: Routledge, 1996), 183-200; *God, Humanity and the Cosmos: A Textbook in Science and Religion*, edited by Christopher Southgate, Celia Deane-Drummond et al (Harrisburg: Trinity Press International, 1999), 35-39. For a technical introduction, see JD North, *The Measure of the Universe: A History of Modern Cosmology* (New York: Dover Publications, Inc, 1965 (1990)); Charles W Misner, Kip S Thorne and John Archibald Wheeler, *Gravitation* (San Francisco: W H Freeman and Company, 1973), part VI; Steven Weinberg, *Gravitation and Cosmology: Principles and Applications of the General Theory of Relativity* (New York: John Wiley & Sons, 1972), part V.

6.   In inflationary scenarios, the present expansion may be accelerating, instead of decelerating, due to the presence of the 'cosmological constant'; an optional theoretical term which can be added to Einstein's field equations. It represents a 'pressure'-like effect which increases the rate of expansion of the universe, but it doesn't radically change the far future scenarios depicted here.

7.   See John D Barrow and Frank J Tipler, *The Anthropic Cosmological Principle* (Oxford: Clarendon Press, 1986), Chapter 10; see also William R Stoeger SJ, 'Scientific Accounts of Ultimate Catastrophes in Our Life-Bearing Universe', in *The End of the World and the Ends of God: Science and Theology on Eschatology*, edited by John Polkinghorne and Michael Welker (Harrisburg: Trinity Press International, 2000).

stars or black holes.[8] In 10^{31} years, protons and neutrons will decay into positrons, electrons, neutrinos and photons. In 10^{34} years, dead planets, black dwarfs and neutron stars will disappear, their mass completely converted into energy, leaving only black holes, electron-positron plasma and radiation, and all carbon-based life-forms will be extinct. The upshot is clear: 'Proton decay spells ultimate doom for . . . *Homo sapiens* and all forms of life constructed of atoms . . .'[9] In short, if big bang cosmology is correct, the parousia is not just 'delayed', it never happens.

3. Methodological challenge: emergence and constraints

Can we not just ignore the negative predictions of scientific cosmology while still playing by the methodological rules which define the field of 'theology and science'? After all, it is this methodology which stresses that fundamentally new processes and properties have emerged phenomenologically again and again in the development of the physical universe and the evolution of life, including consciousness and self-conscious agency at least on planet Earth. These could not have been predicted in advance of their emergence, and yet they have had a profound effect on the physical world—why else would we be in an ecological crisis, for example? So who can say what will develop in the future, or what effect life could have on the universe itself? Moreover, there are metaphysical options which are consistent with the emergence of the radically new, including Whiteheadian meta-physics, physicalism, ontological emergence, etc. Perhaps one or more of them may offer other reasons for confidence in the future in spite of the predictions of big bang cosmology. The problem here is that the same methodological framework which has played an essential role in making it possible for the field of 'theology and science' to grow so richly over the past four decades prevents us from 'side-stepping' the crucial issues raised by cosmology for Christian eschatology. To see this we need to summarise this methodology.

---

8.   If the universe is closed, then in 10^{12} years the universe will have reached its
      maximum size and re-collapse back to a singularity like the original hot big bang.
9.   Barrow and Frank J Tipler, *The Anthropic Cosmological Principle*, *op cit*, 648.

3.1 Methodology in theology and science: brief overview

Advances made in 'theology and science' over the past four decades have been possible because of a remarkable new methodology which arose early in this period and which has proven stunningly catalytic. The methodology, broadly referred to as 'critical realism', includes three major arguments, two of which I will summarise here.[10]

One, that the sciences and the humanities, including theology, form an epistemic hierarchy which ensures both constraint (against 'two worlds' views) and irreducibility (against reductionism), and that within this hierarchy, each level involves similar methods of theory construction and testing and, in particular, that theological methodology is analogous to scientific methodology (though with several important differences). I am drawing directly on the pioneering writings of Ian Barbour[11] as well as on those of Arthur Peacocke,[12] Nancey Murphy,[13] Philip Clayton,[14] John Polkinghorne,[15] and many others, each of whom has contributed to our growing understanding both of the hierarchy and the analogy.

Two, the idea of an epistemic hierarchy is that the disciplines can be placed in a series of levels which reflect the increasing complexity of the phenomena they study. Lower levels place epistemic constraints on upper levels, but upper levels cannot be reduced entirely to lower levels. Thus, physics as the bottom level places constraints on biology: no biological theory should contradict physics, and so on up through the other sciences and humanities. On the other hand, the processes, properties, and laws of biology cannot be reduced without remainder

10. The third argument is that language is intrinsically metaphorical. Critical realists also defend a referential theory of truth warranted in terms of correspondence, coherence, and utility.

11. Ian G Barbour, *Religion in an Age of Science*, Gifford Lectures; 1989-1990 (San Francisco: Harper & Row, 1990).

12. Arthur Peacocke, *Theology/or a Scientific Age: Being and Becoming—Natural Divine and Human*, Enlarged Edition (Minneapolis: Fortress Press, 1993). See particularly Fig 3, 217, and the accompanying text.

13. Nancey Murphy, *Theology in the Age of Scientific Reasoning* (Ithaca: Comell University Press, 1990).

14. Philip Clayton, *Explanation from Physics to Theology: An Essay in Rationality and Religion* (New Haven, Conn.: Yale University Press, 1989), 11.

15. John C Polkinghorne, *The Faith of a Physicist: Reflections of a Bottom-up Thinker* (New Jersey: Princeton University Press, 1994).

to those of physics, and again on up through the other sciences and humanities. Though scholars differ on the precise ordering of the disciplines, and the role that cross-disciplinary fields like genetics plays in the scheme, the idea of an epistemic ordering like this is crucial both to warding off the philosophical claims of reductionism and a 'dualistic' (or even more foliated) ontology of 'levels'. The argument for viewing theological method as analogous to scientific method can be both a description of the way many theologians actually work and a prescription for progress in theological research. Here doctrines are seen as theories, working hypotheses held fallibly and constructed in light of the 'data of theology'—now including the discoveries and conclusions of the social, psychological and natural sciences. Theological theories are held seriously but tentatively, and they are open to being tested against such data.[16]

In order to make even more explicit the ways in which science can (and should) influence theology, let me combine the two ideas we have discussed—epistemic hierarchy and analogous methodology—into a single diagram (Figure 1, focusing here on paths 1–5 only). Here I will consider physics and its effects on theology. One could do a more complicated diagram with physics, biology and theology, for example, and one would need to include the influences of physics on both biology and theology, as well as the influences of biology on theology, etc.

As Figure 1 suggests, there are at least five ways or 'paths' by which the natural sciences can affect constructive theology. (1) Theories in physics can act directly as data which places constraints on theology. So, for example, a theological theory about divine action should not violate special relativity. (2) Theories can act directly as

---

16.   There are, of course, important differences between the methods of theology and the natural sciences. One is that theologians lack criteria of theory choice which are agreed-upon in advance and which fully transcend the influences of the theories under dispute. Another difference involves the extent to which beliefs influence both the relevancy and the interpretation of data, and the power of imagination, analogy and models in theory construction. A third difference is that, as in the social sciences but unlike the natural sciences, much of the data for religious scholars come from subjects; in effect, religious scholars are typically seeking to interpret the interpretation of others—what Phil Clayton calls the problem of the 'double hermeneutic'. Murphy, drawing on Lakatos, has underscored the importance of 'novel facts' in settling disputes and the avoidance of ad hoc as a sign of epistemic progress in theology.

data either to be 'explained' by theology or as the basis for a theological constructive argument. For example, t = 0 in big bang cosmology may be explained theologically via creation *ex nihilo*. Note: the theological explanation should be considered a part of theology, and not as an explanation lying within the domain of science. (3) Theories in physics, after philosophical analysis, can act indirectly as data for theology. For example, the contingency of the universe can serve within natural theology as evidence for the existence of God. Similarly an indeterministic interpretation of quantum mechanics can function within theological anthropology as providing a precondition at the level of physics for the bodily enactment of free will. (4) Theories in physics can also act indirectly as the data for theology when they are incorporated into a fully articulated philosophy of nature (eg process philosophy). Finally, (5) theories in physics can function heuristically in the theological context of discovery as a source of theological inspiration.

3.2 Why we cannot ignore cosmology in thinking about eschatology

We are now prepared to see clearly why the problem of eschatology and cosmology is 'forced' on us by the same methodological framework which has played an essential role in making it possible for the field of 'theology and science' to grow so richly over the past four decades. Thus while our methodological framework includes an epistemological hierarchy of emergent properties and processes to counteract the challenge of epistemological reductionism, it also insists on constraints by lower on higher levels, thereby guarding against total disciplinary autonomy which kept theology isolated and compartmentalised from the sciences during the reign of neo-orthodoxy. In particular, theology may not simply ignore the results of physics. Since scientific cosmology (ie big bang cosmology, inflationary big bang, quantum cosmology, etc) is part of physics (ie relativistically correct theories of gravity applied to the universe), the predictions of 'freeze or fry'—or their scientific replacements in the future—must place constraints on and challenge what theology can claim eschatologically. No easy appeal to contingency, quantum physics, chaos theory, ontological unpredictability, Whiteheadian novelty, emergence, the future, or metaphysics alone will be sufficient to solve this problem.

To their credit, a handful of theologians have recognised this problem, though they have not attended carefully to an adequate response. According to Wolfhart Pannenberg, '(T)he question of eschatology . . . points to one of the most obvious conflicts between a world view based on modern science and the Christian faith'.[17] Jurgen Moltmann argues that 'Christian eschatology must be broadened out into cosmic eschatology, for otherwise it becomes a gnostic doctrine of redemption . . . (I)t is impossible to conceive of any salvation for men and women without 'a new heaven and a new earth. There can be no eternal life for human beings without the change in the cosmic conditions of life.'[18] And for Ted Peters,

> the biblical symbol of the new creation is being interpreted here to refer to a point in the future where . . . the cosmos will undergo transformation and emerge as the everlasting kingdom of God . . . (But) should the final future as forecasted by the combination of big bang cosmology and the second law of thermodynamics come to pass . . . then we would have proof that our faith has been in vain. It would turn out to be that there is no God, at least not the God in whom followers of Jesus have put their faith.[19]

4. Eschatology and cosmology within 'theology and science': the surprising lack of engagement

Given all that has been said so far, one might expect there to be a vast literature on our subject, especially among those scholars who focus on 'theology and science'. In truth, relatively little has been written on the subject. What there is can be divided into two groups. The first includes those who have given passing discussions of resurrection,

17. Wolfhart Pannenberg, 'Theological Questions to Scientists', in *The Sciences and Theology in the Twentieth Century*, edited AR Peacocke (Notre Dame: University of Notre Dame Press, 1981), 12, 14-15. Reprinted in Wolfhart Pannenberg, *Toward a Theology of Nature: Essays on Science and Faith*, edited by Ted Peters (Louisville, Ky: Westminster/JohnKnox Press, 1993), 24, 26-7.

18. Jurgen Moltmann, *The Coming of God: Christian Eschatology*, 1st Fortress Press, edited and translated by Margaret Kohl (Minneapolis: Fortress Press, 1996), 259-61.

19. Ted Peters, *God as Trinity: Relationality and Temporality in the Divine Life* (Louisville, Ky: Westminster/John Knox Press, 1993), 175-6, 17.

eschatology and cosmology. The second includes those few scholars who have focused much more sustained attention.

4.1 Tangential treatments of resurrection, eschatology and cosmology

Process philosophy is frequently described as highly compatible with science; Whitehead himself clearly had early quantum physics and relativity in mind when working on his philosophical writings. One might expect process scholars to be heavily engaged in our subject, but they leave it relatively untouched.[20] Moreover, from the theological

---

20.   See for example Barbour, *Religion in an Age of Science*, 241. See note #37, p 288, for references to this by other process thinkers. Similarly, Cobb and Griffin suggest that the resurrection of Jesus might provide 'special evidence' for life after death in this sense, but they conclude that the relation between Christian eschatology and Whiteheadian philosophy is unsettled; 'there remains a profound mystery which even Whitehead's intuition could not penetrate'. John B Cobb, Jr and David Ray Griffin, *Process Theology: An Introductory Exposition* (Philadelphia: Westminster Press, 1976), 124. See also Marjorie Hewitt Suchocki, *God, Christ, Church: A Practical Guide to Process Theology* (New York: Crossroad, 1982), Chapters. 11, 17; John F Haught, *Science & Religion: From Conflict to Conversion* (New York: Paulist Press, 1995), 174-78. See also John F Haught, *The Promise of Nature: Ecology and Cosmic Purpose* (New York: Paulist Press, 1993), 124-25, 130; John F Haught, 'Evolution, Tragedy, and Hope', in *Science & Theology: The New Consonance*, edited Ted Peters (Boulder, Colorado: Westview Press, 1998), especially 238, 240. There is at least one notable exception: Lewis Ford makes what I would consider an actual empirical prediction about the cosmological future which we should note clearly here: 'I envision an endless series of expansions and contractions of the universe, in which all the outcomes and achievements of each cosmic epoch are crushed to bits in a final cataclysmic contraction, to provide a mass/energy capable of assuming a novel physical organization in the next expansion . . . Only in some such fashion will it be possible for God to pursue his (sic) aim at the actualization of all pure possibilities, each in its due season . . .' Ford's argument is extremely valuable since it can be tested against contemporary scientific cosmology. Unfortunately, though, it would seem to be falsified: in standard big bang cosmology, one cannot extrapolate 'beyond' the final 'crunch' of the closed model to further expansions and contractions, and the open model never recollapses and never ends. Of course, just as with $t = 0$, one might suggest that, for the closed model in a quantum cosmology, the actual universe, being governed ultimately by quantum gravity, would 'bounce', as Ford envisions. This option is certainly worth pursuing, particularly since without the commitment to

perspective adopted in this paper, what is prominently missing is a discussion of the bodily resurrection of Jesus.

Trinitarian theologians, particularly those who stress prolepsis, might be a second place where a thorough engagement with cosmology would be found. Again, however, the engagement is somewhat tangential, although significantly more detailed than that of process theologians. Since the 1960s, Wolfhart Pannenberg has given detailed support of the bodily resurrection and historicity of the empty tomb narratives, and argued that all Christian theology depends on the future coming of God.[21] He is one of the few theologians to openly acknowledge the challenge science brings to this view, as I have cited above. But in his *Systematic Theology*, Pannenberg argues that the Christian claim that the world will have an end can neither be supported by science, *nor need it be in opposition to it* (my italics). The biblical view of an imminent end, and the scientific view of a remote end in the closed model, may not even 'relate to the same event . . . Even if they do, it is only in the sense of very different forms of imminence.'[22] This move clearly lessens the tension between eschatology and cosmology, but the cost seems to be a return, at least briefly, to a 'two worlds' approach atypical of Pannenberg's overall agenda. Mark Worthing has proposed that we understand the parousia as a renewal or transformation of the universe as a whole. This, in turn, shifts the discussion from the end of the world to the concept of eternity as the real issue in relating science and theology. We are led to

---

the bodily resurrection taken in this paper, an eschatology of universal new creation is not part of what Ford requires for his theology. It might be that an endless universe such as he imagines would be consistent with both science and process theology. Lewis Ford, 'Get This Title', in *Hope and the Future of Man*, edited by EH Cousins (Philadelphia: Fortress Press, 1972), quoted in AR Peacocke, *Creation and the World of Science: The Bampton Lectures, 1979* (Oxford: Clarendon Press, 1979), 349.

21. Wolfhart Pannenberg, *Systematic Theology*, translated by G W Bromiley (Grand Rapids, Mich.: Eerdmans, 1998), Vol 3, Chapter 15, especially Section 1, 531. Pannenberg claims that the future of God's reign is already present in the ministry of Christ and the church, but this claim anticipates and depends crucially on its eschatological confirmation. Throughout his writings Pannenberg will insist that Christian theology must not be in contrast to or conflict with natural science, and that the deity of God depends on the eschatological consummation of the world.

22. Pannenberg, *Systematic Theology*, Volume 3, 589-90. Pannenberg is apparently referring to the closed big bang model and not the open model, which, though possessing a finite past, is infinite in size and will continue forever into the future.

consider 'the future of the universe . . . (as) taken up into the eternality of the Creator'.[23] Denis Edwards also conceptualises redemption not only as the forgiveness of sins but as a transformation of the cosmos. Drawing on the writings of Karl Rahner, Edwards suggests that we hold in tension scientific and eschatological differences and live with 'the lack of synthesis' at least for the time being.[24] Ted Peters calls for 'temporal holism' in which the cosmos as a unity of time and space is both created proleptically from the future and redeemed eschatologically by God's future initiative which we know proleptically in Jesus Christ.[25] But Peters, unlike Worthing and Edwards, is ruthlessly honest about the challenge from science. 'Should the final future as forecasted by (scientific cosmology) come to pass . . . then we would have proof that our faith has been in vain. It would turn out to be that there is no God, at least not the God in whom followers of Jesus have put their faith.'[26]

4.2 Polkinghorne: a more detailed treatment of resurrection, eschatology and cosmology

Of those few scholars who have given a more detailed treatment of resurrection, eschatology and cosmology,[27] I will focus here specif-

---

23. Mark W Worthing, *God, Creation, and Contemporary Physics, Theology and the Sciences Series* (Minneapolis: Fortress Press, 1996), 177-78, 198.

24. Denis Edwards, *Jesus the Wisdom of God: An Ecological Theology* (Homebush, Australia: St Pauls, 1995), especially 145-52. See also Denis Edwards, *Jesus and the Cosmos* (New York: Paulist Press), 22.

25. Peters, *God as Trinity*, 168-173. See also Ted Peters, *God—the World's Future: Systematic Theology/or a Postmodern Era* (Minneapolis: Fortress Press, 1992), 134-39, especially 134. 'My hypothesis, then, is the following principle of proleptic creation: God creates from the future, not the past.'

26. Peters, *God as Trinity*, 175-76. See also George L Murphy, 'Cosmology and Christology', *Science and Christian Belief* 6/1 (October 1994): 23

27. A longer account would include the writings of Arthur Peacocke here (see Russell, 'Bodily Resurrection, Eschatology and Scientific Cosmology: The Mutual Interaction of Christian Theology and Science'). In my view, Peacocke affirms objective but not (necessarily) bodily resurrection, remaining open to what I have called 'personal resurrection' (the resurrected Jesus includes personal continuity but not necessarily material continuity with Jesus of Nazareth), thus avoiding the full brunt of the challenge from cosmology dealt with in the present paper. That Peacocke favours a 'personal' over a 'bodily' interpretation seems

ically on the writings of John Polkinghome. From his early writings[28] to recent work[29] John Polkinghome has argued for the bodily interpretation of the resurrection of Jesus and the historicity of the empty tomb. Our resurrection, in turn, is far more than being remembered by God. Instead, it is like a mathematical pattern recreated on some other material medium, achieving 'continuity without material identity' in the 'new environment'. How will God create this new environment? Here we see the crucial importance of the empty tomb for Polkinghome: Just as Jesus' body was transformed into the risen and glorified body, so the 'matter' of this new environment must come from 'the transformed matter of this world'. '(T)he new creation is not a second attempt by God at what he [sic] had first tried to do in the old creation . . . (T)he first creation was *ex nihilo* while the new creation will be *ex vetere* . . . the new creation is the divine redemption of the old . . . (This idea) does not imply the abolition of the old but rather its transformation.'[30]

There are clues about this new creation, this 'new heaven and new earth'. Themes of continuity and discontinuity in the gospel accounts of the resurrection of Jesus indicate something of what the transformed, eschatological 'matter' will be like. Accordingly, science 'may have something to contribute' to our understanding of this transformation. This includes the significance of relationality and holism; the concept of information in addition to the familiar ideas of matter and energy; mathematics; and a dynamic view of reality.

In my opinion, Polkinghome's suggestions about eschatology as creation *ex vetere* and the role science might play in discovering continuities through the transformation are completely 'on target' and point us in the correct direction. Again, what is needed is a methodological clarification for how we are to proceed if we are to test the worth of these ideas.

---

particularly clear in his discussion of eschatology as 'beyond time and space' as suggested by Dante's beatific vision. See Peacocke, *Theology/or a Scientific Age*, 279-88, 332, 344-45; Peacocke, *Creation and the World of Science*, Chapter VIII.

28.   John Polkinghome, *The Way the World Is* (Grand Rapids: Eerdmans, 1983), Chapter 8.

29.   See for example Polkinghome, *The Faith of a Physicist*, chapter 6; John C Polkinghome, *Serious Talk: Science and Religion in Dialogue* (Valley Forge, Pa.: Trinity Press International, 1995), chapter 7.

30.   Polkinghome, *The Faith of a Physicist*, 167.

5. The way forward: a new methodology to meet the challenge: The mutual creative interaction of Christian theology and natural science

It seems clear that if one assumes the bodily resurrection of Jesus and connects this with an eschatology of cosmological transformation, one runs into a direct contradiction with the predictions of contemporary scientific cosmology. In short, an open big bang universe which will never end would seem to contradict belief in a universe which will be transformed into the new creation by an act of God. It is equally clear that if we remain with the current methodology in 'theology and science', we are left with no other options than to accept the contradiction and perhaps wait until science produces a different cosmology.

To move us beyond this impasse, I propose we expand our methodology in order that our theological commitments might play some modest role in the way scientific theories are constructed. This may not be enough to solve our problem, but without it, I doubt whether we can circumvent the contradiction we now have. I also believe that an expanded method is, from an informal point of view, already in place. Making it explicit should be helpful for a variety of problems in theology and science, including our current one.[31] In Figure 1, paths 6, 7, and 8 describe the proposed movement from theology to science.[32]

31. Note: In one sense I am merely summarising and expanding on what has already been discussed by Barbour, Murphy, Clayton and many others, including feminist and post-modernist critics of science. In another sense I am offering a constructive proposal which could make the 'theology and science' interaction much more explicit and, even more importantly, help us assess its true value to both communities.

32. First, though, I want to stress that by 'influence' I am in no way appealing to, or assuming that, theologians speak with some special kind of 'authority', whether based on the Bible, church dogma, magisterial pronouncements, or whatever. Quite the contrary; the overall context should be an open intellectual exchange between scholars based on mutual respect and the fallibility of hypotheses proposed by either side and based on scientific or theological evidence. Instead, the case I wish to make is that such influences have occurred historically and that they continue to occur in the contemporary scientific research. It is first of all, then, a descriptive claim, but it has a mildly prescriptive component as well: I believe a more intentional exploration of such influences could be fruitful for

Path (6): It is well known that theological theories provide some of the philosophical assumptions which underlie scientific methodology. Historians and philosophers of science have shown in detail how the doctrine of creation *ex nihilo* played an important role in the rise of modern science by combining the Greek assumption of the rationality of the world with the theological assumption that the world is contingent.[33] Path (7): Theological theories can act as sources of inspiration in the scientific 'context of discovery', ie in the construction of new scientific theories. An interesting example is the subtle influence of atheism on Hoyle's search for a 'steady state' cosmology.[34] Finally path (8), theological theories can lead to 'selection rules' within the criteria of theory choice in physics guiding the work of individual scientists or teams of scientists.[35] If one considers a theological theory

---

science as they have been theology, and that they could be particularly fruitful for the 'theology and science' interaction.

33. For example, to view nature as created *ex nihilo* implies that the universe is contingent and rational, and these views provide two of the fundamental philosophical assumptions on which modem science is based. By the creation *ex nihilo* tradition I mean to include its long and complex development by Jewish, Muslim and Christian theologians and philosophers during what is often called the Patristic and Middle Ages. Of course other sources of these assumptions were contributory, but it is important to remember that the doctrine of creation *ex nihilo*, has, in historical fact, served in this way. See for example Michael Foster, 'The Christian Doctrine of Creation and the Rise of Modern Science', in *Creation: The Impact of an Idea*, edited by Daniel O'Connor and Francis Oakley (New York: Charles Scribner's Sons, 1969); Eugene M Klaaren, 'Religious Origins of Modem Science: Belief in Creation in Seventeenth-Century Thought' (Grand Rapids: Eerdmans, 1977); *God and Nature: Historical Essays on the Encounter Between Christianity and Science*, edited by David C Lindberg and Ronald L Numbers (Berkeley: University of California Press, 1986); Gary B Deason, 'Protestant Theology and the Rise of Modern Science: Criticism and Review of the Strong Thesis', CTNS Bulletin 6.4 (Autumn 1986); Christopher B Kaiser, *Creation and the History of Science*, The History of Christian Theology Series, No 3 (Grand Rapids, Mich.: Eerdmans, 1991).

34. For an extremely careful and recent account of the extra-scientific factors at play in cosmological debates in this century, including the implicit role of religion, see Helge Kragh, *Cosmology and Controversy: The Historical Development of Two Theories of the Universe* (Princeton: Princeton University Press, 1996).

35. In a similar way, John Barrow uses the Anthropic Principle, not as an argument for design, but as a way of allowing biology to place constraints on physics (ie conditions that are required if the evolution of life is to be possible), and these

as true, then one can delineate what conditions must obtain within physics for the possibility of its being true. These conditions in turn can serve as reasons for an individual research scientist or group of colleagues to choose to pursue a particular scientific theory.

The asymmetry between theology and science should now be quite apparent: theological theories do not act as data for science, placing constraints on which theories can be constructed, as scientific theories do for theology. This safeguards science from any normative claims by theology. It does not, though, mean that theology cannot act to provide criteria for theory choice or inspiration for the construction of new scientific theories, as the older unidirectional relation between theology and science described (ie in which the sole task is the theological interpretation of scientific results). Together these eight paths portray science and theology in a much more interactive, though still asymmetric, mode. I call this the 'method of creative mutual interaction'.

6. Guidelines for new research in eschatology and science

6.1 Overall arguments

Given the expanded methodology described above we are prepared to engage in a two-fold project: 1) Following paths 1–5, we construct a more nuanced understanding of eschatology in light of physics and cosmology, emphasising the transformation of the universe by God beginning with the bodily resurrection of Jesus and continuing through the work of Christ in church, world, and cosmos; and 2) following paths 6–8, we begin a process of searching for a fresh interpretation of, or possibly revisions of, current scientific cosmology in light of this eschatology and its philosophical implications. If such a project is at all successful, it might eventually be possible to bring these two trajectories together at least in a very preliminary way to give a more coherent overall view, than is now possible, of the history and destiny of the universe in light of the resurrection of Jesus and its eschatological completion in the parousia.

This project is clearly a long-term undertaking, requiring the participation of scholars from a variety of fields in the sciences,

---

constraints led Barrow to the discovery of new explanations of hitherto disparate phenomena in physics.

philosophy, and theology. How are we then to proceed? My sense is that we first need some guidelines that will help point us in a fruitful direction. The analogy I have in mind is the following: we are looking for the proverbial 'needle in the haystack' (revised cosmology and eschatology) but we face, instead, a vast field of haystacks (each a different set of possible alterations). It would be useless to just start with the first one at hand. We should find a way to make an 'educated guess' as to which haystack(s) might contain the needle, and then we can start the lengthy search through them. We need guidelines to orient our search in a promising direction. Using them, we can eventually begin the lengthy process of exploring specific ways to enter into the research. For now, the guidelines must suffice.

6.2 Guidelines for constructive theology in light of science

We start with guidelines for theological reconstruction in light of science. Note: These guidelines do not apply to the converse project, scientific research in light of theology. That asymmetry is essential to the methodology here being pursued.

6.2.1 Guidelines 1–3 for paths 3 and 4

Guideline 1: Reject the argument from analogy and its representation as nomological universality regarding the future, but accept them regarding the past and present.[36]

The point of departure for our search for a theologically revised and scientifically informed eschatology will be the idea of creation *ex vetere*: the universe as we know it now will be transformed by an act of God, beginning with the bodily resurrection of Jesus and continuing until the new creation is universal.[37] But cosmology seems to pose an insur-mountable challenge to eschatology based on our choice of the 'hardest case'—the bodily resurrection of Jesus. The challenge can be

---

36.   Note: throughout this paper I am using the term 'present' without discussing the challenge from special relativity. I return to that problem in future work. For now, one response (frequently given) is to use observers floating with the cosmological expansion and defined on an appropriate hypersurface.

37.   Clearly this claim is one held in faith, and its primary characteristic is apophatic: we do not know to any degree of detail what the new creation will be like nor how to make its present and future reality intelligible even with the theological 'hermeneutical circle', let alone when we take the natural sciences on board—as we must.

sum-marised as follows: If the predictions of contemporary scientific cosmology come to pass—the universe continues to expand forever, all material structures decay to elementary particles, and these particles and their ambient radiation cool inevitably towards absolute zero —then the parousia is not just 'delayed', it will never happen. The logic of 1 Corinthians 15 is then inexorable: if there will never be a general resurrection, then Christ has not been raised from the dead, and our hope is in vain. Note, however, the challenge can also be seen as coming from theology to science: if it is in fact true that Jesus rose bodily from the dead, then the general resurrection cannot be impossible. This must in turn mean that the future of the universe will not be what scientific cosmology predicts.

We seem to be at loggerheads. How are we to resolve this fundamental challenge? My response is to recognise that the challenge is not technically from science but from the assumptions which we routinely bring to science. It is not that the predictions of scientific cosmology are wrong in a technical sense, but that we need not assume they necessarily hold. The claim that they do necessarily hold is based on two closely related philosophical assumptions which we routinely make about science: the future will be 'just like' the past (the argument from analogy) and the same laws of nature which describe the past and present describe the future (nomological universality).[38] Thus we typically assume that because contemporary scientific cosmology describes the future of the universe as 'freeze', then that is what will happen, and this generates the challenge addressed here.

But Christian theology assumes that God is free to act in radically new ways, not only in human history but in the ongoing natural history of God's creation, the universe. Now the laws of nature which science discovers reflect God's faithful ongoing action as the continuous Creator of all that is. This is the theological basis for our accepting the philosophical assumptions of analogy and universality when it comes to what science says about the past and present of the universe, including the entire scientific framework of big bang cosmology, evolutionary biology, and so on. But if God has acted in a

---

38.   Clearly the term 'just like' refers strictly to the most fundamental characteristics of nature, and the phrase 'laws of nature' means the actual regularities in nature whose representations in current scientific theories are always provisional and open to revision and rejection.

radically new way, beginning at Easter, and if God will continue to act
to bring forth the continuing transformation of the universe in the
future, then the 'freeze or fry' prediction for the cosmological future is
simply not applicable. Faith in God's new action thus challenges the
assumption that the future which science projects will be the actual
future of the universe, while accepting and welcoming all that we
know through science about God's action over the fifteen billion year
history of the universe.

Guideline 2: Reject methodological naturalism regarding the future
but accept it regarding the cosmic past and present. Any eschatology
which we might construct must be informed by and consistent with
the scientific description of the past history of the universe; that is, it
must be constrained by methodological naturalism in its description of
the past.[39] By this I mean that, to the extent that it embraces a scientific
account of the universe, it should not invoke God in its explanation of
the (secondary) causes, processes and properties of nature.[40] Methodological naturalism may not apply to the cosmological future, though,
since presumably there will continue to be occasions of divine action,
such as those surrounding the Easter events, which cannot be captured
within the confines of a purely natural or secondary-cause explanation.

Note: This guideline separates this proposal as sharply as possible
from such approaches as 'intelligent design' which are critical of
science for not including agency in its mode of explanation of the past
history of life on earth.

Guideline 3: Metaphysical options for the past, present and future:
reject some, allow others.

In revising contemporary eschatology there is a variety of metaphysical options from which we may chose. On the one hand, since
eschatology starts with the presupposition of God, it rules out some
options, such as reductive materialism and metaphysical naturalism.
By taking on board natural science, other metaphysical options become

---

39.   According to methodological naturalism, the explanation of natural properties and
      processes will be in terms of other natural properties and processes. Note:
      methodological naturalism at the level of science in no way rules out a theological
      explanation of these same properties and processes at the level of theology. What
      methodological reductionism does rule out is the use of 'God' (or even 'agency')
      within physics and biology to explain natural processes, as in 'intelligent design'.

40.   It is crucial to note that the commitment to methodological naturalism (and
      methodological reductionism) does not carry any ontological implications about
      the existence / non-existence of God (ie it is not 'inherently atheistic').

unlikely candidates, including Platonic or Cartesian ontological dualism (eg 'soul/body' dualism, 'mind/matter' dualism). On the other hand, there are a wealth of metaphysical options which are compatible with science and Christian theology in its various contemporary forms and which are widely deployed in the current literature in theology and science. These include physicalism, emergent monism, dual-aspect monism, ontological emergence, pan-experientialism (Whiteheadian metaphysics), and others. The point here is that the metaphysical options are limited by the focus on natural science but they are not forced or determined either by science or by theology, and thus represent live options worth further exploration.

6.2.2 Guidelines 4, 5 for paths 1 and 2

Guideline 4: 'Relativistically correct eschatology': reconstruct eschatology in light of contemporary physics. Although we will set aside the predictions big bang offers for the cosmic future, we must be prepared to reconstruct current work in eschatology in light of contemporary physics—specifically relativity and quantum physics—as well as what cosmology tells us about the history of the universe. I will refer to this project as the attempt to construct a 'relativistically correct Christian eschatology'.

Guideline 5: Big bang and inflationary cosmology: 'limit conditions' on any reconstructed eschatology.

Guideline 5 states that standard and inflationary big bang cosmologies, or other scientific cosmologies (such as quantum cosmology) that should be considered place a tight 'limiting condition' on any possible eschatology. All we know of the history and development of the universe and life in it will be data for the new cosmology. If we eventually find that eschatology might, in turn, offer suggestions to constructive scientific research, current scientific cosmology will still act as a constraint or 'limit condition' on such revisions.

6.2.3 Theological reconstruction following these guidelines

Guideline 6: 'Transformability' and the conditions for its possibility (the 'such that' or 'transcendental'[41] argument): guideline 6 is a formal argument and takes the form of a transcendental or 'such that' argument: it asserts the existence of those characteristics which make it possible for the universe to be transformed by God's new action. Thus, if we assume theologically that God will transform the universe into the new creation, then it follows that God must have created the universe such that it can be transformed by God's action; God has already given it precisely those conditions and characteristics which it needs in order to be transformed by God's new act. These conditions and characteristics will be clues to what will be called elements of continuity below. A simple analogy would be to argue that an open ontology provides a precondition for the enactment of voluntarist free will, but it certainly is not the sufficient grounds for it. Guideline 6 might also shed light on which conditions and characteristics of the present creation we do not expect to be continued into the new creation, emphasising what we will describe as elements of discontinuity between creation and new creation.

A consequence of this guideline is the assertion that science can be of immense help to the theological task of understanding something about the transformability of the universe. Physics and cosmology might play a profound role in our attempt to sort out what is truly essential to creation (the elements of continuity) and what is to be 'left behind' in the healing transformation to come (the elements of discontinuity) if we begin with an eschatological perspective on the new creation.

With this guideline in place we can take the next step and ask just what those elements of continuity and discontinuity might be, and in the process, enter into the conversation with physics and cosmology (and eventually the other sciences as well).

Guideline 7: Continuity within discontinuity: inverting the relationship. What, then, actually constitutes such elements of continuity and discontinuity? In the literature on theology and science so far, the philosophical theme of 'emergence in time' has been crucial in discussions of the development of the universe and the evolution of life on earth. This theme presupposes that 'discontinuity' in natural

---

41.   I am grateful to Kirk Wegter-McNelly for stressing the appropriateness of this
       term in describing guideline 2 (private communications).

processes, or the occurrence of the genuinely novel, takes place within the underlying theme of 'continuity' in nature. Now, however, when we come to the task of eschatology, I propose that we invert the relation: the elements of 'continuity' will occur within a radical and underlying 'discontinuity'. In essence, I believe that if 'discontinuity within continuity' characterises emergence or continuous creation (*creatio continua*), then 'continuity within discontinuity' best characterises creation as eschatological transformation (*creatio ex vetere*).

This has important implications on our search for candidates. First, this inversion eliminates 'non-interventionist objective special divine action'[42] as a candidate since this approach is based on 'emergence' and does not involve a transformation of the whole of nature. Indeed, these approaches presuppose that it is the continual operation of the usual laws of nature that makes objective special divine action possible without the need for a violation or suspension of these laws. But the bodily resurrection of Jesus, his corporeal appearances to the disciples, and his ascension to the presence of God, direct us towards a much more fundamental view: a radical transformation of the background conditions of space, time, matter and causality by a new act of God, and with this a permanent change in the fundamental laws of nature.

---

42. *Quantum Cosmology and the Laws of Nature: Scientific Perspectives on Divine Action, Scientific Perspectives on Divine Action Series,* edited by Robert John Russell, Nancey C Murphy and Chris J Isham (Vatican City State; Berkeley, Calif: Vatican Observatory Publications; Center for Theology and the Natural Sciences, 1993); *Chaos and Complexity: Scientific Perspectives on Divine Action, Scientific Perspectives on Divine Action Series,* edited by Robert John Russell, Nancey C Murphy and Arthur R Peacocke (Vatican City State; Berkeley, Calif: Vatican Observatory Publications; Center for Theology and the Natural Sciences, 1995); *Evolutionary and Molecular Biology: Scientific Perspectives on Divine Action,* edited by Robert John Russell, William R Stoeger SJ and Francisco J Ayala (Vatican City State; Berkeley, California: Vatican Observatory Publications; Center for Theology and the Natural Sciences, 1998); *Neuroscience and the Person: Scientific Perspectives on Divine Action,* edited by Robert John Russell, Nancey Murphy, et al (Vatican City State; Berkeley, California: Vatican Observatory Publications; Center for Theology and the Natural Sciences, 1999); *Quantum Mechanics: Scientific Perspectives on Divine Action,* edited by Robert John Russell, Philip Clayton, et al (Vatican City State; Berkeley, California: Vatican Observatory Publications; Center for Theology and the Natural Sciences, 2001).

We also break with 'physical eschatology', 'evolutionary eschatology', 'liberation eschatology', etc. Finally, since continuity will be part of an eschatology of transformation, we eliminate neo-orthodox ('two-worlds') eschatology, which does not take science into account epistemologically, and we eliminate 'supernaturalist' eschatology, 'spiritualised' eschatology, and other eschatologies which presuppose a complete ontological break between 'this world and the next'.

6.3 A final note

Our project also involves the question of whether such revisions in theology might be at all informative to contemporary science—at least for individual scientists who are working in theoretical science, who share eschatological convictions such as developed here and are interested in whether theological ideas might stimulate a creative insight into research science. I hope to suggest ways which this make take place in future writings, following paths 6–8. However, I want to stress that in following these paths, scientists should set aside the preceding guidelines, which only apply to theological research and paths 1–5. I also want to stress once again that if such suggestions led to theoretical proposals in science, it would be up to the scientific community to test them and determine their worth. Of course, philosophical and theological arguments often play an indirect role within science as theories are constructed and assessed, particularly when a judgment between competing theories is inconclusive because the empirical evidence is insufficient (eg big bang and steady state cosmologies during the period of the 1950s and early 1960s). My point is that the 'context of justification' should function as autonomously as possible in relation to 'the context of discovery'.

7. Conclusions: directions for future research

In this paper I have attempted to tackle the 'hardest case' for 'theology and science' today: the apparent falsification of Christian eschatology—when based on the bodily resurrection of Jesus, understood in relation to the 'empty tomb traditions', and placed within the context of the transformation of the universe into the 'new creation'—by the 'freeze' future predicted by scientific cosmology. I hope I have shown how the challenge is unavoidable given the methodology that defines the field of 'theology and science', one which has led to its enormous success over the past four decades.

I hope that the approach outlined here, with its expanded methodology for 'theology and science', and its commitment to producing creative new insights in both fields through this expanded interaction, will prove itself in actual test cases in the future.[43] I welcome all who wish to participate in such a grand, and perilous, venture!

---

43. Again, see Russell, 'Bodily Resurrection, Eschatology and Scientific Cosmology: The Mutual Interaction of Christian Theology and Science', and Russell, 'Eschatology and Physical Cosmology: A Preliminary Reflection', for some preliminary thoughts about research programs in science.

Figure 1

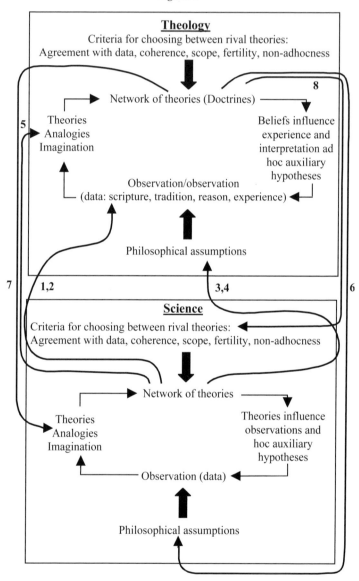

9

Sin and Atonement

Peter Lockart

1. Introduction

As I begin this task of reflection on sin and atonement, it seems important to consider the words of Ted Peters. He states, 'I will suggest that the way we think about sin can in itself be sinful, because to think of sin in a strictly trivial fashion allows us to go on blindly participating in and contributing to social dynamics that wreak widespread suffering in this world'.[1] I would push Peters' view a little further and suggest that the process of reflection, trivial or otherwise, will be affected by my sinful being and probably reflects something of a personal need of self-justification. Furthermore, engaging in this process contributes to the consequences of sin in the world in ways that may be beyond my understanding.

At the same time as this I also believe that theological reflection is doxological. Thus, it is my prayer that what I do, however impaired, will be a witness to the one true God, Father, Son and Holy Spirit. Hence, as I begin I would acknowledge that the very task in which I engage is paradoxical, both glorifying God and revealing something of the world's estrangement from its Creator.

As Jesus is dying on the cross he cries out, 'Father, forgive them; for they do not know what they are doing' (Lk 23:34). Jesus' cry from the cross encapsulates the human situation. Jesus declares that humanity is guilty of something, even though *they do not know what they are doing*, and that humanity is in *need* of God's forgiveness. This combination of the creature's guilt, even in ignorance, and God's willingness to forgive this guilt is the focus of this paper.

---

1. Ted Peters, *Sin: Radical Evil in Soul and Society* (Grand Rapids: Eerdmans: 1994), 7.

The biblical witness speaks of our guilt in terms of sin, turning away from God, and the reconciliation that takes place between God and humanity as atonement. In our modern age the elevation of the place of the individual has caused a tendency within the church to view this reconciliation between God and the creature as an entirely personal matter reliant on the faith of the individual. The main contention of this paper is that the action of God in Jesus Christ takes place in the context of the community. It is a communal event. Thus, the individualism of the Christian faith found in the modern church does not bear a true reflection of God's revelation through the scriptures and therefore may in fact be inappropriate.

The starting point for this discussion will be to examine the revelation of sin. This will be done primarily in the context of the incarnation of Jesus Christ. Jesus' life, death and resurrection take place within the life of God's chosen people, Israel, and as such 'The universality of sin is discovered . . . in the light of the revelation of human destiny by the law and by the crucified and risen Christ'.[2] This universality of sin will also be examined in the context of our human estrangement from the true meaning of our being.[3] In addition, the notion of original sin will be examined. Thus, it will be argued that the revelation found in the incarnation, and the Old Covenant, is that the predicament of sin applies to the whole creation.

This predicament is addressed in the person of Jesus Christ and through him a New Covenant is established between God and the creature.[4] This reconciliation between God and the creature forms the focus of the second section of the paper. Firstly, this will be discussed through the examination of the atonement itself and then in considering the new *being* for humanity established in the person of Jesus Christ. The extent of the atonement will also be examined in relationship to the universal estrangement from God and the meeting of this estrangement in the atonement.

The third major section of the paper will briefly examine the state of the church in the twenty-first century and the need for a greater

---

2.   Wolfhart Pannenberg, *Anthropology in Theological Perspective* (Edinburgh: T&T Clark, 1985), 137.

3.   Sin 'is universal, tragic estrangement, based on freedom and destiny in all human beings, and should never be used in the plural. Sin is separation, estrangement from one's essential being. That is what it means.' Robert C Kimball, *Theology of Culture* (New York: Oxford University Press, 1964), 123.

4.   Cf Luke 22:20; 1 Corinthians 12:25; Hebrews 8:8,13, 9:15, 12:24.

understanding of sin. As part of this discussion the eschatological vision that is given to the church will be considered, as will the church's doxological response to its life in relationship to the Triune God.

The scope of the paper will draw into the discussion many aspects of theological consideration and for this reason will not explore some of the issues in detail. However, the aim is to follow the theme of the universal nature of the atonement as a response to the universal nature of sin and to consider this in the light of the place of the church in the world in our contemporary setting.

1. The revelation of sin

1.1 The incarnation of Jesus Christ

God reveals the truth of human existence and the truth of God's will for the creation most fully through the incarnation of the eternal Word of God, Jesus Christ (Jn 1:1ff). Yet not only is the incarnation of Jesus Christ the ultimate revelation of God's love for the world, but the incarnation also stands as God's action of reconciliation between God and the creation. The necessity of this act of reconciliation by God points clearly to the fact that the creature was in need of reconciliation, in other words that the creature had turned away from God. Furthermore, it shows that humanity could not rectify this situation through our own actions. Thus, the starting point for our understanding that humanity is sinful is found in the incarnation of Jesus Christ.

Karl Barth expresses this truth of human existence as revealed through the incarnation, saying:

> The man of sin, his existence and nature, his why and whence and whither, are all set before us in Jesus Christ, are all spoken to us directly and incontrovertibly: Thou art man! This is what thou doest! This is what thou art! This is the result! We hear Him and we hear this verdict. We see Him, and in this mirror we see ourselves, ourselves as those

who commit sin and are sinners. We are inescapably
accused and irrevocably condemned.[5]

Barth seems to capture something of Paul's contention in his letter
to the Romans, 'All have turned aside, together they have become
worthless' (3:12). Hence, Barth argues that Jesus' incarnation and life
reveal humanity to be sinners and that our sin is irreconcilable by our
own actions.[6] Barth asserts that the pinnacle of humanity's depravity
is expressed in the crucifixion of Jesus when the creature kills the
Creator.[7]

There can be little doubt that the incarnation of Jesus Christ does
teach us about our predicament, and in the mirror of Jesus' life of
perfect obedience[8] we are confronted by our sinfulness. However,
Wolfhart Pannenberg is right to critique Barth's view,[9] asking, 'Are
those who refuse to believe in Christ also spared the confrontation
with the distortion of their human destiny as seen in the structure of
their own behaviour?'[10] This is a valid question. Ted Peters, reflecting
on the human state of being, speaks of a process of revelation through
which we come to know that we are sinners.[11] It can be argued that
this process of 'waking up' to our own depravity does not necessarily
need the revelation of Jesus but is given its true meaning in
confrontation with the revelation of Jesus Christ's life, death and
resurrection. Sin is a concept that is grounded in the context of our
guilt before God and 'therefore it can only be known and understood

---

5.   Karl Barth, *Church Dogmatics* (Edinburgh: T&T Clark, 1985), 1932ff IV/1, 390,
      cited in J Webster, *Barth's Moral Theology: Human Action in Barth's Thought*
      (Edinburgh: T&T Clark, 1998), 68.

6.   This is consistent with Augustine in his *Treatise on Nature and Grace, against
      Pelagius.* (P Schaff (editor), *Nicene & Post-Nicene Fathers of the Christian
      Church*, Vol 5 (Grand Rapids: Eerdmans, 1971), 122.

7.   '. . . man really and finally revealed himself as guilty before God by killing God . .
      .' (Barth, *op cit* I/2, 92).

8.   The 'Scriptures speak of "sinlessness" only in the case of the Lord himself.' GC
      Berkouwer, *Sin* (Grand Rapids: Eerdmans, 1971), 487. Cf 2 Corinthians 5:21; 1
      Peter 2:22; John 8:46 Hebrews 7:26; 1 Peter 1:19ff.

9.   'Only when we know Jesus Christ do we really know that man is the man of sin,
      and what sin is and what it means for man.' Barth, *op cit*, IV/1, 389.

10.   Pannenberg, *op cit*, 92.

11.   'As we grow and come into our own personal consciousness, we wake up to find
      ourselves already within the state of sin' (Peters, *op cit*, 24).

in relation to God'.[12] Thus, whilst it is logical to accept that people can be aware of a discord within their lives and the world around them, Jesus' incarnation is the ultimate revelation of what this discord or evil may actually be about.

1.2 Sin and the law

The revelation of our sinful state through the condescension of the Word of God takes place in the context of God's covenant with God's chosen people, the Israelites. The Old Testament points continually at God's faithfulness to this covenant, and as part of this 'there is found the promise of a Saviour who will be raised up out of the people'.[13] In seeking a broader understanding of the sinful state of the creature, revealed in the coming of Jesus Christ, it is therefore necessary to examine the Old Testament witness, in particular the relationship between sin and the law, and the concept of original sin that has developed within the church.[14]

According to Paul 'through the law comes the knowledge of sin' (Rom 3:20).[15] Thus the law reveals sin.[15] In fact it could be argued that the very existence of the law indicates that humanity is sinful.[16] This is consistent with Paul's assertion that 'sin was indeed in the world *before the law*' (Rom 5:12). However, the association of sin with the law has at times led people to view sin as acts that 'break' the law of God. Yet whilst it is true that such acts point at our sin, and these acts may be referred to as 'sins', these acts are not by definition sin.[17] This is an important distinction to make.

---

12. Berkouwer, *op cit*, 154.
13. Thomas Torrance, *Space, Time and Resurrection* (Edinburgh: The Handsel Press, 1976), 29.
14. It is generally accepted that the concept of 'original sin' is based on the idea of 'the fall' found in Genesis 3 and finds its beginnings as a doctrine in the writings of St Augustine.
15. Cf *The Heidelberg Catechism*, Question and Answer 3.
16. Paul Tillich asserted that, 'He who needs a law which tells him how to act or how not to act is already estranged from the source of the law which demands obedience'. Tillich, *Systematic Theology* (Digswell Place: James Nisbet, 1968), 54.
17. 'If one speaks of "sins" and refers to special acts which are considered as sinful, one should always be conscious of the fact that "sins" are expressions of "sin". It

This view is supported in both the Old and New Testaments. Sin is not predominantly about behaviours and morality. Rather sin is about the source of these behaviours that springs from within us. In examining the Old Testament Pannenberg concludes that when talking about sin,[18] whilst the transgression is always in view, repentance is not merely about the deed but what lies at the root of these deeds.[19] Similarly in the New Testament the issue of sin is more about what causes us to turn away than the actual actions in and of themselves.

> According to Romans 7:7ff sin does not consist merely of individual offenses . . . It precedes all human acts as a power that dwells within us, that possesses us like our own subjectivity as it overpowers us. It is a state of alienation from God. Yet this alienation does not come about without our cooperation and therefore our own—even if divided—consent. [20]

Hence, sin is something that both precedes and underlies the concept of transgressions against God's law.

Thus, the place of the law within the Jewish tradition, and later in Christian thinking, was not primarily to provide a way to please God but rather to reveal humanity's estrangement from God. Ted Peters reflects on this issue saying, 'What codes and commandments do is help us to avoid committing sins. Or, perhaps better, codes and commandments help us to identify our sins when we commit them.'[21] It is this role of the identification of sin that seems central to the place of the law within Christianity. As Calvin suggests, 'Now, the law has power

---

    is not the disobedience to a law which make an act sinful but the fact that it is an expression of man's estrangement from God, from men, and from himself.' Tillich, *op cit*, 53.

18.   The words *hamartia*, *hattat't* and *'awon* all point to a common root in the motivation of the doer. 'Thus the pslamist prays for a clean heart (51:10), and Jeremiah (32:39) and Ezekiel (11:19; 36:26) hope that in the coming age of salvation God will give us a new and different heart that will not contend against his commands'. W Pannenberg, *Systematic Theology* Vol 2 (Grand Rapids: Eerdmans, 1994), 239.

19.   *Ibid*, 239.

20.   *Ibid*, 262.

21.   Peters, *op cit*, 23.

to exhort believers. This is not a power to bind their consciences with a curse, but one to shake them off their sluggishness, by repeatedly urging them, and pinch them awake to their imperfections.'[22]

The place of the law as revelational in the Christian tradition often seems to have become lost in the desire of Christians to obey the law and thereby please God. This confusion over the part that the law plays in the Christian faith can lead to the assumption that people can respond appropriately to the law, thereby justifying themselves. This concept was expressed in the mind of Pelagius. However, in response to this St Augustine developed the doctrine of original sin. It is to this concept of original sin that we now turn.

1.3 The problem of original sin as inheritance

Given that sin precedes the law, and that the law acts primarily as an indicator of sin, the question of what sin is and where it originates is a crucial one. The church has long considered the concept of the fall of Adam in the Genesis 3 to explain the problem.[23] Paul suggests as much in Romans when he asserts that sin came into the world through one man and that all have sinned and fallen short of the glory of God (Rom 5). Augustine picked up these arguments as he developed his doctrine of original sin. However, whilst helpful, these traditional explanations of the origins of sin can be problematic. Hence, a deeper exploration of the concept of the fall, the meaning of sin and how it is transmitted is needed.

Genesis 3 is often referred to as providing the starting point of sin within humanity. Genesis 3 describes a protohistorical event in which the first man, Adam, disobeys God and because of this all of humanity suffer the consequences Adam's action.[24] This historical approach to the passage can lead to ideas of determinism, thus robbing humanity of any autonomy or responsibility for sin. On the other hand, 'Dehistoricizing Adam . . . lifts the concept of Adam's sin out of the idiom of causality, in which to be a sinner is to be the recipient of alien guilt. Adam is not our predecessor but our type; Adam's successors are simply those who follow the "rude and perverted" order manifest in

---

22. Calvin *Institutes*, 2.7.14.

23. Eg 'The Augsburg Confession states that after the fall of Adam all men were both conceived and born in sin.' Berkouwer, *op cit*, 467.

24. Cf *Heidelberg Catechism*, Question and Answer 7.

him.'[25] This concept of Adam being our type turns us away from a discussion of causal links[26] and into one of what the passage reveals about humanity, sin and its consequences.

If Adam is our type, then Adam's transgression must also teach us something of what sin actually is. Augustine argued that concupiscence was at the heart of the matter.[27] However, it is probably more appropriate to understand concupiscence as a manifestation of sin. It is a sin, but this means that the root and core of sin may still remain hidden.[28] Another view has been that *hubris* is at the centre of human sin.[29] Pannenberg also notes that Reformation theology saw unbelief as the root of sin.[30] These concepts of original sin are descriptive of the human condition as opposed to trying to establish a reason or justification for human sinfulness. Bonhoeffer reminds us, 'It is not the purpose of the Bible to give information about the origin of evil but to witness to its character as guilt and as the infinite burden of man.'[31] Thus, whilst some idea of what lies at the heart of sin can be argued, what seems more important is that, for whatever motivations, 'Adam' puts himself in the place of God[32] and thereby denies some element of the truth of the meaning of his existence.[33]

This idea that sin has ontological and teleological implications is paramount. John Zizioulas says, 'viewed from the point of view of

25. Webster, *op cit*, 73.

26. Berkouwer argues that nowhere in Scripture can a causal explanation of man's sin be found. Berkouwer, *op cit*, 25.

27. 'According to Augustine, the perversion of sinful desire rests on a perversion of the will. In assessing priorities, the will sets lesser (worldly) good above the supreme good (God) and even uses the latter as a means to attain the former'. Pannenberg, *Systematic Theology,* Vol 2, *op cit*, 243.

28. *Ibid*, 241.

29. *Hubris* 'is sin in its total form, namely, the other side of unbelief or man's turning away from the divine centre to which he belongs. It is the turning towards one's self as the centre of one's self and one's world'. Tillich, *op cit*, 58.

30. Pannenberg, *Systematic Theology,* Vol 2, *op cit*, 251.

31. Dietrich Bonhoeffer, *Creation and Fall* (London: SCM Press, 1959), 65.

32. 'The fall results from the claim of created man to be the ultimate point of reference in existence (to be God), it is, in the final analysis, the state of existence whereby the created world tends to posit its being ultimately with reference to itself and not to an uncreated being, God.' J Zizioulas, *Being as Communion* (Crestwood, NY: St Vladimir's Seminary Press, 1985), 102.

33. Bonhoeffer speaks of this in terms of Adam losing his *creatureliness*. Bonhoeffer, *op cit*, 73.

ontology, the fall consists in *the refusal to make being dependent on communion*, in a rupture between truth and communion'.[34] Through sin humanity denies communion with God and as such is also separated from the meaning of our existence as God's creatures. 'We may thus (also) understand sin as our human weakness relative to our destiny.'[35] It can be argued that God created humanity with a purpose and that the presence of sin indicates that humanity has lost sight of this purpose. So it is that, 'All of us sin because we think we can attain a full and true life thereby'.[36] Therefore, in denying the truth that our existence as creatures is to be in communion with God, we also deny something of the purpose of our existence within God's creation.

The story of Adam is played out in each one of us, but there always remains an element of human responsibility in our own predicament. Paradoxically, though, if an individual had the power to deny the force of these structures it would mean that Pelagius was right.[37] The problem with this, as Augustine so rightly asserted, is that if a person could live without sin 'then Christ is dead in vain'.[38] Nonetheless, the idea of sin serves the purpose of 'absolving the Creator from responsibility for evil and its consequences in his good creation'.[39] Thus, the Genesis story acts as revelation pointing to, amongst other things,[40] the mystery of human sin and the brokenness of the creature's existence in God's *good* creation.

It has been a confronting issue for the church to explain why all creatures share the brokenness of human existence demonstrated in Adam. Augustine explained the continuing problem of sin within the creation, suggesting that the propensity for sinning is hereditary. It is passed from one generation to the next.[41] Throughout the history of the church theologians have sought both to expand upon and

---

34.   Zizioulas, *op cit*, 102.

35.   Pannenberg, *Systematic Theology*, Vol 2, *op cit*, 258.

36.   *Ibid*, 263.

37.   *Ibid*, 256.

38.   Schaff, *op cit*, Vol 2, 122.

39.   Pannenberg, *Systematic Theology*, Vol 2, *op cit*, 264.

40.   For example, Pannenberg says that the real point of the Genesis story 'is an explanation not of the origin of sin but of the origin of death and of the difficulty involved in work and reproduction' (*ibid*, 263).

41.   Ted Peters, *Playing God: Genetic Determinism and Human Freedom* (New York: Routledge, 1997), 85.

challenge Augustine's ideas. Anselm propounded one of the more significant theories. 'Anselm thought he could give an explanation along Augustinian lines with the thesis that each newly created soul owes to God the original righteousness that had been given to humanity as a species and that had been lost through Adam's fall.'[42]

However, what becomes immediately apparent is that if sin is linked to the notion of inheritance 'it comes to have a "naturalistic, deterministic and even fatalistic ring"'.[43] More recently, notions of genetic determinism have also entered this discussion of the transmission of human evil.[44] Pannenberg argues that there is no necessity for the concept of the inheritance of original sin at all:

> The universality of human sin was thought to be dependent on its transmission from generation to generation. It was overlooked, however, that the Augustinian discovery of the link between love of self and concupiscence itself implies a structure of human conduct that is common to all individuals. Materially, then, no theory of human inheritance was needed.[45]

He goes on to suggest that 'a doctrine of original sin rests on a combination of the supraindividual aspects of sin and the individual setting in the social context'.[46] Pannenberg's view seems far more acceptable than that of the traditional notions of inherited sin. Thus, the universality of human sin can be explained through a myriad of factors that include both those within the grasp of the individual to control as well as those outside it.

The truth of Adam's turning away is repeated in each person and thus there can be little doubt that all have turned aside from God (Rom 3:9ff). In this we have denied the truth of our being. This means that all people are subject to sin and its consequences. Any notion of speaking of sin as individual acts misses the point and trivialises the situation. Sin is about the very way humans exist in relationship to their Creator. 'Human beings do not first become sinners through their own actions

---

42.   Pannenberg, *Systematic Theology*, Vol 2, *op cit*, 254.
43.   Webster, *op cit*, 72.
44.   Eg Peters, *Playing God*, *op cit*, Chapter 3.
45.   Pannenberg, *Systematic Theology*, Vol 2, *op cit*, 247.
46.   *Ibid*, 255.

and by imitating the bad example of others; they are already sinners before any action of theirs.'[47] Hence, it has been shown that Genesis points to a state of sin that applies to all people. It is universal. However, this universality of sin does not necessarily require sin to be an inherited trait.

1.4 The universality of sin

To this point it has been argued that sin is something that affects all human beings and in fact affects our *being* as humans. However, as Berkouwer puts it, this 'confession of original sin may not function and cannot function as a means of excusing ourselves or of hiding behind another man's guilt'.[48] Whilst using the excuse of original sin is inappropriate, so too is blaming other factors.[49] One of the greatest difficulties for most people seems to be actually accepting responsibility for their own actions. A fact that is attested to by trends in litigation in the modern world. It is far easier to acknowledge the presence of evil in the world than to acknowledge that *I* as an individual participate in that evil. Thus, in arguing that sin is a universal, it should still be asserted that no one can absolve themselves of their culpability.

It can also be asserted that sin pervades all that we do. The all-pervasiveness of sin covers the scope not just of all people but of all of the actions in which we engage. John Calvin asserted this view in his *Institutes*:

> We must strongly insist upon these two points: first, that there never existed any work of a godly man which, if examined by God's stern judgment, would not deserve condemnation; secondly, if such a work were found (something not possible for man), it would still lose favour—weakened and stained as it

47. Pannenberg, *Anthropology in Theological Perspective*, *op cit*, 119-120.
48. Berkouwer, *op cit*, 435.
49. 'As much as the reality of evil strikes us, however, the blame is typically put on others—on more or less specific others, or preferably on anonymous structures and pressures in the social system.' Pannenberg, *Systematic Theology*, Vol 2, *op cit*, 237.

is by the sins with which its author himself is surely burdened.[50]

Although this is a rather negative view of the human predicament, Calvin's view is certainly not an isolated one.[51] Part of the problem of sin is that it is not just that humans do what is perceived to be sinful but that everything humanity does is tainted by sin. Therefore, the reality of sin is something that applies to 'the whole phenomenon of human life and that may be known even without the premise of God's revelation, even if this revelation is necessary to bring its true significance to light'. [52]

In this understanding of human reality there is no place for moralism that does not accept the solidarity of our situation. 'Sin's universality shows such a moralistic attitude to be hypocrisy.'[53] This also impacts on any notion that there are different levels of sin. Whilst it may be helpful in terms of human community to postulate that some transgressions are worse than others, in the end these transgressions are merely the expression of the deeper issue of sin.[54]

Overall, it must be said that sin is a problem for the whole creation and that whilst this problem is expressed through the actions of the creature, the expressions of sin are not in themselves the main problem. The revelation of Christ and the scriptures open up to us a fuller knowledge of our sin but this knowledge is somewhat of a paradox. As creatures, humans cannot be absolved from their involvement in sin. We are responsible, yet at the same time the forces

---

50.   Calvin, *Institutes* 3.14.11.

51.   Cf Romans 3:9-18.

52.   Pannenberg, *Systematic Theology,* Vol 2, *op cit*, 236.

53.   *Ibid*, 238.

54.   'It is not uncommon for a theologian to argue in the following way: all human sin is equal because all human sin is infinite. All sin is against God, and because God in infinite and eternal, our sin has infinite and eternal consequence, and hence it is wrong to limit our evaluation of a sinful act to its finite or temporal scope. This may very well be true regarding our relationship to God, but it still seems to me that at the level of inter-human relationships we can profitably discriminate.' Peters, *Sin: Radical Evil, op cit*, 10-11.

involved seem to dictate that sin is a reality that cannot be overcome by human efforts. The Creator alone can resolve the problem of sin.[55]

2. The reconciliation between the Creator and the creation in and through Jesus Christ

2.1 The atonement and the high priesthood of Christ

God's answer to the human predicament is Jesus Christ. The claim of Paul in his letter to the Romans is that Christ died 'once for all' (Rom 6: 10). It is this idea that leads to the notion that what Christ did has implications for all people and for all time. Paul states clearly that he believes that 'just as one man's trespasses led to condemnation for all, so one man's act of righteousness leads to justification and life for all' (Rom 5:18). Through the person of Jesus Christ the sin that affects all of humanity is met, not just in Jesus' death on the cross but also through his life of active obedience to the Father. This process of reconciliation between God and the creature is what has been traditionally referred to as the atonement and takes place in the context of the cultic life of Israel.

In God's covenant with Israel God established means by which reconciliation could take place between a sinful people and a faithful God. The pinnacle of this process for the Israelites was the Day of Atonement, *yom kippur* (Lev 16).[56] In his actions on this day the high priest would intercede for all of Israel.

> When the high priest entered into the holy presence of Yahweh in the sanctuary, that he might present all Israel in his person to God, we can say, as Calvin puts it in his commentary on Hebrews, all Israel entered in his person.
>
> Conversely, when he vicariously confessed their sins and interceded for them before God, God

---

55. As Luther discovered, 'no final peace could be found by the effort to achieve righteousness'. R Niebuhr, *The Nature and Destiny of Man*, Vol 2 (London: Nisbet, 1943), 192.

56. Cf J Torrance, *Worship, Community and the Triune God of Grace* (Carlisle: Paternoster Press, 1996), 37 ff.

accepted them as his forgiven people in the person of their high priest.[57]

The offering of the priest accounted for the sins of all of Israel, corporately[58] and as individuals. Thus, through the cultic life of Israel reconciliation between God and God's people was achieved.

It is claimed that this process of atonement found in the Old Testament is consistent with the actions of Christ as witnessed to in the gospel of St John and the letter to the Hebrews. Jesus acts vicariously for humanity as our high priest. However, unlike the high priest of the Old Covenant, Jesus acts on behalf of the whole creation, not just the people of God.

This process of reconciliation through Jesus begins with the incarnation. The eternal Word of God became human and fully identifies with us in our state of estrangement from God. Yet as Thomas Torrance points out, as he lived this life, as flesh of our flesh and bone of our bone, Jesus lived in perfect obedience to his Father's will, even to the point of death.

> He (Jesus) condescended in great humiliation to unite himself with us in our weakness, corruption and damned existence, living within it all the life of unsullied purity, truth and holiness in such a way as to atone in life and death for our sin and guilt, overcoming all the estrangement and separation that it involved between man and God, and in such a way therefore as to resurrect in himself our human nature in union and communion with the Father.[59]

In this full identification with humanity and our sinful being, Jesus is able to stand as our representative before God.

During his life of obedience to the Father it is clearly demonstrated that Jesus is acting on our behalf. For example, in John we hear that he is baptised by John the Baptist with a baptism for the repentance of sin. Jesus knew no sin but in his baptism of repentance he identifies

---

57.   *Ibid*, 38.

58.   Eg Leviticus 4.

59.   Torrance, *Space, Time and Resurrection, op cit*, 49.

himself with our need of repentance.[60] Likewise as the Holy Spirit descends upon him at his baptism God demonstrates that what he is doing is not for Jesus' sake but for ours (Jn 1:29ff). Jesus, the eternal Word of God, is ever one with the Spirit, so it is for our sake that the accommodation of Holy Spirit in Jesus' sinful flesh takes place.

Acting in a reflection of the high priest of Israel, Jesus gathers around him twelve disciples and consecrates himself through prayer for his task.

> As long before Elijah had gathered together twelve stones representing the twelve tribes of Israel to build an altar for sacrifice, Jesus gathered twelve living stones, such as the rock Peter, and built them round Himself the Lamb of God to be offered in sacrifice. Upon this Twelve, the reconstituted Israel, He was to build His church, and so he formed and fashioned them into a foundation, in a profound sense, one Body with Himself.[61]

This action of Jesus is confirmed and extended in his so-called 'high priestly prayer' of John 17. Jesus prays that all those who come to believe may be one with each other and with him (Jn 17:20ff). Thus Jesus acts vicariously, 'He is at once the *One* and the *Many*'.[62]

Hence it can be said that Jesus is the mediator of the New Covenant. 'He stepped into the conflict between the covenant faithfulness of God and the unfaithfulness of man and took that conflict into His own flesh as the Incarnate Son and bore it to the very end.'[63] There is an exchange that takes place through what Jesus does.

---

60. '. . . He became a curse for us. He was not a sinful man. But inwardly and outwardly His situation was that of a sinful man. He did nothing that Adam did. But he lived a life in the form it must take on the basis and assumption of Adam's act. He bore innocently what Adam and all of us in Adam have been guilty of. Freely he entered into solidarity and necessary association with our lost existence. Only in this way "could" God's revelation to us, our reconciliation with Him, manifestly become an event in Him and by Him.' Barth, *op cit*, I/2, 152.

61. Thomas Torrance, 'The Atonement and the Oneness of the Church', *Scottish Journal of Theology*, Vol 7 (1954): 248.

62. *Ibid*, 250.

63. *Ibid*, 251.

It is the *mirifica commutatio* of which Calvin speaks.[64] Jesus stands in our place, and thus in his *being* and *doing,* who we are and what we do is exchanged with who he is and what he does. Jesus' actions are consistent with the high priest of Israel and so it can be said of Jesus Christ that he is the one 'whom God put forward as an atoning sacrifice through (Jesus') faithfulness by means of his blood' (Rom 3:25).[65]

The concept of the atonement does not sit comfortably with all people, and there remains a variety of understandings of the atonement that have not been examined in this paper. For example, the feminist theologian Mary Grey traces some of the concepts that have developed in both Eastern and Western churches through the centuries.[66] Grey's analysis that the emphasis on the cosmic dimensions in the East and the juridical and legal dimensions in the West are not necessarily incongruent but can be drawn together is fair.[67] However, her suggestions for a feminist approach to the concept seem to discount the way that God brings about the atonement in the person of Jesus Christ.

As Hengel points out, 'The theme of expiation in the sense of "purifying the land" from evil and disaster or of "assuaging" the wrath of the gods was part of the *lingua franca* of the religions of late antiquity'.[68] But whilst what happens in Christ is consistent with the cultic life of Israel, it also is different.

> For example, it spoke not of atonement for a particular crime, but of universal atonement for *all* human guilt. Furthermore, it was decisive that God's grace was given, not as the result of the heroic action of a particular man, but by God himself, through

---

64. *Institutes* IV:17.2.

65. For a discussion on this translation of '(Jesus') faithfulness' see (BW Longenecker, 'Pistis in Romans 3:25: Neglected Evidence for the "Faithfulness of Christ"?' *New Testament Studies,* Vol 34 (1993): 478-480, here 479.

66. Mary Grey, *Redeeming the Dream: Feminism, Redemption and Christian Tradition* (London: SPCK, 1989), 110ff.

67. *Ibid,* 113-114.

68. Martin Hengel, *The Atonement: A Study of the Origins of the Doctrine in the New Testament* (London: SCM Press, 1981), 19.

Jesus, the Son, who was delivered over to death (2 Cor 5:18ff).[69]

Hence, Jesus' action stands in the context of the cultic life of Israel whilst at the same time adding a new dimension to this action.

Ultimately, the reconciliation that takes place between God and humanity in Christ is supremely God's action. Thus, whilst the concept of the atonement may not sit comfortably with all people, we must take seriously the idea that what occurs is consistent with Jesus acting as the high priest for the whole creation. Nonetheless, one of the outcomes that Grey seems to look for is pertinent. She argues for a reconstruction of the word atonement as *at-one-ment*.[70] In this she captures that what is occurring in Jesus is an act of reconciliation. It is not just about appeasing an angry deity because of our wrongdoing. Rather it is about the recreation of the human being in Jesus Christ so that we are *at-one* again with God and each other.

2.2 New being in Christ—the hypostatic union of God and the creature

In looking at sin it has been asserted that sin is something that affects our very *being* as humans. Sin disrupts the communion that God created us for. 'Sin is an "absurd act"; it contradicts our being, and so constitutes something that we cannot do, and yet do.'[71] This 'absurd act' or disruption is something that alters our existence and contradicts the very purpose of our being. 'The essential thing about a person lies precisely in his being a revelation of truth, not as "substance" or "nature" but as a "mode of existence".'[72] Thus, for this situation to be remedied means that the atonement has to include a change in not just our behaviours, but in the nature of our very *being* as humans.

In Jesus, the eternal Word of God, God condescends to become one with the sinful state of humanity. 'Jesus is himself the hypostatic union of the Creator and the creature.'[73] Through this hypostatic union

---

69. *Ibid*, 19.
70. Grey, *op cit*, 126.
71. Webster, *op cit*, 71.
72. Zizioulas, *op cit*, 106.
73. Torrance, *Space, Time and Resurrection*, *op cit*, 75. 'By living the life which Jesus Christ lived in our midst, the life of complete obedience to the Father and of perfect communion with him, the life of absolute holiness in the midst of our sin

between God and the creature, the creature is re-created (2 Cor 5:17). Hence, the atonement points to the truth that human being is *being* in communion with God. Through the coming of Christ into the world God is revealed as a Triune God in God's own being. This truth of God's being is expounded in the Nicene-Constantinopolitan Creed. Thomas Torrance argues that,

> The Chalcedonian Christology needs to be filled out in accordance with its own fundamental position, in a more dynamic way, in terms of the incorporating and atoning work of the Saviour, for the only account the New Testament gives us of the Incarnation is conditioned by the perspective of the crucifixion and resurrection.[74]

Thus, to understand the change that has been wrought in human being through the atonement it is necessary to understand something of the relationship that exists within the Godhead itself.

The truth of God's being is that God exists in communion. The Father, Son and Spirit exist in a perichoretic unity of love. This 'implies that the three persons of the trinity exist only in reciprocal eternal relatedness. God is not God apart from the way in which the Father, Son and Spirit in eternity give to and receive from each other what they essentially are.'[75] In John 17 Jesus' prayer is that we be one with him as he and the Father are one. Thus, 'Our human nature is set within the Father-Son relationship of Christ'.[76] We are made to be a part of this relationship as we are drawn into Christ's life by the power of the Holy Spirit. Zizioulas reminds us that Christology is essentially conditioned by Pneumatology.[77] So it is that through the power of the Holy Spirit and in Christ we enter into the very life of the divine Trinity.

---

and corruption, and by living it through the whole course of our human existence from birth to death, he achieved within our creaturely being the very union between God and man that constitutes the heart of atonement, effecting man's salvation and restoration to communion with God the Father.'

74.   Torrance, 'The Atonement and the Oneness of the Church' *op cit*, 247.

75.   C Gunton, *The One the Three and the Many* (Cambridge: Cambridge University Press, Cambridge, 1993), 164.

76.   Torrance, *Space, Time and Resurrection*, *op cit*, 69.

77.   Zizioulas, *op cit*, 111.

Thus, through Jesus, humanity enters into the truth of what we are meant to be and, in this, humanity is saved from the consequences of our rejection of God.

> When Christ says He is the truth and at the same time the life of the world, He introduces into truth a content carrying ontological implications. If the truth saves the world it is because it is life. The Christological mystery, as declared by the Chalcedonian definition, signifies that salvation as truth and life is possible only in and through a person who is ontologically *true*, ie something which creation cannot offer, as we have seen. The only way for a true person to exist is for being and communion to coincide. The triune God offers in Himself the only possibility for such an identification of being with communion; He is the revelation of true personhood.[78]

In this we cannot follow Jesus' example but only be changed by God's gracious action for our sake. As Zizioulas asserts, the creature can only be saved though the one who is fully divine and fully human. Christ must be God to be our saviour.[79]

God's affirmation that this reconciliation has taken place is the resurrection of Jesus. 'Resurrection is atonement in its creative and positive result and achievement, in the recreation and final affirmation of man and the assuming of him by grace into union and communion with the life and love of God himself.'[80] Jesus' appearance on the Easter dawn is God's 'Yes!' to the recreation of human being in Christ. 'It is a creative event within the creation.'[81] For those who are alive in Christ Jesus there is now no condemnation as he intercedes for us and we are made joint heirs with him (Rom 8:1, 17, 34). In the resurrection

78. *Ibid*, 107.
79. *Ibid*, 108.
80. Torrance, *Space, Time and Resurrection, op cit*, 56.
81. *Ibid*, 31.

it is revealed that 'union with God is the end and goal of the atonement'.[82]

In this view of the resurrection traditional views of human being come into question. Torrance argues against the idea that humans are made up of a body and an immortal soul and goes on to assert,

> It is the fulfilment of God's covenant mercies in the incarnation and resurrection that confers immortality. Christ only has immortality and we receive out of his fullness. The general resurrection is absolutely dependent on the resurrection of Jesus Christ himself, for it is in his death and resurrection that God has dealt with death and guilt and hell once and for all.[83]

What is at stake in the atonement is not the salvation of souls from hell but the opening up of God's eternity to the created being. The fallen creature is redeemed. Thus, in the resurrection and ascension of Christ the new being that is established in him is made available for all.

The atonement brings *new being* for humanity. It is a change in the nature of human existence that finds our definition in true communion with God. Just as God's own being is communal so to it must be said that the truth of the creation is that it too has its being in communion. 'The mystery of being a person lies in the fact that here otherness and communion are not in contradiction but coincide. Truth as communion does not lead to the dissolving of the diversity of beings into one vast ocean of being, but to the affirmation of otherness in and through love.'[84] In this relationship of love the creature is free to be in union with the other without losing their particularity of being. Hence, the atonement means that in Christ humanity is invited into the hypostatic union between Father, Son and Spirit. In Christ and through the Spirit the creature enters into the life of God.[85]

---

82. *Ibid*, 67.
83. *Ibid*, 35.
84. Zizioulas, *Being as Communion, op cit*, 106.
85. 'For the sake of His infinite love He has become what we are in order that He may make us entirely what He is' (Ireneaus).

2.3 Is there a limit to God's grace?

Thus far it has been asserted that the atonement, which reconciles God and humanity, has universal implications. Jesus addresses the discord in human being because he is true in his being human.[86] Pannenberg argues that 'The universality of sin . . . is a presupposition for the universality of the redemption wrought by Christ'.[87] However, whilst it is generally agreed that God's action in Christ does have universal implications there is a question as to whether all people access this grace and are thereby saved.

This issue of who is saved has been a part of the debates within the Reformed church. Some of this debate has taken place in the context of the teachings of John Calvin.[88] 'In several places he (Calvin) maintains that while Christ's atonement is universal, the gift of saving faith is limited to the elect.'[89] Bell argues that Calvin is able to make this claim because 'he did not link the doctrines of election and atonement in a logical developmental order of cause and effect'.[90] According to Bell, it seems that Calvin believed that whilst the atonement is effective for all it only extends to those who by faith embrace the gospel.[91] Hence, it can be argued that although the redemption of the creation in the atonement has universal connotations, the limitation on God's saving grace may be the reception and acceptance of that grace.[92]

However, there is a danger in such an approach, because faith itself can become a new kind of works. Righteousness could be seen as being achieved through the veracity, or purity, or authenticity of a person's belief. In such a scheme of belief 'legal repentance' can become the key to salvation.

---

86. John 14:6, 'I am the way, and the truth, and the life.'

87. Pannenberg, *Anthropology in Theological Perspective*, *op cit*, 120.

88. It should be noted here that since the Synod of Dort it has been agreed that Calvin taught a limited doctrine of Atonement. (MC Bell, 'Calvin and the extent of the Atonement', *Evangelical Quarterly*, Vol 55 (1983): 115).

89. *Ibid*, 118.

90. *Ibid*, 121.

91. *Ibid*, 119.

92. 'Our reconciliation to God is both objective (Christ does something for us that we could not do for ourselves) and subjective (we have to embrace and make our own the forgiveness made available in him)' (John Polkinghorne, *Science and Christian Belief* (London: SPCK, 1994), 138.

> Legal repentance says: 'Repent, and if you repent
> you will be forgiven!' as though God our Father has
> to be conditioned into being gracious! It makes the
> imperatives of obedience prior to the indicatives of
> grace, and regards God's love and forgiveness and
> acceptance as conditional upon what we do—upon
> our meritorious acts of repentance.[93]

God's saving action within the creation is just that: God's action. Thus, as Torrance goes on to argue, evangelical repentance is quite different from 'legal repentance'. He states 'repentance is our response to grace, not a condition of grace'.[94] Thus, any suggestion that our acceptance of God's action is what makes the atonement efficacious on an individual level is highly questionable. Repentance is a part of our response to God's grace. It is not the thing that activates God's grace.

Whether a person can actively and deliberately reject God's grace and thereby deny their participation in God's saving action is another question worthy of consideration. To answer such a question would, in part, depend on what it means to be a participant in God's divine life and God's saving action. In addition to this, it must be considered whether God's unconditional love can encompass and forgive active rejection of God, which seems to be what sin is all about in any case. Hence, it would seem that whilst there is a plausible case to be argued that a person may be able to deny their inclusion in God's action of grace, it seems more likely that God's salvation may still encompass all people.

In addition, if we accept that what God does in Jesus Christ has ontological implications for the whole creation, then it seems that the atonement must be effective in some way for all people. In the atonement the whole being of creation is altered through reconciliation with God. 'Atonement can in the end mean no less than the reconciliation of all creation, at its different levels of response, with true structures and laws of its constitution—that is, with the love of God which is the principle of the harmony of life with life.'[95] Under a situation of total guilt the creature has the certainty of total forgive-

---

93.   J Torrance, *Worship, Community and the Triune God, op cit*, 44.

94.   *Ibid*, 44.

95.   RF Barry, *The Atonement* (London: Hodder & Stoughton, 1968), 171.

ness.[96] Understanding what it means that the atonement is effective for all people is another question and is also a different question to whether or not these people are saved. What we can say, however, is that the atonement does have universal implications.

God confirms the fulfilment of Christ's actions in the resurrection. As Thomas Torrance suggests, the only thing comparable to the resurrection of Jesus is the original creation of the universe through the eternal Word of God.[97] The ongoing mystery of sin confronts us, but as Barth says, sin is a 'reality that has already been accused, condemned and abolished in Jesus Christ: its existence is that of a defeated reality, an "impossible possibility"'.[98] Sin has been defeated in Christ. Thus the place of the church in the world is not to engage in an arbitrary process of determining who is 'in' and who is 'out', but in proclaiming that the unconditional grace of God has come into the world though the atoning action of Jesus Christ.

3. The proclamation of the church

3.1 The state of play in the church and world

The theme of this paper that sin and atonement have universal implications leads us into questioning how sin and atonement are understood and interpreted in the current context. In his book *Humanism: The Wreck of Western Culture* the sociologist John Carroll pronounces, 'Our culture is past cruelty. It is wrecked. It is dead.'[99] This drastic diagnosis of the condition of Western culture is one that implicitly concerns the church. Firstly, because the church both embraced and sustained the philosophy of humanism, which Carroll cites as being the root of the problem. And, secondly because of the current trend of congregations in the West in embracing the remnants of this culture in an attempt to make the church 'relevant', or 'useful', or even just 'attractive', to the general populace.

Humanism has the tendency to elevate the place of humanity and of the individual. 'It attempted to replace God by man, to put man at

---

96. Tillich, *op cit*, 66.
97. Torrance, *Space, Time and Resurrection*, *op cit*, 59.
98. Webster, *op cit*, 67.
99. J Carroll, *Humanism: The Wreck of Western Culture* (London: Harper Collins, 1993), 1.

the centre of the universe, to deify him. Its ambition was to found a human order on earth, in which freedom and happiness prevailed, without any transcendental or supernatural supports—an entirely human order.'[100] In a sense *I am that I am* has been replaced in humanism by *I* the individual. 'Authority is not in God, who comes into a person's life with a mission; it is rooted in a person's psychological needs.'[101] This seems to reflect the very essence of sin.

James Torrance identifies the fact that this individualism, which grew from humanism, has collapsed into narcissism,[102] a collapse that is typified by a preoccupation with the self:

> . . . my rights, my liberty, my pursuit of happiness. Religion then becomes a means towards self-realization. All the interest is in self-esteem, self-fulfilment, self-identity, self-realization, the human potential movement and possibility thinking, leading either to the nihilism of post-modernism or neo-gnosticism of the New Age movement which identifies the self with God.[103]

In this culture the search for personal meaning and identity has supplanted being in the world as God intended. One of the consequences of this shift has been the loss of higher conscience.[104] This loss is typified by the parent who watches through the lens of a video

---

100. Ibid, 2.

101. C Ellis Nelson, *How Faith Matters* (Louisville: Westminster/John Knox Press, 1989), 38. Cited in D Capps, *The Depleted Self: Sin in a Narcissistic Age* (Minneapolis: Fortress Press, 1993).

102. Torrance cites Allan Bloom *The Closing of the American Mind* (New York: Simon & Schuster, 1987).

103. J Torrance, *Worship, Community and the Triune God*, *op cit*, 30.

104. Kierkegaard told an anecdote of a wager that expressed this loss of conscience. 'Two English lords were riding along when a man whose horse had bolted galloped past shouting for help. One lord said to the other: "A hundred pounds he falls off!" "Taken," was the immediate reply, at which they wheeled their horses, spurred them on, and galloped past the runaway horse to open the gates and prevent anything getting in its way . . . The dismal message in this story is that humanist will has atrophied to nothing, now it has lost its higher conscience, the "I am" has degenerated into that of a chronic invalid watching life from the window of the hospital.' Carroll, *op cit*, 6.

camera whilst their baby is cruelly attacked by a cat, as was the case on 'Funniest Home Videos'. Capturing the action for personal gain somehow overrode the compassion of the parent who could have dropped the camera to intervene. Humanism has not fulfilled its goal in creating any sort of new order of humanity, and as humanism has developed so too has its influences on the church and its theology.

The most profound influence, in the context of this discussion, has been humanism's contribution to the dissolution of the traditional doctrine of original sin. Pannenberg traces the decline of the doctrine of original sin, suggesting its beginnings in the sixteenth century.[105] 'The decay of the doctrine of original sin led to the anchoring of the concept of sin in acts of sin, and finally the concept was reduced to the individual act.'[106] By the eighteenth century the decline of the doctrine of original sin meant 'the weight that Reformation theology and Protestant piety attached to recognition of sin as a condition of assurance of salvation became truly problematic for the first time'.[107] This deterioration of the concept of original sin to individual 'sins' has not been limited to the Protestant tradition.[108]

Alongside the decline of the doctrine of original sin Pannenberg cites the linguistic decay in the use of the word 'sin' and the growth of moralism. Pannenberg notes that these days the word 'sin' tends to be found only in formal Christian settings and in a 'light-hearted manner' to describe a 'liberation from the prohibition of pleasures associated with traditional morality'.[109] But not only has there been decay in the use of the word 'sin', there has also been a corresponding growth in rigid moralism. In this setting the Bible 'has (too often) been treated, particularly in Protestantism, as a manual of ethics, of moral values, of religious ideas, or even sound doctrine'.[110] This too has been problematic. The moralism that resulted from anchoring the concept of sin in sinful acts fell victim to criticism of a Christian 'Pharisaism that judged the moral failures of others without any psychological or social

105. 'Already in the sixteenth century some groups, particularly the Socinians, described the doctrine of original sin as unbiblical and rejected it as offensive to human sensibilities.' Pannenberg, *Systematic Theology*, Vol 2, *op cit*, 232.
106. *Ibid*, 234.
107. *Ibid*, 232.
108. Tillich, *op cit*, 52.
109. Pannenberg, *Systematic Theology*, Vol 2, *op cit*, 235.
110. J Torrance, *Worship, Community and the Triune God*, *op cit*, ix.

understandings of the causes'.[111] Thus, the demise of the doctrine of original sin contributed to the growth of pietism and the elevation of the actions of the individual as defining the Christian life.[112]

The consequence of humanism, and subsequent philosophies, on the church has been profound. In the case of the growth in moralism, people have used their standing as Christians to judge other groups in the world, to discriminate against them and even subjugate them.[113] In the case of the denial of an overarching concept of sin, a sense of responsibility for one's own actions has been lost.[114] In the case of the emphasis on the individual and the quest for self-identity, churches have become places of self-affirmation and self-fulfilment.[115] The comment that people will only go to church if they can 'get something out of it' reflects this state of play. The church is immersed in the culture of the West and with it continues to reflect that sin is universal, even within the church![116] Hence, the condition of the church in the world testifies to the truth of Martin Luther's reflection that Christians are at once both justified and sinners.

---

111. Pannenberg, *Systematic Theology* Vol 2, *op cit*, 234-135.

112. This has caused a growth in acceptance of what could be considered a Pelagian theology in modern Christendom.

113. 'This kind of mentality that localizes evil in others or in groups easily leads to violent upheavals. A point that differentiates this deep-seated inclination to seek evil in others, and to exculpate oneself or one's group, from the biblical and especially the Christian treatment of evil as sin, is that the latter finds the root of evil in the human individual, and indeed in each individual as such, not in someone else.' Pannenberg, *Systematic Theology,* Vol 2, *op cit*, 237.

114. 'Parishioners will be viewed less as sinners rebelling against the laws of God and human nature, and more as victims, caught in a complex set of personal circumstances and psychosocial conditions over which they may exercise only limited influence and control' D Capps, *The Depleted Self: Sin in a Narcissistic Age* (Minneapolis: Fortress Press 1993), 1.

115. 'Until recent times Protestants had considerable loyalty to their denomination and a sense of accountability to a congregation. In the place of this loyalty has emerged the idea of a congregation as an assembly of like-minded individuals seeking personal satisfaction.' Cited in Capps, *op cit*, 107.

116. Many Christians seem to find it odd to consider that they continue to be sinners once they have 'given their life to Jesus'. And even in the New Testament 'When sin raises its head in the Christian's living the entire New Testament finds occasion for surprise.' Berkouwer, *op cit*, 144.

3.2 The witness of the church

Given that the church itself is imbued with the sin that affects the whole creation, one might question the place of the church in the world and its mission. However, in Jesus' atoning action in the creation, Jesus not only includes the disciples in what he does but also commissions them to proclaim God's love and compassion for the world, and in this to glorify God.[117] Thus, the disciples carry the good news of Christ into the world so that the world might believe and enter into union with God through grace.

This declaration of the good news includes the act of confession and declaration of forgiveness. In this the mystery of our sinfulness is acknowledged. 'Under the power and blessing of the Spirit, confession can be seen as the clearest confirmation of this biblical view of the inexplicability of sin. Confession entails a rejection of any meaningful explanation of sin and a recognition that sin is 'without cause'.[118] The corresponding forgiveness that the church declares gives the sinner hope in their reconciliation with God through Christ. In this way forgiveness is an affirmation of the Christian life in the face of ongoing sin. 'The purpose of forgiveness is to help the sinner, not to prevent the sin.'[119] Hence, the church plays a vital role in the acknowledgment of both sin and atonement through confession and forgiveness.

Another aspect of the church's existence is its communion with God. The promise of the coming of the Holy Spirit is that the church will have access to this union with God now. 'Through the power of the Spirit we have union with the risen Christ here and now and in that union taste already the powers of the age to come.'[120] This communion is both God's gift and will for the church.[121] Knowing God is eternal life (Jn 17:3). It gives us hope in the face of the brokenness that we can see in creation. Pannenberg states:

> In spite of sin and its ramifications, then, we may
> again and again know the original joy in life, joy in

---

117. Cf Matthew 16:13ff; Matthew 28:16 ff; John 21:15ff.

118. Berkouwer, *op cit*, 141.

119. Peters, *Sin: Radical Evil*, *op cit*, 266.

120. Torrance, *Space, Time and Resurrection*, *op cit*, 64.

121. Cf *Basis of Union*, paragraph 1. M Owen, *Witness of Faith: Historic Documents of the Uniting Church in Australia* (Melbourne: Uniting Church Press, 1984), 25.

> the richness, breadth, and beauty of creation and in each new day, joy in the illuminations of the life of the spirit, power for action within the order of community life, and a turning to others and participation in their joys and sorrows.[122]

Thus, in the church the creature has the opportunity to enter knowingly into true unity with the Creator.

This entering into union with God has eschatological implications. Christians can look forward with expectation to the future consummation of God's work. 'Christian hope goes beyond actuality; it takes its rise in trust in the inexhaustible potency of the new world which Jesus Christ embodies and has made.'[123] This hope in the future does not, however, lead to a discounting of the present reality. The church sustains hope for humanity, stimulating resistance to the darkness and nightmares of this world where nations and individuals are idolised through its actions.[124] Any idea that the church itself will bring in the kingdom of God is highly questionable. However, the liberation theologian Gutierrez is right in saying that 'The self-communication of God points towards the future, and at the same time the Promise and Good News reveal humanity to itself and widen the perspective of its historical commitment here and now'.[125] Union with our resurrected Lord is the human destiny and this union begins in the now of God's creation. Thus, the church has the mission of witnessing to the final consummation of God's atoning action in both word and deed.

Through all of these aspects of its life the church glorifies God and proclaims Jesus Christ as its Lord and Saviour and as the hope for the whole creation. The logical response to knowledge of God and the coming kingdom of God is to live in harmony with the revelation of human destiny.[126] 'Faith prompted by grace is satisfied with allowing God to be good. Furthermore, faith prompted by grace permits us to appreciate what is good in other people, eliminating any need to scapegoat them. Faith prompted by grace empowers us to live

---

122. Pannenberg, *Systematic Theology,* Vol 2, *op cit*, 275.

123. Webster, *op cit*, 95.

124. *Ibid*, 96.

125. G Gutierrez, *A Theology of Liberation* (London: SCM Press, 1988), 95.

126. Pannenberg, *Anthropology in Theological Perspective*, *op cit*, 94.

graciously.'[127] In seeking to live graciously, in acknowledging the mystery of sin through confession, in hearing the declaration of forgiveness, the church offers glory to the God who made all things and sustains all things.

4. Conclusion: 'being in communion'

In the title of his book *Being as Communion* John Zizioulas captures a vision of how God wills the creation to 'be'. God's will is that the creature lives in communion with God, a state of *being* in relationship. However, the coming of Christ into the world confirms the truth of Adam's plight that the creature lives outside this union that it was created for, and this is expressed in the concept of sin. Sin is manifested in human behaviours that reject God, but why humans sin remains somewhat hidden. God created humanity and it was good (Gen 2:30). Yet somewhere in the freedom granted to the creature, the creature chose itself over and above God and the nature of human being as opposed to being in communion with God. Having entered into this situation, the revelation of the incarnation is that humanity cannot rectify the problem through its own actions.

The reality of this predicament of sin is met in the incarnation of Jesus Christ and his atoning work for our sake. He is the high priest *par excellence*. In God's unending love Jesus Christ comes to reconcile the creature with Creator and in this remakes our being, a fact affirmed in the resurrection:

> Now on the ground of the resurrection, and its final rejection of all negation of being in judgment, we can really believe that man is, that man is man. He is the creature God made him to be and may not now cease to be what he is. He is man in living communion with the creative Source of life. The resurrection of Jesus Christ and of human nature in him is therefore the foundation and source of a profound and radically new Christian humanism.[128]

---

127. Peters, *Sin: Radical Evil*, *op cit*, 272.
128. Torrance, *Space, Time and Resurrection*, *op cit*, 79.

Jesus' entry into the world is God's eternal 'Yes!' This redemptive act of God sits juxtaposed against the 'No!' of sin found in all people. And because of this, humanity has the opportunity to enter into God's 'Yes!' in the present time and for all time.

What occurs in Christ occurs at a cosmic level, and so as individuals all people partake in the atonement in some way. The church's role in the world should thus be formed not by a mission of 'saving souls', who may in fact already be redeemed and thus be able to partake in God's salvation, but in proclaiming that God's love is unconditional and that we have been saved through grace. In the contemporary context the Western church needs always to critique its actions in the world and not supplant *God's* 'Yes!' with the 'yes' or 'no' of *our belief.* The problems associated in reducing sin to individual acts and the assumption of personal piety and self-righteousness should also be raised and challenged.

In conclusion, it must be said that the individualistic notions of sin and salvation that have developed within the Western church are aberrations from what sin and atonement are actually about. The universal nature of sin means that there is solidarity amongst all people that no individual can surpass. At the same time as saying this, the solidarity of human sinfulness is answered by God's grace in the atoning work of Jesus Christ once for all. In him we come to know the truth of our being in communion. In the end those who come to know this truth can only respond to God's love by living in tune with that love, witnessing to it and glorifying God the Father, Son and Spirit, to whom be all praise now and forever. Amen.

10

Luther's *Finnlandisierung*: A Recent Debate about Salvation in Reformation Thought

Duncan Reid

In the last decade the work of a circle of Finnish Luther scholars has become known in the English-speaking world. Writing about a Luther seminar held in the United States in 1993, Carl Braaten and Robert Jenson report that 'the Finnish delegation was by far the most impressive and interesting new voice'.[1] A recent assessment by Eric Gritsch is even more extravagant: 'The *theosis* thesis in Mannermaa's research has caused neuralgia along the course of nerves in the body of Luther research'.[2] The new interpretation, proposed by what is variously known as the 'Finnish School' or the 'Mannermaa circle'[3] after their founding thinker, Prof. Tuomo Manermaa of the Finnish Academy for Luther Studies in Helsinki, has not however been without its critics. In this paper I intend to outline what is new in the Finnish interpretation, that is, how it differs from the received view of Luther as promoted by the scholars of the 'Luther Renaissance'. Then I shall report on the reaction to the new interpretation, especially as it appears in a very thoroughly researched and carefully written

---

1. C Braaten and R Jenson, 'Preface: The Finnish Breakthrough in Luther Research', in *Union with Christ: The New Finnish Interpretation of Luther*, edited by C Braaten and R Jenson (Grand Rapids: Eerdmans, 1998), vii. I will use this book as my main source for the Finnish school. A valuable summary of the Finnish interpretation has been written by Jeffrey Silcock, 'Luther on Justification and Participation in the Divine Life: New light on an Old Problem', *Lutheran Theological Journal*, 34 (2000): 127-139.
2. E Gritsch, 'Response to Tuomo Mannermaa "Glaube, Bildung und Gemeinschaft bei Luther/ Faith, Culture and Community"', *Lutherjahrbuch* 66 (1999): 197-206, here 198.
3. Braaten and Jenson, *op cit*, vii.

response by Reinhard Flogaus.[4] All this is directly relevant to the theme of this conference, as this debate centres on the concept of *theosis* (or deification) as a way of understanding salvation.

1. The Finnish interpretation

It is perhaps not surprising to learn that the Finnish interpretation has been prompted by ecumenical dialogue, especially (but by no means exclusively) with the Orthodox, for whom *theosis* is fundamental in the understanding of salvation. The dialogue with Roman Catholicism is also clearly an important one for the Finnish school. Even so, it is important to note that the Finnish school is less concerned with doing ecumenical theology than with Luther research, ie re-examination of the sources of Lutheran theology.[5] This has led the Finnish scholars not to make of Luther a Western proponent of Eastern Orthodoxy— indeed, there are still issues to be resolved with regard to the relationship between the Finnish interpretation and contemporary Orthodox thought. Rather, they seek to reread Luther so as to see in him themes that had not been noticed in the standard research. This is achieved by an attempt to comprehend 'the "whole" Luther, without postulating anachronistic differences between "reformatory" and "catholic" or between "modern" and "medieval" aspects of his thought'.[6] The Finnish school argues that the concept of *theosis* in particular is essential for understanding particular loci in Luther's works.[7] This new 'Finnish' Luther is not totally unrecognisable. The key insight that Luther brings to the tradition, according to

---

4.   R Flogaus, *Theosis bei Palamas und Luther: Ein Beitrag zum ökumenischen Gespräch* (Göttingen: V & R, 1997).

5.   Peura's article 'Die Vergöttlichung des Menschen als Sein in Gott', *Lutherjahrbuch* 60 (1993): 39-71, makes virtually no reference to Orthodox or patristic sources. Its focus is *theosis* in Luther's own work. Elsewhere Peura points to the value of ecumenical dialogues in that they 'encourage us to re-examine our own tradition' (S Peura, 'Christus Praesentissimus: The Issue of Luther's Thought in the Lutheran-Orthodox Dialogue', *Pro Ecclesia* 2/3 (1993): 364-371, here 364).

6.   R Saarinen, 'The Presence of God in Luther's Theology', *Lutheran Quarterly* 8/1 (1994): 1-13, here 4.

7.   T Mannermaa, 'Why Is Luther So Fascinating? Modern Finnish Luther Research' in Braaten and Jenson, 1-20, here 13.

Mannermaa, is the theology of the cross,[8] and this modifies the patristic speech of participation in God and union with Christ. The believer must empty him- or herself—here the Finnish school is at one with traditional Luther research—and the one who does so empty themselves for Christ's sake is enabled thereby to become *capax Dei*.[9]

Mannermaa cites *De libertate christiana* as a key source for the notion of participation and *theosis* in Luther's thought. In this text, Luther links the Lutheran tradition into 'the common classical Christian heritage',[10] according to Mannermaa, and does it in a way not always apparent from the perspective of later Lutheranism as defined in the confessional writings, the Augsburg Confession and the Formula of Concord. There are systematic themes in Luther's thought that have been overlaid by interpretation, and which need to be uncovered. Indeed, it can be these hidden themes that make Luther relevant to current concerns. In particular for Mannermaa and his school, it is this theme of participation in the divine nature, this assertion that God comes near to us and gives Godself to us as favour and gift, that is most relevant to ecumenical dialogue.

Mannermaa argues that Luther research in the twenteith century has been dominated, and misled, by its own Kantian presuppositions. This has led scholars to understand Luther as proposing a 'community of willing and affecting' between God and the believer as the foundation for the salvation,[11] and to think of our relationship with God in terms of personal trust. But this, he argues, is a reduction of the claim Luther wants to make.[12] There no place here for salvation locating itself in a sense of the real indwelling of God in the believer, or

---

8. *Ibid*, 10, and Mannermaa 'Justification and *Theosis* in Lutheran-Orthodox Perspective', in Braaten and Jenson, 25-41, here 39.

9. Mannermaa, 'Why Is . . . ', in Braaten and Jenson, 10.

10. *Ibid*, 20.

11. *Ibid*, 7. See also R Saarinen, 'Liberty and Dominion: Luther, Prieras and Ringleben', *Neue Zeitschrift für Systematische Theologie und Religionsphilosophie*, 40 (1998): 171-181.

12. R Saarinen, 'The Presence of God in Luther's Theology', *Lutheran Quarterly* 8/1 (1994): 1-13, here 10. Saarinen is careful to point out that this 'real-ontic' union is less than total fusion of two elements, because it respects the continuing otherness of the elements united, and is thus best described as perichoretic (98). Furthermore, it does not have to import to the discussion a philosophical ontology (10).

an ontological union with Christ. A real union between a human subject and God (or even a real apprehension of God by the human subject) is ruled out by Kantian epistemology. For example, Albrecht Ritschl's distinction between a 'physical' and a 'personal-ethical' relationship with God,[13] which became standard for Luther interpretation for most of the 20th century, means that there can be no 'communion of being' between God and the believer, but only a causal nexus of affecting and being affected. This has in turn led to a forensic understanding of salvation, and an ethical emphasis in the notion of discipleship.

However, Mannermaa argues, this is true neither to Luther nor to the best in the Lutheran tradition, according to which 'God, in the very fulness of his essence, is present in the believer. Important here is to recognize that any notion that God himself does not "dwell" in the Christian and that only his "gifts" are present in the believer is explicitly rejected.'[14] According to Mannermaa, Luther knows no distinction between justification and sanctification. As these are inseparable in Christ, so must they be inseparable in the one who is united with Christ in faith and love. Thus justification must be defined in immediate relationship to sanctification through divine indwelling, or in other words, to the patristic notion of *theosis*. The new interpretation reminds us that Luther's own epistemological background was of a classical realist variety,[15] whereby the thing known was present in the knower. Luther himself continued to follow this epistemology even in his Reformation writings, according to the Finnish school.[16]

The difference might be described this way. We can see our discipleship of Christ either in ethical terms, as a 'following' or 'imitation' of Christ, whereby I model my behaviour on that of Christ. Or we can see discipleship in more ontological terms, whereby Christ dwells in me and I am given union with him, so that we share more than a communion of willing and affecting—a union of *being*.[17] As a believer I do not simply follow after, but I really participate in the life of Christ: 'The "divine nature" of the believer is Christ himself. The Christian himself no longer lives, but rather Christ lives in him or

---

13. Mannermaa, 'Justification . . .', in Braaten and Jenson, 27.
14. *Ibid*, 27.
15. Mannermaa, 'Why Is . . .', in Braaten and Jenson, 5.
16. *Ibid*, 6.
17. *Ibid*, 7.

her.'[18] Mannermaa argues that this more ontological understanding (which bears a clear relationship to the emphasis in Luther's eucharistic theology on real presence) better reflects Luther's own understanding of discipleship and salvation. The practicalities of Christian life become more a matter of spirituality than of ethics in this framework, and the patristic notions of *synergeia* (cooperation) and *theosis* (deification) take on a degree of meaning that could find no place in more traditional interpretations. We are, for example, helped in times of temptation not by looking to the example of Christ in his temptation and following him, but by virtue of his (as the one who has been tempted and successfully overcome temptation) dwelling *in* us. We in fact becoming united with Christ, *becoming* Christ as it were, in the concrete situation of temptation that faces us.

Love plays a key role in the Finnish interpretation,[19] though in a way quite different from the scholastic understanding of it. 'The core of Luther's program of Reformation itself can be formulated by saying that the form (ie the living reality) of faith is not divinely elevated human love, as in the scholastic program . . . but is in reality Christ himself.'[20] This is in fact an affirmation, against the scholastic notion of created grace, of the primacy of uncreated grace—or in other words, of the indwelling of God's presence in the believer. This uncreated grace—which has clear links to the Eastern notion of grace as *energeia*—is linked by Mannermaa to faith: 'faith is like the cloud of God's presence in the temple'.[21]

Several of the themes outlined by Manermaa are developed in depth by his associates. Justification is the focus of the paper by Simo Peura, this motif being explicated in a discussion of grace (*gratia* or *favor*) as gift (*donum*). These concepts are seen as mutually interpreting in Luther. The gift is the gift of God's righteousness, bestowed in the event of union with Christ. According to Peura, the standard interpretation of the Formula of Concord suggests an intellectual apprehension of a new relationship with God, a *coram*-relationship,[22]

---

18.   *Ibid*, 18.

19.   *Ibid*, 13.

20.   Mannermaa, 'Justification . . .', in Braaten and Jenson, 36.

21.   *Ibid*, 37.

22.   S Peura, 'Christ as Favor and Gift: The Challenge of Luther's Understanding of Justification', in Braaten and Jenson, 42-69, here 47. Here Peura implicitly calls

but not the substantial change in the believer that union with Christ would imply.[23] This in turn has allowed Lutherans to magnify the gulf between Luther's (supposed) view of justification and the Roman Catholic understanding of the same concept. Peura's emphasis on the real indwelling of Christ, in Luther's own thought, allows no such gulf to emerge. Luther, for Peura, remains firmly within the Catholic tradition of the early and medieval church, except that, in his debate with late scholasticism, he 'abandons the concept of created grace'.[24] Love is the gift, but is only present when the giver is also present. Peura underlines the identity of God's essence and actions *ad extra* when he writes: 'Luther holds all saving divine attributes in the same way: he does not separate God's essential nature ontologically from the divine attributes effecting salvation'.[25] God is essentially identified with God's names, or attributes.[26] These statements would seem problematic from an Orthodox, especially Palamite, perspective, and I will address this issue below. Strangely, in another place Peura seems to allow for a distinction in Luther between God's being and God's doing[27]—a position that I believe could bring Luther much closer to a Palamite understanding of God. Peura emphasises the notion of *cooperatio*[28] in Luther (again with reference to *De libertate christiana*), and *conformitas Christi*[29] There is a movement *into* Christ,[30] whereby the believer *becomes* Christ.[31] In this union with Christ, the justified

---

in question the heart of Ebeling's existentialist reading of Luther. See G Ebeling, *Luther: An Introduction to His Thought* (London: Collins, 1972), 192-209. The Finnish school thus attempts to retrieve an essentialist interpretation. Flogaus supports the Ebeling position, 378.

23.   Peura, 'Christ as Favor', in Braaten and Jenson, 46-7.

24.   *Ibid*, 48.

25.   *Ibid*, 49.

26.   *Ibid*, 50, and Braaten, 'Response', 74.

27.   Peura, 'Christ as Favor', in Braaten and Jenson, 65; cf S Peura, 'What God Gives Man Receives: Luther on Salvation', in Braaten and Jenson, 76-95, here 82, where the same distinction is allowed for human beings—as it is in Palamite thought—between person and property.

28.   Peura, 'Christ as Favor', in Braaten and Jenson, 57-8.

29.   *Ibid*, 60.

30.   *Ibid*, 62.

31.   Braaten, 'Response to Simo Peura', in Braaten and Jenson 74; cf W Elert on the *Christusbild (Der Ausgang der altkirchlichen Christologie: Eine Untersuchung*

believer receives the gift of Christ's attributes, primarily Christ's righteousness before God. The theology here is clearly Lutheran in its sensibility, but Peura is emphatic that this gift or favour does not come about without the real indwelling of Christ, and real union with Christ. Furthermore, to say this—although it may be at variance with later Lutheran thinking, even at variance with the sentiments of the confessional writings in places—is, he argues, true to Luther's own perception of salvation. It is, in other words, a proper return to the sources, according to Peura, laying aside the Kantian filter through which Luther and the confessional writings have been read for over a century. In saying all this, Peura emphasises the common catholic heritage Lutherans hold with other Christians of the Eastern and Western traditions. Lutherans may speak, with the early church tradition, of *theosis*, provided it is always acknowledged that the giver of this state is God.[32] Luther's quarrel with scholasticism and its notion of created grace is that it could lead to the misapprehension that the agent of deification is somehow ourselves.[33] The giver of union with Christ is the Holy Spirit[34] and none other. Union with Christ is thus fundamentally trinitarian and perichoretic.

Antti Raunio extends the discussion into the area of ethics, and argues the believer's ontological participation in Christ brings with it a parallel participation in Christ's attributes. 'The attributes are essential qualities: therefore the Christian participates through them in the divine essence itself . . . the person becomes a participant in the divine nature, which is the love that gives itself to the other.'[35] The 'golden rule' is thus understood not as 'enlightened self-interest', but as transforming the believer into Christ, and into the other person who is also

über Theodor von Pharan und seiner Zeit als Einführung in die alte Dogmengeschichte [Berlin: Lutherisches Verlagshaus, 1957]).

32. Peura, 'What God Gives', in Braaten and Jenson, 84-5.
33. Dr Peura emphasised this in conversation (3 July 1999): part of the the distrust of the language of deification is understandable reserve about Nietzsche's self-deifying *Übermensch*, and before that, Feuerbach's call for theology to be transformed into anthropology (See R Flogaus, 'Die Theologie des Gregorios Palamas—Hindernis oder Hilfe für die ökumenische Verständigung?' *Ostkirchliche Studien* 47 (1998): 105-123, here 119).
34. Peura, 'Christ as Favor', in Braaten and Jenson, 91.
35. A Raunio, 'Natural Law and Faith: The Forgotten Foundations of Ethics in Luther's Theology', in Braaten and Jenson, 96-124, here 113.

seen as Christ. The process is the opposite of the modern affirmation of the autonomous individual. Instead, it is the transformation of the individual, first ontologically, and then as a consequence, ethically.[36] The argument here demands a tight identification of being with attributes, and it is here that again, certain problems emerge, not least in the terminology. When Raunio says that 'Christ possesses divine essences such as wisdom, strength, justice, goodness, freedom and so on', the reader is left wondering not only about the boldness of the identification of essence with attribute, but also the use of the plural itself: surely there is only one divine essence. Despite this problem, the strength of the paper is in drawing out the practical ethical consequences of the Finnish interpretation—one that would find ready support from other strong proponents of what I have elsewhere called the 'identity principle'.[37]

Where Raunio takes the discussion forward, as it were, into the realm of practical ethical consequences, Sammeli Jantunen takes it back into the more foundational area of metaphysics. Luther has little to say explicitly about ontology, Jantunen acknowledges, and this has led his interpreters—especially those of the 'so-called personalist Luther-interpretation (Gerhard Ebeling, et al)' into an explicitly anti-metaphysical reading of his work.[38] But this supposedly anti-metaphysical reading rests, according to Jantunen, on a particular set of metaphysical presuppositions, namely the Kantian distinction between phenomena (in this case, events that are apprehended as the works of God) and the noumenon (God's essence). This interpretation argued that 'God can be present in the world only in his actual effects (especially on the will and the conscience of the believer), which are to be differentiated categorically from his being'.[39] But Luther does not, according to Jantunen, deny an analogy of being and goodness between God and

---

36. Cf Jantunen's *'agere sequitur esse'*. S Jantunen, 'Luther and Metaphysics: What Is the Structure of Being According to Luther?' in Braaten and Jenson, 129-160, here 144.

37. D Reid, *Energies of the Spirit: Trinitarian Models in Eastern Orthodox and Western Theology* (Atlanta: Scholars Press, 1997). Cf C LaCugna, who in my opinion asserts this identity principle far too strongly (see D Reid, 'The Defeat of Trinitarian Theology: An Alternative View', *Pacifica* 9 (1996): 289-300), but whose contribution, perhaps as a consequence, offers a very clear and definite causal link between trinitarian theology and ethical praxis.

38. Jantunen, 'Luther and Metaphysics', in Braaten and Jenson, 129.

39. *Ibid*, 131, fn 5.

the world, nor does he deny the validity of philosophical concepts, so long as they are 'bathed' or baptised so as to receive a new and different meaning from the the significance they normally carry in philosophical discourse.[40] It is this *nova vocabula* that breaks open the syllogistic reasoning of scholasticism,[41] but not in a way that does away with metaphysics as such. Here again, being and attribute ('goodness') are held close together, and yet they are not simply identified with one another. Jantunen in fact allows a distinction between being and act in Luther, so that being remains behind the outward action. With regard to the issue of participation, Jantunen argues that while William of Ockham had denied the ontology of participation, Luther's Ockhamist teachers were not always consistent in the absence of a reliable alternative ontology.[42] Other authorities who did assume such an ontology, notably Augustine, were held in high regard and had their own influence. Ockham understood creaturely being as the outworking of God's *creatio continua*, and the scholars of the Luther Renaissance emphasised this element in Luther's work by replacing being (*Sein*) by becoming (*Werden*).[43] But this leads us to read Luther within a particular, rather skewed metaphysical framework, according to Jantunen: we either fail to notice Luther's references to being and participation, or read into them a lesser significance than their author intended.

2. Reaction to the Finnish interpretation

Reinhard Flogaus has responded to the Finnish interpretation in a book on salvation as *theosis* in Palamas and Luther. Flogaus sets himself the question: are Luther and Orthodoxy closer than previously thought, as the Finnish interpretation would seem to suggest? His book is characterised by the thoroughness of German scholarship at its very best, and is unquestionably a major contribution to Palamas research, making extensive use of the full scope of the primary sources as well as a range of contemporary Palamas scholars, both Eastern and Western. Flogaus parallels this Palamas research with an exhaustive examination of relevant texts in Luther. Flogaus is careful to reject a

---

40.   *Ibid*, 132.
41.   *Ibid*, 132, fn 24.
42.   *Ibid*, 148-153.
43.   *Ibid*, 142-4.

number of older Protestant assessments of both *theosis* and
justification. *Theosis*, for example, can no longer be dismissed as self-
deification,[44] and justification is not to be presented primarily in
forensic terms.[45] Even so, Flogaus makes a number of criticisms of the
Finnish interpretation of Luther. Here I do not follow Flogaus's own
lengthy discussion of what he sees as the points of disjunction between
Palamas and Luther, but offer my own summary of the criticisms of
the Finnish interpretation that emerge throughout the book.

Flogaus argues there is a problem of a lack of parallelism between
Orthodox and Lutheran terminology. There are very few allusions to
deification in Luther,[46] far less references to union with God than to
union with Christ, in terms of 'becoming Word' (*Wortwerdung*).[47]
Further, the question of salvation may have been less important for
Palamas than previously thought. Uppermost in Palamas's own mind
was the question of our knowledge of God.[48] Linked to this is the
relative importance of the key concepts in the different traditions.
While the Protestant understanding of salvation must engage with
theosis,[49] justification has no place in either Orthodox liturgy or
theology.[50] Luther's theology is uncompromisingly a theology of the
cross, as indeed the Finnish school readily admits, while the cross
—and thus christology—seems to have little role in the Eastern
doctrine of *theosis*. To this it has to be admitted that the Finnish interpretation has largely focused on Luther rather than Palamas.[51] It
critiques the older readings of Luther by Ebeling and others in the
hope of going beyond what it sees as an essentially closed, and
therefore ecumenically unhelpful, interpretation. On the whole, it has
not yet actively explored a convergence of Luther with specifically
Palamite thought. For this reason, the problem of being and act
continues to be raised in a way that would seem not to be amenable to
Palamite thought. When Flogaus quite properly asks whether Lutheranism and Orthodoxy are closer than previously thought, there is a
sense in which he is going beyond the brief of the Finnish school.

---

44. Flogaus, *Theosis*, 5.
45. *Ibid*, 7.
46. *Ibid*, 37, 375.
47. *Ibid*, 341-2.
48. *Ibid*, 56-63.
49. *Ibid*, 409.
50. *Ibid*, 30.
51. An exception is the contribution to the debate by H Kamppuri.

There is a gradualism implicit in the Palamite notion of *theosis*, and this contrasts strongly with the either/or (*or* both/and) of Luther's more dialectical approach to salvation.[52] The notion of growth or progress of created nature towards God is foreign to Protestant thought, according to Flogaus. There is indeed a tension here between the now (*in re*) and the not yet (*in spe*), but this is a dialectical tension, in which the justified human person is both sinner and just. Where Luther would have us understand ourselves as at once, dialectically, both sinners and justified, Palamas sees us as on a journey from here to there, from sinners to saints. But again, this may be too simple a contrast, as Flogaus unwittingly shows. In Luther also he sees a tension between the now and the not yet, between that which is *in re* and that which is as yet *in spe* (but which will be *in re*). There is, in other words, a progression in Luther, just as in Palamas there can be a fullness of the creature's being in God, here and now. In any case, Peura has pointed out that 'synergism in no way threatens justification: God's imputative act does not depend on human cooperation'.[53] Rather, justification can be seen as the start of the process of sanctification.

Flogaus accuses the Finnish school of positing a Luther who is a consistently mystical theologian.[54] Against this view, he proposes a break between the early Luther and the later writings in which a mystical theology is more and more strongly rejected.[55] Even Luther's early thought is marked by an emphasis on christology not found in Palamite thought. From the end of the 1520s, we see in Luther emerging distinctions between grace and gift (the continuing iden-tification of which is important to Peura's argument), and between justification and sanctification. These distinctions cannot be restricted, as Mannermaa would have, to later Lutheran writings—it is there in

---

52. Flogaus, *Theosis*, 410. See also R Flogaus, 'Einig in Sachen *Theosis* und Synergie', *Kerygma und Dogma*, 42 (1996): 225-243, here 235.

53. Peura, 'Christus Praesentissimus', 369.

54. Erich Vogelsang ('Luther und die Mystik', *Lutherjahrbuch* 19 (1937): 32-54) argues that there is a consistent approach to mysticism throughout Luther's mature work, and that Luther's criterion for valid mysticism is experience (as opposed to speculation). If defensible, this argument would place Luther close to contemporary Palamism in its understanding of mystical encounter with God. See AM Allchin, 'The Appeal to Experience in the Triads of St Gregory Palamas', *Studia Patristica* (*Texte und Untersuchungen*, 93) 8 (1966): 323-328.

55. Flogaus, *Theosis*, 312, 376-7.

Luther himself. To this charge we have to acknowledge that Luther did indeed, as Flogaus argues, move away from the German mystical tradition during the course of his working life.[56]

Finally, Flogaus asks: Is deification a helpful concept for us nowadays? Contemporary christology looks to the humanising of humanity rather than its deification (Küng, Jüngel).[57] Our end in Christ is to become true human beings. Also for Luther the end of salvation is not to become gods, but servants. According to Flogaus, Luther wants us to be united not with God, but with Christ, the *verus homo*, and in a way that 'would make deification obsolete'.[58] But this might not be so far from the state to which Palamas is calling us, if we are to take seriously what his modern interpreters have said. The whole point of the essence-energies distinction, as regards salvation, is to maintain the ultimate ontological distinction between the deified human person and the eternal persons of the Trinity. We are to become, like Christ, children of God, but not trinitarian hypostases, for we are children of God by adoption and grace. Christ alone is child of God (*pais theou*) by nature. Even so, Flogaus's question raises a much larger issue as to whether discourse about union is in any way helpful to a postmodern mindset. Does such discourse serve simply to assimilate, and thus erase, difference? We are rightly suspicious of such erasures of difference—including the difference between God and humanity. We need also to be suspicious of any erasure of difference between two different and perhaps incommensurable theological systems.[59]

Flogaus's treatment of Palamite thought is not without its problems. There are, for example, occasional cases of special pleading, as when Flogaus sees contradiction to the rules of logic as dialectic in Luther but oxymoron in Palamas.[60] More seriously, Flogaus sees Palamas's thought as neo-Platonic[61]—and then seems surprised that it regards human beings as closer than the angels to God, on the grounds that we are embodied and thus, unlike the angels, have the benefit of aesthetic, sensual knowledge.[62] So Flogaus harbours the suspicion

---

56.   *Ibid*, 361.
57.   *Ibid*, 13, 15-6, 364. See also Flogaus, 'Einig in Sachen *Theosis* und Synergie', *Kerygma und Dogma*, 42 (1996): 225-243, here 226.
58.   Flogaus, *Theosis*, 364.
59.   *Ibid*, 65.
60.   *Ibid*, 292.
61.   *Ibid*, 128.
62.   *Ibid*, 141, 145.

(despite his own disclaimers in other places) that the Palamite doctrine of *theosis* may just be yet another expression of the ancient and ever-present Greek tendency to bridge the gap between the divine and the human.[63] Flogaus's more recent accusation that the teaching of Gregory Palamas and its doctrinal consequences are now the major reason for continuing alienation between East and West is, in my opinion, and for reasons explored elsewhere, far too simple.[64]

Also problematic is Flogaus's charge that the Finnish school, in common with other Scandinavian scholars,[65] makes use of a *Grundmotiv*, a single hermeneutical key to the interpreting of Luther. The Finnish school claims in fact to free Luther scholarship from an older tendency to interpret Luther through particular hermeneutical keys—for example the forensic understanding of justification or the *coram*-relationship[66]—and see Luther in a new light, as a mystical theologian.[67] It is precisely such interpretations of Luther through a single hermeneutical key that the Finnish scholars, for their part, are calling in question.[68]

Despite his references to the energies of the Spirit as the means of deification,[69] Flogaus in the end sees the energies as offering *theosis* in

---

63. *Ibid*, 52.

64. R Flogaus, 'Die Theologie des Gregorios Palamas—Hindernis oder Hilfe für die ökumenische Verständigung?' *Ostkirchliche Studien* 47 (1998): 105-123, here 109.

65. Flogaus, *Theosis* , 34. He has G Aulen and A Nygren in mind.

66. Ebeling, *Luther*, sees this as 'the very basis of of Luther's mode of thought' (193) and that it 'determines his thought' (223).

67. An important source is Erich Vogelsang, 'Luther und die Mystik', *Lutherjahrbuch* 19 (1937): 32-54. I am grateful to Dr Peura for this reference (conversation 3 July 1999).

68. As Carl Braaten recognises in his response to Peura, in Braaten and Jenson, 74. See also R Saarinen, 'Liberty and Dominion: Luther, Prieras and Ringleben', *Neue Zeitschrift für Systematische Theologie und Religionsphilosophie*, 40 (1998): 171-181, here 171: ' . . . the Kantian line (sc of interpretation) is problematic in its tendency to reduce the many-sided phenomena of religion and theology to moral notions and value-judgements'. By contrast, Eric Gritsch welcomes Mannermaa's discovery of a 'hermeneutical key' to understanding Luther; see E Gritsch, 'Response to Tuomo Mannermaa "Glaube, Bildung und Gemeinschaft bei Luther/ Faith, Culture and Community"', *Lutherjahrbuch* 66 (1999): 197-206, here 199.

69. Flogaus, *Theosis*, 81-3, and his criticisms of D Wendebourg, 190, 228-9.

the form of a relationship with the divine essence rather than with a specific trinitarian hypostasis, viz the hypostasis of the Spirit.[70] This becomes for Flogaus one of the two great weaknesses of the Palamite *theosis* doctrine.[71] I have argued elsewhere (and Flogaus also seems to support this position in places[72]) that the energies, because of their relationship with the hypostasis of the Spirit, are mediated by the Spirit, and thus give us access not to divine essence as such, but to the trinitarian God.

The other great weakness Flogaus sees in Palamism is an inner-divine subordination of energies to essence, on the grounds of a causal relationship between essence and energy. This is simply not a sustainable charge. One of the achievements of the trinitarian theology of the 4th century was the insight that causation does not necessarily involve a relationship of inferiority or subordination. The first trinitarian hypostasis is the source or cause (*aitia*) of the second, but it does not follow that the second is subordinate to the first. The trinitarian theology of the 4th century was quite prepared to think of the second person as caused, but rejected the suggestion that this implied subordination. This has also become an important principle of political life: an adult person (and in many circumstances this increasingly applies to children as well), though 'caused' by his or her parent, is not consequently considered subordinate as a political agent. By the same logic, the divine energy may have its cause in the divine essence, but still be no less divine. Flogaus correctly sees two ontological levels (*Seinstufen*) in Palamas' doctrine of God,[73] in which the *ousia* is the *aitia* of the energy. This is helpful in saying that energy is in fact a way of God's being God, though causally dependant upon some other way of God's being God that is beyond it. But it in no way implies subordination.

Despite these problems, Flogaus's book justifies its modest subtitle 'contribution to ecumenical conversation' in several ways. First, Flogaus uncovers strong evidence for Palamas's reliance on key texts in Augustine—whom he calls the 'spiritual father' of Palamas's chris-

---

70. Flogaus, *Theosis*, 210-1, where Flogaus sees the special role of the Spirit in *theosis* as a 'nicht mehr intergierbares Relikt aus der Tradition'; cf 202-3.

71. *Ibid*, 284.

72. *Ibid*, 95, 115, 181-3, 219, 259-60.

73. *Ibid*, 274.

tology.[74] While this might give some discomfort to the original proponents for the 20th century Palamas Renaissance, it also suggests an unexpected meeting point for Eastern and Western thought in Augustine. Second, both Palamas and Luther are presented as opponents of scholasticism.[75] This can be seen in their understanding of grace as uncreated grace, and their non-speculative approach to the knowledge of God. The theology of grace is developed by Palamas in a way that precludes created grace,[76] and Luther rejects the scholastic understanding of grace as created *habitus*.[77] Similarly with regard to theological speculation—neither for Palamas nor for Luther is this a reliable way to God. Luther's famous dictum that one becomes a theologian 'not by understanding, reading or speculating, but by living'[78] may, in fact, stand much closer to Palamas's ascetic way than Flogaus is willing to allow. Admittedly, Luther's characteristic addition 'and much more by dying and being damned' ('*immo moriendo et damnando*') is a sentiment foreign to Palamas. The same might also be said for God's *absconditas sub contrario* in Luther[79]—this may not be a point of disagreement with Palamas, but of commonality with what Vladimir Lossky called the antinomic method.[80] Neither for Luther nor for Palamas[81] do we human beings possess an 'organ of sense' for the discernment of God's presence. For both, God's presence is given by God alone, through the hypostasis of the Spirit. For Palamas, deification is effected by the energies of the Spirit; for Luther, union

---

74. *Ibid*, 243. See also 98-100, 109, 149, 243, 248, 256, 258, 277. Flogaus also points out where Palamas is at variance with Augustine, for example (an example of relevance to this discussion) where Palamas distinguishes between the Spirit and the Spirit's gift (of grace), Augustine had explicitly identified Spirit as the gift (Flogaus, *Theosis*, 259-60), and the whole Western tradition has followed him in this identification.

75. And also, it could be said, both have an at least ambivalent relationship with humanism. See K-H zur Mühlen, 'Korreferat zu Tuomo Mannermaa "Glaube, Bildung und Gemeinschaft bei Luther"', *Lutherjahrbuch*, 66 (1999): 207-218.

76. Flogaus, *Theosis*, 159-60, 279.

77. *Ibid,* 373.

78. Cited in Flogaus, *Theosis*, 292-3.

79. *Ibid*, 292, 349.

80. V Lossky, *The Mystical Theology of the Eastern Church* (New York: St Vladimir's Seminary Press, 1976).

81. Flogaus, *Theosis*, 177, 272.

with Christ is a work of the Spirit.[82] Finally, the theology of the cross is seen as Luther's innovation, but this is nowhere linked to the Orthodox understanding of *askesis*—which, if not seen primarily as a human activity but as a divine intiative in the believer—may offer a point of contact with the *theologia crucis*. Both are theologies, undertaken—each in its own way—*sub cruce*.

3. The problem of act and being

To my mind the key problem in the Finnish interpretation—as I have hinted already—is that of being and act, or essence and attributes.[83] What I want to say here is tentative, because I write as an outside observer, neither Lutheran nor Orthodox, but involved in sympathetic dialogue with both. Mannermaa, in reference to 2 Peter 1:4, writes: '. . . the presence of Christ means that the believer participates in the "divine nature". And when participating in God's essence, the Christian also becomes a partaker of the properties of the essence.'[84] This statement, and others like it, are common in the works of the Finnish school. While it clearly seeks to make common cause with a patristic notion of *theosis*, and thus with contemporary Orthodox thought, it also seems to contain elements problematic to contemporary Orthodox theology. Elsewhere, Peura argues,[85] Luther himself is at odds with the neo-Kantian interpretation of Luther, which characteristically separates God's being (*esse*) from God's effects or works (*Wirkungen*). This renders the 'effects' less real than the essence, but paradoxically places the essence beyond our reach: knowledge of God, and even more so union with God, become impossible. The Palamite distinction between essence and energies is superficially like the Kantian distinction between being and act. But it is a mistake to think that Palamism posits an unknowable God in the way Kant asserts God's essential intellectual unknowability. For Palamism, God is indeed in essence beyond knowability, but is really (and immediately) apprehended and known in God's energies.

---

82. *Ibid*, 311. (See R Prenter, *Spiritus Creator* [Philadelphia: Westminster Press, 1953]. This is another Scandinavian treatment of Luther that could presumably also be accused of taking a single-issue approach, this time in terms of pneumatology.)

83. Flogaus, *Theosis*, 377.

84. Mannermaa, 'Justification', in Braaten and Jenson, 34.

85. Peura, 'Christ as Favor and Gift'.

Palamite scholars make a clear distinction between essence (or super-essence) and energies in God, and this would seem to run parallel to the Kantian distinction between being and act that is so anathema to the Finnish scholars. This would seem to mean the Finnish interpretation, though initiated by ecumenical dialogue with the Orthodox, remains ecumenically problematic. If anything, Kant might have offered a point of contact. By contrast, the Finnish interpretation seems to present us with an uncompromising version of the identity principle, ie the identity of God's inner trinitarian being with God's trinitarian actions *ad extra*. If my reading of contemporary Orthodox theology is correct, this would not be an acceptable methodological axiom. And yet there is ambiguity on both sides: Palamite scholars are not always as consistent as we might like them to be, and the Finnish Luther scholars at times seem to allow a notional distinction between God's being and God's actions. Luther himself, as Flogaus acknowledges, allows a distinction in God between *quidditas* and *qualitas*,[86] which would indeed suggest a parallel with the Palamite distinction between essence and attributes.

I suggest the problem may be one of terminology as much as anything else. The Palamite position alternates between speaking of essence (*ousia*) and super-essentiality (*hyperousiotes*), when referring to the ungraspable, transcendent side of God. It is uncomfortable with any notion of divine essence as a Kantian noumenon or thing-in-itself. God's essence is beyond knowing, and also beyond linguistic description—hence the paradoxical term 'super-essence'. Contrary both to Palamas's opponent Barlaam and to Kant, however, this position does not imply an agnosticism about the inner being of God. God allows Godself to be really known. *Theosis*, as Flogaus points out, is not something that leads to (or arises out of) theoretical knowledge (*Wissen*) of God, but to knowledge (*Kennen*) by acquaintance—it is the outcome of experience (*peira*).[87] Palamite thought is insistent that God can be and is known personally through the energies (or acts, attributes, names, etc), even though these are not final encapsulations of divinity. Through the energies the believer really and ontologically participates in the divine life, and knows God through this existential participation. Palamite writers use this concept to interpret the 2 Peter

---

86.   Flogaus, *Theosis*, 377.
87.   *Ibid*, 159.

1:4 statement about participation in the divine nature. 'Divine nature' here is understood to includes both God's actions and the divine life that transcends the actions. Palamism has its own safeguard against self-deification by placing the initiative with God the Holy Spirit, and through the gradualism that Flogaus finds incompatible with Luther's thought, the notion of *epektasis*, or continual reaching out and movement ever deeper into the life of God in a never-ending pilgrimage of salvation. When the Finnish scholars assert the identity of God's being and actions (attributes, names, etc), they are also saying that we participate in the divine being of Christ and know the divine being through that participation. Both positions assert we know God, we know the divine nature, over against a Kantian scepticism about that which lies beyond the perceptible world. Both positions assert a participatory way of knowing, over against any purely intellectual knowing—the reverse side of which is necessarily an arena of not-knowing. Not-knowing is located on the side of God's essence, and it refers to that in which we do not participate. Palamite theology maintains the distinction, but asserts that our not-knowing is subsumed under a participatory knowing through the energies or works of God *ad extra*. The Finnish scholars deny the distinction in order to deny the Kantian proposition that there is a realm of the inherently unknowable, namely the realm that is beyond sense perception, and that God resides in this dimension.

There is no doubt that the Finnish Luther scholars are still working within a Western theological framework. Flogaus may well be correct in saying that *theosis* means something different for Palamas than it does for Luther, though we should not forget we are dealing with Flogaus's interpretations of Palamas and Luther.[88] Ecumenical dia-

---

88. An example of how the same term can be used with different connotations is Luther's expression 'the joyful (or wonderful) exchange' (*commercium admirabile*, or *fröhlicher Wechsel*). Flogaus reads this to mean 'the exchange of the sin of the Christian for the righteousness of Christ' (*Austausch der Sünde des Christen gegen die Gerechtigkeit Christi*, Flogaus, *Theosis*, 301), and his argument in the following pages is bounded by this definition. By contrast, an Anglican commentator on the *theosis* theme in his own tradition uses Luther's term to explicate a sermon passage from Lancelot Andrewes, but in a fully ontological sense: 'Here already is the marvellous interchange of human and divine which the whole Christian mystery celebrates' (AM Allchin, *Participation in God: A Forgotten Strand in Anglican Tradition* [London: DLT, 1988], 17). The

logue with the Orthodox has led the Finnish Luther scholars to reinterpret the sources of their own theology. But the theological terminology still needs to be clarified if this dialogue is to be taken further. There are points in the discussion where the Finnish school still seems to be speaking at cross-purposes to the Orthodox —assuming that I understand both positions correctly. The point in common is that both the Finnish Lutherans and the Orthodox are stating, in their own ways, that the utterly transcendent God is knowable through participation, and that this participation is to be understood not intellectually but experientially, and salvation is understood ontologically, as union. Where Palamite theology sees this participation and *theosis* occurring through the mediation of the Holy Spirit (and in practice through the energies of the Spirit), the new thinking within Lutheran circles locates the mediation in Christ —access to whom, however, is given by the Spirit.

The Finnish school offers a new, open-ended reading of Luther. It can be accused of emphasising a single hermeneutical motif, though this is not its intention, and in reality other interpretations lend themselves to the same accusation. Flogaus, while acknowledging the value of the new interpretation, has cautioned against its hasty and uncritical reception. I leave it to scholars more familiar with Luther than I to comment on whether the Finnish interpretation can be justified. In any case the debate will not be concluded in a hurry. The take-home message from the debate is the reminder that the meaning of any text is in front of the text, between ourselves as readers and the text itself. What Luther intended is not available to us, except through what he has written. New readings are not only possible but inevitable. As Eric Gritsch puts it at the end of his article, 'Mannermaa . . . tries to be simultaneously committed to the literal meaning of Luther texts and to a theological sensibility for the sake of possible new insights derived from this ever so richly endowed reformer'.[89] We will inevitably read

---

question that occurs to me here, is: did Luther really intend a meaning as limited as that which Flogaus reads into it?

89. Gritsch, 'Response to Tuomo Mannermaa', 206.

It is to Dr Juntunen that I owe the humorous notion of Luther's *Finnlandisierung* (personal correspondence, 8 June 1999)—the significance of which I hope will be apparent from the paper as a whole. I am also particularly grateful for the time Dr Peura gave me for a meeting and conversation in Helsinki, 3 July 1999.

11

Saving Grace and the Action of the Spirit outside the Church

Denis Edwards

Archeological evidence suggests that human beings have been present in Australia for more than 50,000 years. A mere four hundred years ago, in 1605, Pedro Ferdinandez de Quiros, a Portuguese in the service of Spain, set off to discover the great south land, *terra australis*. He believed that he had been called to bring saving faith to the inhabitants of the place he called the South Land of the Holy Spirit, *Australia del Espiritu Santo*. De Quiros was convinced that the inhabitants of the south land were children of God, but he imagined them living in the darkness of unbelief. He hoped to bring them the good news of salvation in Christ. The indigenous peoples of Australia had certainly not heard the gospel. But what does this mean in terms of a Christian theology of salvation? Did salvation arrive only with the European missionaries or was it already at work in Australia? Was the Spirit present only once the gospel was preached, or was the Spirit present and active amongst the people of Australia for 50,000 years before Europeans saw their first kangaroo?

These same questions can be asked of the first human beings. Did they emerge in a world of grace? The ancestors of humans were various species of *Australopithecines* who evolved in Africa more than four million years ago. *Homo erectus* emerged about two million years ago, with a much larger brain than other species. They were the first hominids to use fire, to run like modern humans, to hunt consistently, to make stone tools according to plan, and to range beyond Africa. Various archaic species of *Homo* followed, including the Neanderthals, who lived between about 135,000 years ago and 34,000 years ago. Modern humans evolved about 120, 000 years ago, and gradually replaced other species such as Neanderthals.

Richard Leakey points out that we have little evidence about the consciousness of early humans. The first evidence of deliberate burial is that of a Neanderthal of a little more than 100,000 years ago. Leakey sees Neanderthals as having a reflective consciousness, but one that would have been less developed than that of modern humans, which has benefited greatly from the emergence of modern language. What about the self-awareness of *Homo erectus?* Leakey suggests that it would be surprising if late *Homo erectus* 'did not have a level of consciousness significantly greater than that of chimpanzees'. He says of *Homo erectus* that their 'social complexity, large brain size, and probable language skills' all point to a developed level of consciousness. But he acknowledges that we are not certain whether they possessed a form of spoken language and we cannot be sure that they possessed a form of human-like self-awareness.[1]

Clearly there is no way of pinpointing when our ancestors first came to any kind of religious experience. But, I will put the case that the Spirit was first given to human beings long before Pentecost, long before the ecstatic utterances of the prophets of ancient Israel and long before the call of Abraham and Sarah. The Spirit was with the people of Australia 50,000 years ago and the Spirit was there in the very emergence of the human. The Spirit was present not simply as enabling the process of evolution from within, but as surrounding and embracing early humans in self-offering love. Humans evolved in a world of grace. The Spirit of God was the ambience for the emergence of the human. The theological story of the emergence of the human is the story of emergence into a gracious universe.

In presenting this line of thought I will begin with Karl Rahner's position that the experience of the Holy Spirit is co-extensive with human history. Then in a second step, I will ask about the relationship between this universal experience of the Holy Spirit and the Christian conviction about salvation in Christ. Finally I will offer some brief reflections on the relationship between the experience of the Spirit and non-Christian religious traditions.

1. The universal experience of the Holy Spirit

Can we human beings experience the Spirit of God? This is clearly a fundamental question for the life of faith and for theology. The answer is not obvious. On the one hand there are Christians who testify to ecstatic, charismatic or mystical experiences of the Spirit. On the other

---

1.   Richard Leakey, *The Origin of Humankind* (London: Phoenix, 1994), xiv-xv.

hand, there are those who argue that because God radically transcends our minds, God can never be one object amongst others of our experience.

What is clear is that psychological and cultural factors necessarily play a significant role in the interpretation of religious experience. This suggests at least a cautious approach to the experience of the Spirit. What is claimed to come from the Spirit may be, at least in part, the product of a human imagination. It may also be a delusion. This is not to deny the possibility of religious experience, but to argue that religious experience is necessarily filtered through the personality of its recipient. It can find expression only in human imaginations and in human words and symbols. These are always limited and sometimes misleading. They may be pathological. All of this means that there is need for a critical stance when people claim to experience the Spirit, above all when they claim to have a message for others to follow. But none of this caution rules out a theological claim that we can and do experience God's Spirit.

Karl Rahner has articulated such a claim. Furthermore, he insists that this experience occurs in a fundamental way in ordinary human experience of the world. It is not reserved for elites. It is an experience of the Spirit at the heart of daily life. Rahner insists that when we speak of the experience of the Spirit, the experience in question is not of the same order as the experience of created objects, like a door, a book or a tree. It is a much more global experience of transcendence, of openness to the infinite, an experience that occurs as the context and background for all of our specific everyday experiences.

This experience of transcendence, of 'going beyond' the ordinary and everyday, occurs in ordinary everyday knowing. We ask questions. Every specific answer opens up further questions. Our questions have no end. There is a restless, ceaseless searching of our minds that cannot rest in any specific result. Our questions open out towards endless infinity. Whenever our minds move towards an individual object such as a flower, we come to know it in a wider context. What is known and named as an individual object, is known against an unnamed and implicitly-known context. This context involves all possible knowledge. It has no boundaries, reaching out towards the infinite. We can bring this context to explicit awareness, but only by making it concrete and specific. It always escapes our concepts. It is like the horizon that forms the context for our journey, but which, if we focus on it and we move towards it, always springs up again beyond our grasp.

Rahner offers two beautiful images for the experience of infinite mystery that occurs in our everyday knowing. He says that the object of explicit awareness, such as a tree outside the window, is like *a tiny island in the boundless ocean* of the nameless mystery that surrounds it. When I form a concept of a tree, I grasp the tree only against the endless possibilities of things. Rahner's second image is that of seeing a light on a dark night. What we can grasp with our minds are like little lights, and the nameless mystery that surrounds them is like the *night that alone makes visible our little lights and gives then their brightness.*[2]

This experience of openness to mystery occurs not only in human knowing, but also in the free acts of the human will. In all of our specific commitments there is an implicit invitation to give ourselves into a love that is unconditioned. Above all, this implicit invitation is found in the experience of love of another person. Even in the deepest and most satisfying experiences of loving close family and dear friends we come against limitation and loneliness. We recognise that there are hungers of the heart that no human being can finally fill. The partial fulfilment we experience in love of another opens out towards a love that has no limits. It points to the seemingly endless restlessness of human desire and to the unlimited capacity of the human heart.

There is a boundless expanse to the human mind and heart, and this boundless expanse is always there as the context of ordinary knowledge and love. Rahner sees the Spirit of God as dwelling in this openness of the human person. But he insists that the Christian sees this as God's Spirit only through revelation. *Philosophically,* all we say is that there is an unlimited openness of the human spirit, and we may hope that God is the goal of this movement. But, *theologically,* on the basis of the revelation of God's universal salvific will, we can say that it is the grace of God, God's self-communication in the Spirit, which surrounds and sustains the human person. The dynamic openness of the human person is an openness towards the Spirit of God present in self-offering love.

At the heart of ordinary life, there is an experience of transcendence that revelation tells us is in fact an experience of the Spirit of God. This experience is often obscured by preoccupation with the specific things

---

2.   Karl Rahner, 'Experience of the Holy Spirit', *Theological Investigations* XVIII (New York: Crossroad, 1983), 196-197.

that engage our attention. The experience of the Spirit can remain implicit, preconceptual and unnamed—like the light of the sun which we may not see directly because we are concerned with the objects made visible only by its light.[3] Or to return to Rahner's other image, it may be thought of as like the darkness that we do not notice because we are attending to the lights that the darkness makes visible. We can avoid attending to this darkness, but we can also attend to it, and open our minds and hearts to the mystery that surrounds us. We can learn to dwell in this openness to the Spirit in a time of prayer.

Rahner points out that as well as these experiences of transcendence in ordinary knowing and loving, there are also particular times when this ever-present experience of the Spirit is brought more clearly to the forefront of our conscious experience. These are moments that are commonly thought of as religious experiences. They occur when the individual objects of our attention serve to bring to mind the accompanying experience of the Spirit. Everyday experience then becomes a pointer to the ever-present but not always noticed experience of the Spirit.

This happens in positive ways when the object of our experience in its beauty, goodness or mystery points us towards the Spirit of God who sustains it. There are times when an everyday reality becomes transparent to the light of the Spirit shining through it. A person can be caught up in the beauty and mystery of creation, whether in being captivated by a single flower, pondering the exuberance of life in a rain forest or gazing at the stars on a moonless night, and find in this experience a sense of gracious presence. A moment of shared friendship can come as a pure gift, a gift that cannot be controlled or held too tightly, but which brings a sense of being immensely blessed. A new-born child can bring the parents to an absolute wonder and be received as a mysterious God-given gift. There are moments of creativity, in cooking, writing, gardening, building, painting, teaching, parenting and relating, when we can experience the breakthrough to the new as simultaneously from ourselves and as a gift from beyond ourselves.

There are also negative and sometimes extremely painful moments that lead us into mystery, when the everyday realities with which we are concerned break down. There are times when all that supports our

---

3.   *Ibid*, 199.

deepest commitments disappears, and we find ourselves called to an unconditioned trust and know that this is a moment of God's Spirit in our lives. There are times when loneliness takes hold in our hearts, when love is unrequited, when those we love seem far away, when all we feel is absence and emptiness, and this emptiness comes to a solitude where there is a silent presence. There is the experience of being badly damaged by another, when in spite of bitterness and disappointment, we find ourselves with the freedom to forgive and know this freedom as grace. There is the death of those we love, times when loss and grief leave us unspeakably desolate, yet something upholds us even in what seems absolutely hopeless and unendurable.

In the light of the God revealed in Jesus, Christians can find in these experiences the presence of God in the Spirit. In the light of revelation, they can understand what they experience as 'the love of God poured into our hearts by the Holy Spirit that has been given to us' (Rom 5:5). Paul, of course, was talking about the experience of those who were justified by faith, who 'have peace with God though our Lord Jesus Christ'. This raises the important question of the relationship between the experiences of the Spirit and salvation through Christ. If all human beings live in a world of grace, if they experience the Spirit in some way in everyday life, how is this experience connected to the salvation that Christians see as mediated to the world in the life, death resurrection of Jesus Christ?

2. The Holy Spirit and salvation in Christ

The Christian tradition has long struggled with the relationship between the universality of God's saving will and salvation in Christ. The early Christian community was convinced that the boundless love of God revealed in the Christ event is a universal love that breaks through all boundaries and embraces the whole world. At the same time they were convinced that this saving love was given in Jesus Christ, in his life death and resurrection. These two aspects of Christian theology are both represented in the Christian scriptures. The conviction that salvation comes through Christ is expressed in texts such as these: 'For as in Adam all died, so also in Christ shall all be made alive' (1 Cor 15:21); 'I am the way, and the truth and the life. No one comes to the Father except through me' (Jn 14:6); 'There is salvation in no one else, for there is no other name under heaven given among mortals by which we must be saved' (Acts 4:12); 'For there is one God; there is also one mediator between God and humankind, Christ Jesus, himself human, who gave himself a ransom for all' (1 Tim 2:5).

God's universal saving love finds its real expression in the whole person of Jesus Christ, rather than in specific texts. It also finds expression in the biblical figures of both testaments who are neither Jewish nor Christian but are moved by God and open to God. Cornelius was a favourite example for writers in the patristic period. Cornelius is a devout and good Gentile whose prayers and alms-giving were well-pleasing to God long before his conversion and baptism (Acts 10). In Acts 17, we find Paul reflecting explicitly on God's presence to non-Christians: 'What therefore you worship as unknown I proclaim to you . . . the God who made the world and everything in it . . . made all nations to inhabit the whole earth . . . so that they would search for God and perhaps grope for him and find him—though indeed he is not far from each one of us. For "In him we live and move and have our being", as even some of your own poets have said, "For we too are his offspring"' (23-28). God's universal will to save finds its classic expression in First Timothy: 'God our Saviour desires everyone to be saved and to come to the knowledge of the truth' (1 Tim 2:4).

These two insights, that salvation is through Christ and that God wills all people to be saved, have stood in some tension throughout Christian history. At times the stress has been on the possibility of universal salvation. Justin Martyr (c. 100-165) writes of Jewish people who obeyed the Mosaic Law, that 'since they who did those things which are universally, naturally, and eternally good are pleasing to God, they shall be saved in the resurrection'.[4] In response to the question as to whether Gentiles can be saved, he comments that 'Christ is the *Logos* of which all humankind partakes' and that those 'who lived according to reason *(logos)* were really Christian'.[5] Clement of Alexandria (c 150–c 215) insists that God is 'the Saviour of all' and 'as each was disposed to receive it, God distributed his blessings, both to Greeks and barbarians'.[6] Origen (c 185–c 254) teaches that God in every age wanted human beings to be just and 'always provided human beings endowed with reason with occasions for practicing

---

4.   Justin Martyr, *Dialogue with Trypho* 45, translator Thomas Falls, FC 6:215. See Francis Sullivan's *Salvation outside the Church? Tracing the History of the Catholic Response* (New York: Paulist Press, 1992), 14-27.

5.   Justin Martyr, *First Apology*, 46, translator Thomas Falls, FC 6:83-84.

6.   Clement of Alexandria, *Stromata*, 7:2 PG 9: 409-10.

virtue and doing what is right'. He appeals to a beautiful text from the
Wisdom of Solomon: 'In every generation she (the Wisdom of God)
passes into holy souls, and makes them friends of God and prophets'
(7:27).[7]

Alongside this tradition was one that insisted that salvation is given
through Christ and the church and to willfully reject either was to
reject God. This found expression in the saying of Cyprian (c 200–258),
taken up by Augustine (354–430) and others: 'Outside the church, no
salvation.' This teaching was affirmed by the Fourth Lateran Council
(1215), by the Council of Florence (1442) and in the bull *Unam Sanctam*
of Pope Boniface VIII (1302). However, this negative formulation was
not understood to be an absolute denial of salvation for those who
were not Christian. Thomas Aquinas pointed to the possibility of
salvation through an explicit or implicit desire for baptism. Dominican
theologians from the Salamanca school, such as Domingo Soto
(1494–1560), and Jesuits from the Roman school such as Francisco
Suarez (1548–1619) responded to the European discoveries of countless
non-Christian peoples with a theology of the possibility of salvation
through implicit faith.

In one of its most decisive and most important theological
clarifications, the Second Vatican Council taught a positive approach to
the theology of salvation outside the church. The *Constitution on the
Church* says:

> Those too can attain eternal salvation who, through
> no fault of their own, do not know the Gospel of
> Christ or his church, yet sincerely seek God, and,
> moved by grace, try in their actions to do God's will
> as they know it through the dictates of conscience.[8]

This text insists that salvation can come to those who do not know
the gospel and are outside the church through a response to God's
grace that is expressed in fidelity to conscience. It clearly teaches that
grace and salvation exist beyond the confines of the church. That this is
the work of the Spirit is taught explicitly in a parallel text in the
Pastoral Constitution on the Church in the Modern World. The context is
the *Constitution's* description of the way Christians participate in

---

7.   Origin, *Contra Celsum*, 4:7 PG 11:1035-38.
8.   *Lumen Gentium*, 16.

Christ's death and resurrection through the indwelling of the life-giving Spirit. The text goes on to describe how non-Christians share in Christ:

> All this holds true not only for Christians but also for all people of good will in whose hearts grace works in an invisible way. For since Christ died for all, and since the final vocation of humankind is in fact one and divine, we ought to believe that the Holy Spirit offers to all, in a way known only to God, the possibility of being associated with this paschal mystery.[9]

In this text, we are told that it is the Spirit of God who offers saving grace to all people of all times, and this grace is understood as participation in Christ's death and resurrection. Many Christians have thought of salvation as being available not only *though* the death of Jesus but also *after* it. But according to the teaching of the Second Vatican Council, salvation is universally available in the self-giving of God to us in the Holy Spirit. This would mean that we would need to think of salvation being possible throughout the whole history of modern humans going back 120,000 years, and to their ancestors, stretching back, perhaps, to *Homo erectus* of two million years ago. Whenever there has been a human person open to the mystery of God, there the Spirit of God has been present as self-offering love.

This raises the fundamental question: How can the salvation of a woman who lived, for example, 50,000 years ago in Australia be related to Jesus of Nazareth who lived 2,000 years ago? Karl Rahner offers a response to this question. He points out that the Spirit, at work in saving grace throughout human history, is always the Spirit directed towards Christ. The meaning and purpose of the Spirit's work is expressed in God's self-giving to the world in Jesus Christ. It is the Spirit of God who brings about the incarnation and our salvation in Christ, and in this sense the Spirit is the efficient cause of the Christ event. But the whole history of the Spirit's presence in grace is directed towards Jesus Christ. In this sense Christ is the final cause of the Spirit. The Spirit is oriented towards God's explicit self-giving in Christ. The

---

9.   *Gaudium et Spes*, 22.

Spirit bears this goal within. Rahner speaks of this as an intrinsic *entelechy* of the Spirit.[10] This expression from Aristotelian philosophy refers to the inner ordering that directs an entity to its natural goal or completion. The Spirit has an inner ordering and direction towards the goal of God's self-giving in the Word made flesh.

How then, is the experience of the Spirit related to the cross of Christ? Rahner notes that traditional ways of talking about salvation, such as satisfaction, substitutionary atonement and sacrifice, can give the false impression that something happens in the cross that changes God's mind. He believes that such expressions, although legitimate when properly understood, are time-conditioned attempts to communicate something more basic and primary—the mystery of what God has done for us in Jesus. They are *secondary* and *derivative* with regard to the primary experience of salvation in Christ. The cross does not cause a change in God. It does not change God from being a God of wrath to being a God of grace. God does not need appeasing. God is the cause of salvation. It is God's eternal will to save that finds expression in the cross. The death and resurrection are not in any sense a cause of God beginning to love us sinners. They are the consequence, expression and embodiment of this divine love.

Rahner suggests an understanding of the death of Jesus as *symbolic* or *sacramental* cause of our salvation. Jesus' life of self-giving love finds its climax in the surrender to God in his death. This is both the symbol and the accomplishment of God's eternal saving love.[11] Here salvation receives its explicit expression in human history. God's saving grace has been present throughout the whole of human history in the Spirit of God. This presence of the Spirit is always Christ-directed. The saving grace that is already mysteriously present and active in the Spirit is both symbolised and realised in Jesus' life, death and resurrection. The cross is the primary sacramental sign of grace. This specific efficacious *sign* of grace and the *universal reality* of grace are radically and intrinsically linked together. The sign belongs to the essence of grace. In the cross, grace finds historical expression. In this sense the cross is the cause of the salvation which it signifies. Jesus

---

10. Karl Rahner, *Foundations of Christian Faith* (New York: Crossroad, 1978), 316-318. See also his 'Jesus Christ in the Non-Christian Religions,' *Theological Investigations* XVII (New York: Crossroad, 1981), 46.

11. Karl Rahner, *Foundations,* op cit, 283-285. For Rahner's understanding of symbol see his 'The Theology of Symbol', *Theological Investigations* IV (Baltimore: Helicon Press, 1960), 221-252.

Christ is the sacrament of the salvation of the world.

This means that a woman living in Australia 50,000 years ago already lived in a world of grace. This grace was nothing else than the Spirit of God surrounding her, present to her in the openness of her own heart and mind. God freely gives the Spirit as a constitutive dimension of human existence. God has freely chosen to come to us, to embrace our existence and to offer us love. So this woman lives in a graced universe. She, like every human being, can respond to this divine self-offering positively or negatively. She can accept or reject the Spirit. To accept the Spirit is to receive the gift of justifying grace through a form of faith. It might be an implicit faith that finds expression in her care for her children, her compassion for those around her. It may find expression in her fidelity to the promptings of the Spirit in the depths of conscience.

Of course her response might also be sinful rejection of the Spirit. And in any case her existence is touched not by only by the gracious inviting presence of the Spirit, but by the cumulative weight of human sin that enters into the place of her free decision. But, in spite of the inclination to evil that is also part of human existence, this woman lives her life with an always-present experience of the Spirit as the horizon of everyday experience. And in grace she may well embrace this self-offering of love, and find her salvation. From the point of view of Christian faith, when she embraces the Spirit she embraces the Christ-directed Spirit.

3. The Spirit of God and the religious traditions of humankind

In many theological circles, then, including those associated with my own Roman Catholic tradition, it is not in any way controversial to claim that the salvation of Jesus Christ is offered to all people of every age through the ever-present Spirit of God. In fact, this is the explicit and formal teaching of Pope John Paul II, who writes:

> The universality of salvation means that it is granted not only to those who explicitly believe in Christ and have entered the Church. Since salvation is offered to all, it must be made concretely available to all. But it is clear that today, as in the past, many people do not have an opportunity to come to know or accept the Gospel or to enter the Church. The social and

> cultural conditions in which they live do not permit
> this, and frequently they have been brought up in
> other religious traditions. For such people salvation
> in Christ is accessible by virtue of a grace which,
> while having a mysterious relationship to the
> Church, does not make them formally part of the
> Church but enlightens them in a way which is
> accommodated to their spiritual and material
> situation. This grace comes from Christ; it is the
> result of his sacrifice and is communicated by the
> Holy Spirit. It enables each person to attain salvation
> through his or her own free cooperation.[12]

But if salvation is indeed understood as universal in outreach, then this raises the further question of how a Christian theology might view the role of other religions in mediating salvation. The Second Vatican Council addresses other religious traditions positively, as a 'preparation for the gospel' and as containing 'seeds of the Word'.[13] It expresses respect for all that is 'true and holy' in these traditions and sees them as often 'reflecting a ray of that Truth that enlightens all people'.[14] But the Council did not offer a Christian understanding of the role of other religions in salvation.

While John Paul II has not pursued this issue directly, he has made a significant theological contribution by his emphasis on the presence and work of the Holy Spirit in non-Christians and in their religions. In his first encyclical, he spoke of beliefs on non-Christian religions as being an 'effect of the Spirit of truth' operating outside the visible confines of the Christian church.[15] He challenged missionaries to respect everything 'wrought in the human being by the Spirit, "which blows where it wills"'.[16] Later, he addressed the people of Asia in a radio broadcast: 'I have come to Asia to be a witness to the Spirit who is active in the history of peoples and of nations.' Reflecting on the Day of Prayer for Peace at Assisi with leaders of religious traditions, he

---

12. *Redemptoris Missio*, 10. Translated as *On the Permanent Validity of the Church's Missionary Mandate* (Homebush, NSW: St Paul, 1991), 23.

13. *Ad Gentes* 3, 11.

14. *Nostra Aetate*, 2.

15. *Redemptor Hominis*, 6. Translated as *Redeemer of Man* (Homebush, NSW: St Paul, 1979), 20-21.

16. *Ibid*, 12, 36-37.

said: 'Every authentic prayer is called forth by the Holy Spirit, who is mysteriously present in the heart of every person.'[17] In his encyclical on the Holy Spirit, he again speaks of the universality of the Spirit's presence and action. He says that we need to go back behind the last two thousand years: *'We need to go further back,* to embrace the whole of the action of the Holy Spirit even before Christ—*from the beginning,* throughout the world, and especially in the economy of the Old Covenant.'[18] He reminds his hearers of the Second Vatican Council's teaching that the Holy Spirit acts 'outside the visible body of the church'.[19]

Finally in his encyclical on mission he returns to this theme of the universal presence and action of the Spirit:

> The Spirit, therefore, is at the very source of the human being's existential and religious questioning, a questioning which is occasioned not only by contingent situations but by the very structure of his or her being . . . The Spirit's presence and activity affect not only individuals but also society and history, people, cultures and religions. Indeed the Spirit is at the origin of the noble ideals and undertakings which benefit humanity on its journey through history . . . Again, it is the Spirit who sows the 'seeds of the Word' present in various customs and cultures, preparing them for full maturity in Christ . . . Thus the Spirit, who 'blows where he wills' (cf John 3:8), and who 'was already at work in the world before Christ was glorified', and who has 'filled the world, holds all things together (and) knows what is said' (Wis 1:7), leads us to broaden our vision in order to ponder his activity in every time and place. I have repeatedly called this fact to mind, and it has guided me in my meetings with a

---

17.   See Francis Sullivan, *Salvation outside the Church? op cit,* 190, 193.

18.   *Dominum et Vivicantem,* 53. Translated as *The Holy Spirit in the Life of the Church* (Boston: St Paul, 1986), 91.

19.   *Ibid.*

wide variety of peoples.[20]

He insists that the church's relationship with other religions is to be governed by a two-fold respect—respect for the human person's quest for answers to the deepest questions and respect for the action of the Spirit in the human person.

This body of teaching might be summarised in the following six points: 1. The Spirit of God is at work universally in all times and places and for every person; 2. This Spirit is always the Spirit of Jesus Christ; 3. The Spirit offers every person salvation, an offer that each person can accept or reject; 4. The Spirit is present and active not only in individuals, but in societies, cultures and religions; 5. The Spirit sows the 'seeds of the Word' that are present in various cultural and religious practices; 6. Christians are called to discern and ponder the presence and action of the Spirit in other religious traditions.

Clearly, what we encounter in another tradition may be the gift of the Spirit. It may be a 'seed of the Word'. Does this mean that such an aspect of the tradition may be a mediation of salvation? While this question is not answered by John Paul II, he does state: 'Although participated forms of mediation are not excluded, they acquire meaning and value *only* from Christ's own mediation, and they cannot be understood as parallel or complementary to his.'[21]

This raises a question for Christian theology: Is it appropriate for a Christian, who believes that salvation comes through Christ, to understand that non-Christian religious figures or institutions may constitute participatory forms of mediation in salvation? I believe that the answer to this question can only be yes. As Karl Rahner has pointed out, once it is granted that a non-Christian shares in salvation, then one cannot deny that such a person's religion may have a positive contribution to make to salvation without understanding salvation in 'a completely ahistorical and asocial way'.[22] Salvation is always a gift of God, but if it is to impact on humanity then it has to find embodiment in history and community. The experience of saving grace will arise, in some cases, in and through religious figures, texts and rituals and may well find expression in the language and practices of one's own religious tradition. A religious figure, text or ritual may be

---

20.   *Redemptoris Missio*, 28, 29.

21.   *Ibid*, 5, 18.

22.   Rahner, *Foundations of Christian Faith*, *op cit*, 314.

not only revelatory but also a means of salvation, because it may give expression to the presence and action of the saving Spirit of God.

I believe that this theology of the Spirit offers an all-important foundation for a Christian approach to inter-religious dialogue. I find the traditional typology, exclusivism, inclusivism and pluralism, of little help in the contemporary situation.[23] All too often a complex theological position is distorted by making it fit one of these types. And I find none of these categories satisfying. Each of them seems to demand a higher perspective, a standpoint above the individual traditions—from which the traditions are co-related and evaluated. In particular I think that the pluralist position often takes the point of view of enlightenment reason to make *a priori* judgments about what is common to the religions, and I do not think that this is a tenable or helpful position. It does not allow the traditions to emerge in their proper specificity and otherness.[24]

I would argue that inter-religious dialogue ought not to proceed in *a priori* fashion. Christians, for example, ought not to decide in principle and before the dialogue has taken place that their Hindu partners are either included within Christianity or excluded. Dialogue, if it is to be genuine, must be tradition-specific. Christianity is committed to the belief that God's self-revelation and salvation are irrevocably given to the world in Jesus Christ. But there is no reason from within Christian faith to suggest *a priori* that Jesus either excludes or includes other religions as such. Of course specific beliefs and practices of another religion may be found to be congruent or incongruent with Christian faith in Jesus Christ. But this is a matter to be discovered in

---

23. This typology has certainly facilitated discussion over the last twenty years. It was popularised by Alan Race in *Christians and Religious Pluralism* (London: SCM, 1983). For other important approaches to these issues see Paul F Knitter, *No Other Name? A Critical Study of Christian Attitudes towards the World Religions* (Maryknoll, NY: Orbis, 1985) and Jaques Dupuis, *Towards a Christian Theology of Religious Pluralism* (Maryknoll, New York: Orbis, 1997). On the pluralist approach, see John Hick and Paul Knitter (editors), *The Myth of Christian Uniqueness: Towards a Pluralistic Theology of Religions* (Maryknoll, NY: Orbis, 1987).

24. At this point I am in agreement with Gavin D'Costa's argument. I also agree with his contention that a tradition-specific trinitarian approach actually achieves some of the aims of the pluralist position. See his Gavin D'Costa, *The Meeting of Religions and the Trinity* (Edinburgh: T&T Clark, 2000).

dialogue, not decided prior to genuine conversation. If a Christian is to enter into inter-religious dialogue, then she can do so only on the basis of the living Christian tradition. But at the heart of this tradition is the trinitarian understanding of the Spirit and the Word/Wisdom of God. In the Christian doctrine of the Spirit there is a commitment to the idea that the Spirit is like the wind, blowing where she will. Christians believe that the Spirit cannot be contained within the confines of the church. The Spirit may well challenge Christians from outside Christianity. The Spirit may speak to Christians from what is *other* in another tradition in a way that appears new and confronting.

As Jacques Dupuis and Gavin D'Costa point out, this provides a trinitarian basis for a Christian openness in dialogue to another tradition. This is a radical position. The Spirit who is at the heart of the Christian community may be addressing the Christian community in prophetic ways from another religious tradition. The Christian church, if it is to be faithful to its own identity as a Spirit-led church, must be attentive to what the Spirit has to say from the other tradition. It will need to attend to God's giving of God's self 'through the prayers, practices, insight, and traditions found within other traditions'. This facilitates a stance before other religions that is both 'critical and reverential'.[25] But for the Christian this can only mean a genuine discernment of spirits that cannot be done in the abstract or in principle, but only in the concrete engagement of humble and patient dialogue.

This discernment of spirits is necessarily tradition-specific. For a Christian, this discernment is always a testing in the light of Christ—whether it be a matter of discerning the promptings of the Spirit within the Christian community, the listening for the Spirit in conversation with another religious tradition, or in reading the signs of the times in the social and cultural life of the wider community.

In Jesus, Christians find the Wisdom of God revealed in the midst of humanity. They understand this Wisdom of God as radically with us in Jesus of Nazareth, in the specificity and uniqueness of his person, his liberating words, his prophetic deeds, his life death and resurrection. They see Jesus as the human face of God. They believe all of this to be the work of the Spirit. They believe that the Spirit was always directed to the Word made flesh. It is to be expected that in other religions the experience of the Spirit will find expression in an

---

25.   *Ibid*, 115.

explicit way in holy persons, rituals and texts. These may constitute a Spirit-given Word that Christians can understand in relationship to the Word made flesh. They may constitute Wisdom from God that Christians can understand in relation to Jesus the Wisdom of God. These persons, rites and texts may give expression not only to human limitations but also to sin—as is also the case for Christianity. But through the grace of the Holy Spirit they may also be expressions of the Wisdom of God that Christians find revealed in Jesus of Nazareth.

3. Conclusion

The story of the Spirit that begins with the big bang continues as the story of grace. The Creator Spirit who fills the universe is from the very beginning the Sanctifier, the bringer of grace. The Spirit is not only the Creator Spirit but also the Bearer of Grace. From the beginning, the Spirit is present to human beings in self-offering love. The Spirit of God graciously accompanies and celebrates every emerging form of life. This same Spirit delights in the emergence of creatures who can respond to the divine self-offering love in a personal way. They are to be offered the gift of transforming and sanctifying grace. A grace-filled universe awaits their arrival. Alongside this story of grace there is also a tragic story of the wilful rejection of grace. Human beings are born into a world of grace, but are also drawn towards violence and evil. In the midst of such a world, the Spirit offers freedom and salvation in a way that Christians understand as anticipating, and as directed towards, the Christ event. Whenever humans emerge who were capable of religious experience and implicit faith, they emerge into a graced world.

12

Salvation in the Otherwordly?

Hans Schwarz

In 1973 at the World Conference on Mission and Evangelism of the World Council of Churches in Bangkok, the motto 'Salvation Today!' was advanced. The same motto has also been accentuated in liberation theology. Here Gustavo Gutiérrez captured the attention of theologians with the classic *A Theology of Liberation: History, Politics and Salvation*, first published in 1972. Gutiérrez makes it clear that 'it is important to keep in mind that beyond—or rather, through—the struggle against misery, injustice and exploitation the goal is the *creation of a new humanity'.*[1] Gutiérrez is adamant in pointing out that the intrinsic eschatological structure of the Christian faith is not to be spiritualised. Neither its present nor its future aspects should be related merely to spiritual realities, since their origin and goal have definitely historical bearings. For instance, when prophets announce the kingdom of peace, this presupposes the establishment of justice on earth. Similarly, the coming of the kingdom and the expectation of the parousia necessarily imply historical, temporal, earthly, social and material realities. Spiritualisation of faith, however, tends to forget the human consequences of the eschatological promises and the power to transform unjust social structures. The elimination of misery and exploitation therefore can be understood as a sign of the coming kingdom.

Indeed, we can learn with Gutiérrez from the Old Testament that God is a history-making God, and salvation is spoken of in terms of a re-creation of history. Especially King David captured the focus of the promissory history of Israel. The hope for the re-establishment of the Davidic kingdom was kept alive by the prophets and continued well

---

1.   Gustavo Gutiérrez, *A Theology of Liberation: History, Politics, and Salvation*, fifteenth anniversary edition with a new introduction by the author. Translated and edited by C Inda and J Eagleson (Maryknoll, NY: Orbis: 1988), 81.

into the New Testament times. Telling for this hope is the remark of Cleopas, one of the two disciples of Jesus who were going to Emmaus, when he lamented about the crucified Jesus: 'But we had hoped that he was the one to redeem Israel' (Lk 24:21). The redemption addressed here is not unrelated to the redemption enunciated in the Benedictus which includes also salvation 'from our enemies', which originally had a political connotation.[2] Since the this-worldly materialisation of the hoped-for kingdom never materialised as the disappointed hopes in the Persian King Cyrus II, Zerrubbabel, and Bar Kochba show, there occurred an increasing spiritualisation of salvation. Even Jesus stated according to John 18:36: 'My kingdom is not from this world.' However, the Pauline imperative to 'not let sin exercise dominion in your mortal bodies' (Rom 6:12) indicates that the hoped-for kingdom never became so other-worldly that it had no impact on this life. Paul was convinced that already here we 'might walk in newness of life' since we are 'dead to sin and alive to God in Christ Jesus' (Rom 6:4,11).

Nearly two thousand years have elapsed since Paul made these claims. Yet what has happened to the final realisation of the kingdom? Should we side with Martin Werner and others who tried to explain the whole development of the Christian dogma from the fact that the eschaton and the parousia did not come as expected?[3] If we do, we would simply have to abandon the notion of salvation, since, I am sure, most would agree that the Christian dogma is not synonymous with salvation. Yet another avenue was pursued especially in the nineteenth century, namely to think of salvation in evolutionary terms.

---

2. Cf Eduard Schweizer, *Das Evangelium nach Lukas (NTD)* (Göttingen: Vandenhoeck & Ruprecht, 1986), 256 and 28, who in his exegesis makes the connection between Luke 24:21 and Luke 1:68, and points to the initial political meaning of liberation 'from our enemies' (Lk 1:71).

3. Cf Martin Werner, *The Formation of Christian Dogma: An Historical Study of Its Problem*, translated with an introduction by SGF Brandon (New York: Harper, 1957), 47, 71f, and other places. Werner attempts to describe the process of the formation of the Christian dogma as a process of de-eschatologising the main apostolic doctrine caused by the crises that emerged when the parousia was more and more delayed.

1. The evolutionary concept of salvation

The theory of evolution, forever connected with the name of Charles Darwin and expressive of the progressive spirit of the nineteenth century, is essentially focused on the present and attempts to delineate laws according to which the present emerges from the past. When we read Darwin's *Origin of Species*, however, we notice on the one hand his focus on the present. But then we detect that, in the conclusion at least, Darwin also pointed to the future by writing: 'And as natural selection works solely and for good of each being, all corporeal and mental endowments will tend to progress toward perfection.'[4] Two words are significant in this statement: 'progress' and 'perfection'. Indeed, the discerning eye will notice some kind of development in nature, whether one follows Darwin's theory or talks about successive new creations. Therefore Darwin concludes: 'From the war of nature, from famine and death, the most exalted object which we are capable of conceiving, namely, the production of the higher animals, directly follows.' Of course, in the *Origin of Species* Darwin did not yet focus on humanity.

But in his autobiography, Charles Darwin pondered: 'Believing as I do that man in the distant future will be a far more perfect creature than he is now, it is an intolerable thought that he and all other sentient beings are doomed to complete annihilation after such long-continued slow progress. To those who fully admit the immortality of the human soul, the destruction of our world will not appear so dreadful.'[5] This kind of reasoning, that if life finally succeeds to emerge it cannot be simply snuffed out, was reiterated more than a century later by Frank J Tipler and John D Barrow in their book *The Anthropic Cosmological Principle*. They start with the observation that there are a number of improbable accidents that are totally unrelated to each other. Their occurrence is necessary so that on the basis of carbon-containing molecules an observer can appear in our universe. This leads them to three different anthropic principles. The weak principle asserts: 'The observed value of all physical and cosmological quantities are not

4. Charles Darwin, *The Origin of Species by Means of Natural Selection or the Preservation of Favoured Races in the Struggle of Life* (Chicago: Encyclopaedia Britannica, 1952), 243 (in the conclusion) for this and the following quote.

5. Francis Darwin, editor, *The Life and Letters of Charles Darwin, Including an Autobiographical Chapter* (1888) (New York: Johnson Reprint, 1969), 312, in an excerpt of an undated letter.

equally probable, but they take on values restricted by the requirement that there exist sites where carbon-based life can evolve, and by the requirement that the Universe be old enough for it to have already done so.'[6] The strong anthropic principle goes another step further and asserts: 'The Universe must have those properties which allow life to develop within it at some stage in its history.'[7] Finally, Tipler and Barrow also formulate the final anthropic principle that says: 'Intelligent information-processing must come into existence in the Universe, and, once it comes into existence, it will never die out.'[8] This means, once life has emerged, it is implausible that it should simply die out again.

In a more recent publication with the telling title *The Physics of Immortality: Modern Cosmology, God, and the Resurrection of the Dead*, Tipler becomes more explicit about why life will not just cease to exist. Tipler knows that the future of the universe is such that life as an information process cannot continue forever in its present form, that is, as a carbon-based organism. If life as an information process that can sustain communication is to continue at all, it must continue to exist on some other basis. Tipler is convinced that in the not-too-distant future computers will possess the capability for autonomous information processing and communication, and finally even will be able to reproduce themselves. Since Tipler understands a person as an entity capable of autonomous information processing and communication, and since computers will be able to assume these functions, he sees the only possibility of future 'life' on the basis of computers. Tipler tells us that the extinction of humanity is the logically necessary consequence of eternal progress. Since we are finite beings, we have definite limits. Our brains can only contain a limited amount of information. Since the advance of life to the Omega Point is a fact, the furthermost developed consciousness must one day be a non-human one. But everything that we as individual beings contribute to culture will survive our individual death. The next step of intelligent life will be information-processing machines. The closer we move to the Omega Point, the more computer capacity is available to store our present world and to

6. John D Barrow/Frank J Tipler, *The Anthropic Cosmological Principle*, second edition (Oxford: Clarendon Press, 1988), 16.

7. Barrow/Tipler, 21.

8. Barrow/Tipler, 23.

simulate it exactly. Finally there will also be the possibility of simulating all possible visible universes, namely of simulating 'virtual' universes. At the end, 'not only are dead being resurrected, but so are people who have never lived.'[9] All people and all histories that could have existed will then indeed exist.

The dead will be resurrected as soon as the capacity of all computers in the universe is so large that the capacity required for the storage of all possible human simulations is only an insignificant fraction of the total capacity. According to Tipler, the resurrection will occur immediately before the Omega Point is reached. Unlike Teilhard de Chardin, Tipler no longer talks about alpha and omega, since God is not the enveloping higher dimension but the endpoint, the Omega Point of our processes. Since Tipler's physical reductionism is unaware of its own limitations, Tipler can propound eternal progress, which means that 'knowledge will grow without bound, per capita wealth will increase to infinity'.[10]

Tipler pays little attention to the law of entropy which states that in an isolated system the non-convertibility of energy never decreases, but either remains constant or increases. Evolution does not contain a salvational prospect in itself. Considering the immensity of our universe, it is difficult for us to visualise that as a system the universe is not a *perpetuum mobile*, an arrangement that continuously keeps running. Even if the end of time and change is billions of years away, all processes within our universe move toward a point at which they will stop. Since the material on which evolutionary concepts are built is finite, the salvation which evolutionary models offer confronts finitude. When we consider another avenue of millennial hope, salvation is not simply thought of as an extension of the material. Here the other-worldly and the this-worldly seem to merge.

2. Millennial concepts of salvation

Today millennial ideas are more widespread than ever in Christian conservative circles (ie among evangelicals, fundamentalists, and Pentecostals), even though they are largely ignored by mainline churches. Both Christian and secular utopias, from the hope of an inner-worldly realisation of the kingdom of God to the attempt to

---

9.   Frank J Tipler, *The Physics of Immortality: Modern Cosmology, God, and the Resurrection of the Dead* (New York: Doubleday, 1994), 223.
10.   Tipler, 104.

build an egalitarian society, have received their main impetus from the Christian notion of the community of the faithful which is radically renewed historically and societally in visible form prior to judgment day. Millennialism, coming from the Latin 'one thousand years,' or chiliasm, meaning the same in Greek, stands for the expectation of a visible reign of Christ with the believers before the immediate coming of the end of the world.

Though millennialism is a distinctive Christian teaching, its roots go back beyond Revelation 20:1-15 to Jewish apocalyptic traditions. As Eusebius of Caesarea tells us, Papias stated that 'there will be a period of some thousand years after the resurrection of the dead, and that the kingdom of Christ will be set up in material form on this very earth'.[11] Eusebius leaves no doubt that he has little use of this this-worldly progression of the kingdom towards salvation. When Eusebius was composing his church history, the Christian faith had already become an officially accepted religion in the Roman Empire. There was no need any more to hope for a future millennium in which the evil forces were subdued. This was still the case in early Christendom, as we can gather from Barnabas, Papias, or Justin Martyr who advocated some kind of millennialism. While the fortunes of the Christians certainly turned around with Emperor Constantine, the church did not become, as Augustine once thought, 'the kingdom of Christ and the kingdom of heaven'.[12] Moreover, there seemed to be a continuous conflict between the church and the worldly authorities, not to mention within the church itself, as numerous schisms show. Therefore it came as no surprise that, with the turn of the first millennium, millennial ideas were revived on a larger scale.

After long studies and meditations in the wilderness of the Calabrian mountains, Joachim of Fiore, a Cistercian monk, had some kind of revelation at a Pentecost celebration between 1190 and 1195. During the revelation he discovered the meaning of the last book of the Bible and the correspondence of the Old Testament with the New. In his exposition of the Book of Revelation, he distinguished between those items that had already come to fulfilment and others where

---

11.   As quoted by Eusebius of Caesarea, *Church History* 3.39, in *NPNF* 23:317.
12.   Augustine, *City of God* 20.9, edited and translated by RW Dyson (Cambridge: Cambridge University Press, 1998), 988.

fulfilment was still outstanding. In a prophetic way he outlined the future stages of a providential development of history.

In analogy to the seven days of creation he saw the history of salvation as a sequence of seven ages, each lasting one millennium.[13] Using the forty-two generations (six ages times seven generations) leading up to Jesus (Mt 1:1-17), he divided the old covenant into seven parts: six ages with seven generations which precede Christ and then Christ, who signifies the seventh epoch. In analogy to that, the new covenant is also divided into seven parts, six ages each with seven generations. Each generation lasts thirty years, corresponding to Jesus' age at his death. These calculations show that the new covenant will last 1260 years. After that, comes the seventh epoch, which is the time of the Spirit. While the old covenant is the time of the Father, characterised by law and fear, the new covenant of the Son lasts till AD 1260 and is characterised by grace and faith. The third and final epoch was inaugurated already by St Benedict (ca. 480–ca. 515) and is characterised by love and the Spirit. In many different ways and with numerous metaphors Joachim presents these three different ages.

Joachim, who believed that he belonged to the second epoch, 'did not draw any revolutionary conclusions from the implications of his historico-eschatological visions'.[14] While he saw his own time as a century of radical decay, he projected a messianic leader who would bring about spiritual renewal for the sake of the kingdom of Christ, and who would disclose to all people that which hitherto had been disguised in significant figures and in the sacraments. But his hope was not materialistic, anti-ecclesiastic, or anti-institutional, as with some of his successors. He regarded even the thousand years of the new epoch to be only symbolic. Joachim opted more for a radical spiritualisation of the world during the time of the Spirit than for an earthly renewal.

Later followers of Joachim were less patient than he, and also more inclined to give his thoughts a material base. For instance, the Franciscan Spirituals in the thirteenth and fourteenth centuries attempted without compromise to fulfil the laws of the kingdom of

---

13. For the following cf Medard Kehl, *Eschatologie*, 183-4.
14. So Karl Löwith, *Meaning in History*, 151, and Bernhard Töpfer, *Das kommende Reich des Friedens: Zur Entwicklung chiliastischer Zukunftshoffnungen im Hochmittelalter* (Berlin: Akademie-Verlag, 1964), 48-103, especially 102-3, who shows that Fiore's monastic idealism stayed within the boundaries of the church and did not exhibit any revolutionary impetus that was going to change the world.

God in the present age. This brought them into tremendous conflicts with the Dominicans, who pursued similar ideas. It also led them into open confrontation with the imperial messianism of Emperor Frederick II and with the institutional Roman Catholic Church. While the Dominicans denounced them, and both church and state persecuted them, the idea of a total renewal and cleansing of this earth persisted.

Ernst Bloch asserts that Joachim drew up 'the most momentous social utopia of the Middle Ages', because it abolishes both church and state.[15] Its third age is an age of 'universalised monastic and consumer communism, an "age of free spirit"'.[16] Bloch sees the fundamental principle of Joachimism in the 'unconcluded revelation'.[17] He appreciates the active fight of Joachimism against the social principles of a Christianity that since the time of Paul had associated itself with the class-conscious society. Consequently, it had to compromise its message. According to Bloch, this third period of history, as prophesied by Joachim, seemed to emerge in the Soviet Union and, quite naturally, found its archenemy in the clerical domination of the second period. This clerical kingdom does not fully comprehend the third period, or if it does, it denounces it.[18] These extrapolations show how much Bloch is interested in the anticlerical and political-revolutionary implications of Joachim's thought.[19] In Marxist fashion, Bloch also appreciates the 'complete transfer of the kingdom of light from the other world and the empty promises of the other world into history, even though into a final state of history'.[20] According to Bloch, the relegation of our hopes to a better beyond must then cease. Moreover, their attempt to date the projected kingdom of God made the sectarian

---

15. Ernst Bloch, *The Principle of Hope*, 2:509.

16. Ernst Bloch, *The Principle of Hope*, 2:510.

17. Ernst Bloch, *The Principle of Hope*, 2:514.

18. Cf. Ernst Bloch, *The Principle of Hope*, 2:513.

19. Though Joachim's thought had an unmistakably revolutionary character (cf Ernst Benz, *Evolution and Christian Hope: Man's Concept of the Future, from the Early Fathers to Teilhard de Chardin* [Garden City, NY: Doubleday, Anchor Books, 1966], 42), Gerhard Sauter rightly cautions us against Bloch's interpretation of Joachim. The anticlerical and political-revolutionary impulses of Joachim were less direct than Bloch assumes. Cf Sauter, *Zukunft und Verheissung: Das Problem der Zukunft in der gegenwärtigen theologischen und philosophischen Diskussion* (Stuttgart: Zwingli, 1965), 331.

20. Ernst Bloch, *The Principle of Hope*, 2:510.

revolutionaries employ their total energy, which for Bloch is a sign of the true sectarian.

For centuries Joachim's writings were propagated, and pamphlets were written in his spirit and in his name. Even Thomas Müntzer (ca 1490–1525), the apocalyptic utopian and 'new Daniel' who wanted to rigorously enforce God's will in this eschatological end-time, refers to Joachim.[21] In a letter attached to his discourse *On Contrived Faith* (1524) he mentions that his enemies call Joachim's teaching 'with great mockery' the 'Eternal Gospel'. Müntzer holds Joachim in high esteem, though he claims that he does not derive his revolutionary ideas from Joachim, 'but rather from the living speech of God'.[22] Martin Luther and his followers, however, rejected categorically any utopian ideas in the Augsburg Confession of 1530, where they stated: 'Rejected, too, are certain Jewish opinions which are even now making an appearance and which teach that, before the resurrection of the dead, saints and godly men will possess a worldly kingdom and annihilate all the godless.'[23]

Even with this rejection the fire of utopian dreams was not extinguished. Gotthold Ephraim Lessing (1729–81), one of the spiritual leaders of the Enlightenment in Germany, shows a familiarity with a trinitarian periodisation of history and refers to the third age as an age of 'a new eternal gospel'.[24] It is of much more far reaching consequence that even Friedrich Engels, the co-author of the *Communist Manifesto*, declared in 1842:

---

21. Cf the extensive biography by Walter Elliger, *Thomas Müntzer: Leben und Werk*, third edition (Göttingen: Vandenhoeck & Ruprecht, 1976), 444-5.

22. As reprinted in Michael G Baylor, editor and translator, *Revelation and Revolution: Basic Writings of Thomas Müntzer* (Bethlehem: Lehigh University, 1993), 84. Cf also Ernst Bloch, *The Principle of Hope*, 2:512. When Müntzer mentions here that he has read Joachim's *Commentary on Jeremiah*, this is based on a misunderstanding. The *Commentary on Jeremiah* was a pseudo-Joachimite document, printed in Venice in 1516 (cf Baylor, 213 note 20). This shows us what popularity Joachim enjoyed in the 16th century.

23. *The Augsburg Confession* (XVII), in *The Book of Concord*, 38-9.

24. Gotthold Ephraim Lessing, *The Education of the Human Race* (86-9), in *Lessing's Theological Writings*, selections in translation (London: Adam & Charles Black, 1956), 96-7. Though not mentioning Joachim explicitly, he refers to some of the enthusiasts of the thirteenth and fourteenth centuries, who, according to Lessing, have perhaps caught a glimpse of this 'new eternal gospel', and only erred in predicting its arrival as 'so near to their own time'.

> The self-consciousness of mankind, the new Grail,
> around whose throne the nations joyfully assemble . .
> . that is our profession, that we become the Templars
> of this Grail, to gird our swords around our loin, and
> joyfully risk our lives in the last holy war after which
> will follow the millennium of freedom.[25]

In the context of these secularised versions of millennialism we must also mention the idea of the kingdom of God in America, a country that is not called the New World just because it was discovered relatively late. Even August Comte's idea of a tri-partite history as an ascent from the theological through the metaphysical up to the scientific phase is not unrelated to Joachim's notion of the three ages.[26]

Again the Marxian dialectic of the three stages of primitive communism, class society, and the final communism as the realm of freedom and in which the state will have withered away has its antecedents in Joachim's three ages. This is no less true of the phrase 'the Third Reich', as a name for that 'new order' which was to last a thousand years but fortunately only lasted from 1933 to 1945. The messianic self-consciousness of the Nazi ideology can be seen in the fact that Adolf Hitler was called *'der Führer'* (leader) of this Reich ('empire' or 'kingdom') and was greeted by millions with *'Heil!'* (salvation).[27] As Norman Cohn perceptively writes:

> Communists no less than Nazis have been obsessed
> by the vision of a prodigious 'final, decisive struggle'
> in which a 'chosen people' will destroy a world
> tyranny and thereby inaugurate a new epoch in
> world history. As in the Nazi apocalypse the 'Arian

---

25. Karl Marx and Friedrich Engels, *Historisch-Kritische Gesamtausgabe* (Frankfurt am Main: Marx-Engels-Archiv, 1927), 1/2:225-6; quoted in Ernst Bloch, *The Principle of Hope*, 2:515.

26. So Norman Cohn, *The Pursuit of the Millennium: Revolutionary Messianism in Medieval and Reformation Europe and Its Bearing on Modern Totalitarian Movements*, 2nd edition (New York: Harper Torchbooks, 1961), 101.

27. Cf Karl Löwith, *Meaning in History*, 159. It seems strange that in describing Joachim and his idea of the Third Reich, Bloch passes over Hitler and his utopian dreams with silence. Should this indicate that Hitler's program cannot be integrated into a 'principle of hope'?

> race' was to purify the earth by annihilating the
> 'Jewish race', so in the Communist apocalypse the
> 'bourgeoisie' is to be exterminated by the
> 'proletariat'. And here, too, we are faced with the
> secularised version of a phantasy that is many
> centuries old.[28]

While Joachim was still looking for a leader, both the communists and the Nazis thought well enough of themselves to provide this leadership. Yet as soon as finite humanity wants to bring about the conditions of the infinite, of eternal peace and equality, only terrorism results. Even after these dramatic failures, millennialism has not collapsed.

On the religious scene, both the nineteenth and the twentieth century have witnessed the emergence of larger millennial groups. Foremost among these are the Jehovah's Witnesses, who claim that the millennium is a time of testing for those who have not yet found salvation in this life. The Mormons, or the Church of Jesus Christ of the Latter-Day Saints, see the United States as the centre of their millennial hopes. In their creed, point 10, we read: 'We believe that Zion will be founded on the American continent, that Christ will personally rule the earth, that this earth will be renewed and it will gain paradisiacal splendour.'[29] Similarly, the Seventh-Day Adventists expect a premillennial, personal, visible return of Christ at a time unknown but close at hand. After the millennium, from the ruins of the old earth, a new earth will be created as the final place for the immortal saints.

Often millennial expectations have been accompanied by withdrawal from the world. This can be seen in utopian communities, such as the Shakers or the Oneida Community. This leads us to the last group of occasional representatives of religious millennialism, namely pietistic, fundamentalistic, and revivalistic groups. To demonstrate the necessity for conversion, they welcome chiliastic ideas. Periods of great personal and societal anxiety and despair have tended to intensify the hopes in a this-worldly intervention of Christ, as could be seen especially with the turn of the millennium. Especially dispensational premillennialism, with its precise system of a historic progression, has often used the Bible to identify specific current events as the future

---

28.   Norman Cohn, *The Pursuit of the Millennium*, 311.

29.   Creed (10), as quote by Åke V Ström, 'Mormonen', in *TRE* 23:317.

tribulational fulfilment of the Day of the Lord. It also identifies tribulations with the mysterious visions of biblical apocalyptic. Progressive dispensationalists caution that one should observe that in biblical history itself, prophetic fulfilment has always been identified and proclaimed by prophetic authority. Yet this authority is mistakenly claimed by modern doomsday prophets. Moreover, 'the re-employment of literary descriptions in later prophecy and apocalyptic calls into question the assumption that this language gives *one concrete historical scenario* in partially codified form'.[30] This means that we do not have a timetable outlining the millennium. We encounter here only highly symbolic language.

In conclusion, we must say that the secularist form of millennial hopes attempting to bring about earthly redemption from all evils denies its own finitude. It does so by creating in magnitude what it wants to overcome. Both communism and national socialism are telling examples of the wake of blood and terror left behind after both collapsed under their own finite vision. The religious vision that forgets the caution of dispensational premillennialism falls in a similar trap to the secular one. In attempting to escape from this world's troubles and anxieties, we bring about new anxieties and disappointments. Millennial thoughts testify to the human impatience over the not-yet-visible universalisation of Christ's rule. Yet they are unable to bring this rule about or to speed up its progression. They are at the most a pointer to salvation, but should not be mistaken for salvation itself.

Yet does it make sense to hope in salvation, since two thousand years have already elapsed since Christ first came on this earth? Was not Rudolf Bultmann correct when he wrote: 'The parousia of Christ never took place as the New Testament expected. History did not come to an end, and, as every schoolboy knows, it will continue to run its course.'[31] Before we too quickly agree with such a sober assessment, we should note that virtually every religion on earth attests to the

---

30. Craig A Blaising and Darrell L Bock, *Progressive Dispensationalism: An Up-to-Date Handbook of Contemporary Dispensational Thought* (Wheaton, IL: BridgePoint, 1993), 294.

31. Rudolf Bultmann in his programmatic essay 'New Testament and Mythology', in *Kerygma and Myth: A Theological Debate*, edited by Hans Werner Bartsch, translated by RH Fuller (London: SPCK, 1953), 1:5.

notion of a disturbed existential union of humanity and the super-human power(s) in which humanity believes and upon which it feels itself dependent. At the same time every religion is convinced that this union can be re-established and salvation can be regained. Salvation is not just a Christian desire, but also something intrinsic to the human condition. All people have a feeling that things are not the way they ought to be and desire to have them changed.

We should also look beyond the human scale. Even among animals and plants there seems to be a struggle for survival and an attempt to gain the bigger part to thrive and flourish. Buddha correctly understood this craving for life as the source of pain and suffering. Yet what happens if we abolish this craving? Is it really true, as Buddha hoped, that tranquillity will set in? If this were really the case, Nirvana would already be part of this world. Yet Buddha never dared to claim that. Or is it rather as stated in a frequently used saying of the 1970s and which is often wrongly attributed to Bertolt Brecht: 'If there is war and nobody joins it, war will come to you.'[32] Regardless what we try, we cannot escape from negativity. If there is any salvation at all it must be beyond us in the otherworldly.

3. Salvation as a new creation

How can we think of salvation beyond these earthly confines? Some process thinkers, such as Charles Hartshorne and Schubert Ogden argued 'against any subjective immortality, holding that as objectively experienced by God our lives are wholly preserved and cherished forever'.[33] Similarly, John B Cobb, Jr, the most prominent represen-tative of process theology, opts for transcending all separating individuality by a more complete community with other fellow human beings and with all things. 'In this community the tensions between self and Christ decline, and in a final consummation they would disappear.'[34] Cobb has rightly noticed that our destiny is interwoven with the whole cosmos. This cosmos witnesses to temporality and

---

32.   For details and the quotations see Jan Kopf, *Brecht-Handbuch. Lyrik, Prosa, Schriften* (Stuttgart: JB Metzler, 1984), 165.

33.   So Lewis S Ford, *The Lure of God: A Biblical Background for Process Theism* (Philadelphia: Fortress, 1978), 114, who provides us with a good summary of different process positions.

34.   John B Cobb, Jr, *Christ in a Pluralistic Age* (Philadelphia: Westminster, 1975), 258.

perishableness. Moreover, especially our individuality and ego-consciousness contributes to divisions and divisiveness. Christ therefore gains in stature as temporality wanes and separating individuality decreases. John Hick, too, emphasises 'the gradual creation of perfected persons—their perfection consisting . . . in a self-transcending state beyond separate ego-existence'.[35]

Two questions, however, must be asked of these proponents of process ideas: 1) Paul reminded the Corinthians: 'For just as the body is one and has many members, and all the members of the body, though many, are one body, so it is with Christ . . . Now you are the body of Christ and individually members of it' (1 Cor 12:12,27). This means the divisiveness issuing forth from a separate ego-existence is not a Christian virtue, but an aberration. In Christ we are one body, but still distinct as members of that body. Therefore the abandoning of individual distinctiveness is not a necessary part of the salvational process or its goal. (2) Even if we merge into Christ or into God, as some proponents of process thought suggest, it would be unthinkable that we would leave this created universe behind as a butterfly abandons its cocoon. When we ask how this creation is issuing into God, we must give some hint of how such transformation might be possible.

We must refer here to Paul who wrote: 'The last enemy to be destroyed is death. For "God has put all things in subjection under his feet". . . When all things are subjected to him, then the Son himself will also be subjected to the one who put all things in subjection under him, so that God may be all in all' (1 Cor 15:26-28). Paul addresses here the universal reign of God and argues that once Christ has completed the victory over the anti-Godly powers he will subject himself to God who has subjected everything to Christ. In this way, God may be all in all. This does not indicate a merging into God, especially not of humans or of the created world, but the containment of everything that is destructive and anti-Godly. In this manner the contradiction and tension between church and world, immanence and transcendence, time and eternity is overcome. In other words, there is a new creation that transcends the possibilities of this world. Exactly that is the hope that is fostered in virtually all religions.

---

35.   John Hick, *Death and Eternal Life* (New York: Harper & Row, 1976), 249.

For Christians, this is not a pie-in-the-sky hope, but one that to some extent can already be anticipated in this world, as Paul asserted: 'Now that you have been freed from sin and enslaved to God, the advantage you get is sanctification. The end is eternal life' (Rom 6:22). Within our natural this-worldly limitations there is possible a foreshadowing of that in which we believe, redemption. With that kind of twofold anchoring, in the new life in Christ and in the hope for the universalisation of this new life, any delay of the parousia that we might perceive is not a burning issue. Decisive is only faithfulness and steadfastness.

Yet how can we conceive of salvation in the otherworldly? While our new world orders always smack very much like the old ones, Paul talked in radical juxtapositions. Therefore the only pictures we could use are those that Dionysius the Aeropagite indicated when talking about the attributes of God, since evidently this new creation is in uncompromised closeness to God. There Dionysius talked about the negative, the superlative and the causal way. It will be incomparably different, incomparably better and it will be originated by God. This would also mean that the present creation would not stand in the way of redemption, because it would not set the parameters for a new creation. Yet the exact configuration of these parameters we must leave up to God. This ignorance is similar to the ignorance about what would happen from one big bang and big crunch cycle to the next.

Contributors

Brendan Byrne SJ teaches New Testament at Jesuit Theological College, Melbourne.

Denis Edwards teaches Systematic Theology at Catholic Theological College, Flinders University/Adelaide College of Divinity, Adelaide.

Rosalie Hudson is an Aged Care Consultant in Melbourne.

Peter Lockart is a Minister of the Word in the Uniting Church in Australia, Brisbane.

Peter Lockwood teaches Old Testament at Luther Seminary, Adelaide.

Duncan Reid is Dean of the United Faculty of Theology, Melbourne.

Robert J Russell is founder and Director of the Center for Theology and the Natural Science, and Professor of Theology and Science in Residence at the Graduate Theological Union, Berkeley, California.

Ted Peters is Professor of Systematic Theology at the Pacific Lutheran Theological Seminary, Berkeley, California.

Hans Schwarz is Professor of Protestant Theology and Director of the Institute of Protestant Theology, University of Regensburg, and adjunct Professor of Systematic Theology, Lutheran Theological Southern Seminary, Columbia, South Carolina.

Mark Worthing is Dean of Studies and lecturer in Systematic Theology at Tabor College, Adelaide.

Biblical References

Author Index

Subject Index